by Violet Powell

Five out of Six
A Substantial Ghost
The Irish Cousins

Standing, left to right: Hildegarde Somerville, Egerton Coghill,
Aylmer Somerville. *Seated, left to right:* Edith Somerville, Violet
Martin (Martin Ross) at Castletownshend, *circa* 1886.

THE IRISH COUSINS

The Books and Background
of Somerville and Ross

by

VIOLET POWELL

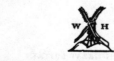

HEINEMANN : LONDON

William Heinemann Ltd

LONDON MELBOURNE TORONTO
JOHANNESBURG AUCKLAND

First published in Great Britain 1970
Copyright © by Violet Powell 1970

434 59953 0

PRINTED IN GREAT BRITAIN
by BUTLER AND TANNER, FROME

For

Tristram and Virginia

FRONTISPIECE showing Hildegarde Somerville, Egerton Coghill, Aylmer Somerville, Edith Somerville, Violet Martin (Martin Ross) at Castletownshend, *circa* 1886

Contents

The Books of Somerville and Ross

Condensed from *A Bibliography of the First Editions of the Works of E. Œ. Somerville and Martin Ross* compiled and edited by Elizabeth Hudson (New York 1942)

An Irish Cousin (1889)
Naboth's Vineyard (1891)
Through Connemara in a Governess Cart (1893)
In the Vine Country (1893)
The Real Charlotte (1894)
Beggars on Horseback (1895)
The Silver Fox (1898)
Some Experiences of an Irish R.M. (1899)
All on the Irish Shore (1903)
Some Irish Yesterdays (1906)
Further Experiences of an Irish R.M. (1908)
Dan Russel the Fox (1911)
In Mr Knox's Country (1915)
Irish Memories (1917)
Mount Music (1919)
Strayaways (1920)
An Enthusiast (1921)
Wheel-tracks (1923)
The Big House of Inver (1925)
French Leave (1928)
The States through Irish Eyes (1930)
An Incorruptible Irishman (1932)
The Smile and the Tear (1933)
The Sweet Cry of Hounds (1936)
Sarah's Youth (1938)
Notions in Garrison (1941)
Happy Days! (1946)
Maria and Some Other Dogs (1949)

Acknowledgements

THROUGHOUT the writing of this book the family and friends of E. Œ. Somerville and Martin Ross have been unfailingly generous with gifts and loans of original material and photographs. At Drishane, Brigadier Desmond Somerville, nephew of E. Œ. Somerville, and Mrs Somerville helped me with family history and geographical background. Their kind hospitality included the privilege of examining Mrs Somerville's decipherment of Colonel Thomas Somerville's much crossed letters from Corfu. Sir Patrick Coghill and Professor Nevill Coghill, nephews of E. Œ. Somerville and literary heirs of both writers, have given continual encouragement, suggested additional lines of research, patiently answered many questions and supplied the photograph for the frontispiece. Miss Muriel Currey, whose typescript of her aunt Martin Ross's diary is annotated with great perception, has helped also in disentangling the two strands of Somerville and Ross's writing. The late Captain Lionel Dawson, R.N., nephew of Martin Ross, gave a vivid idea of life at Ross during its restoration.

From New York, Miss Elizabeth Hudson sent her revealing collection of photographs and letters concerning the later years of E. Œ. Somerville. The bibliographer of Somerville and Ross, and a close friend of the surviving partner, Miss Hudson was kind enough to get in touch with me on her own initiative, and to give her reminiscences of her visits to Drishane.

I must thank my husband, Anthony Powell, for invaluable help and criticism.

The first draft of this book was already written when Mr Maurice Collis' biography, *Somerville and Ross*, appeared, a book which has done so much to increase the reputation of the two writers. I am most grateful to Mr Collis for signposts among the Somerville and Ross papers, although they have sometimes led us to different destinations. Incidentally I misled Mr Collis with information indicating that E. Œ. Somerville's birthplace on Corfu could be identified.

In thanking all those who have helped in many different ways, I can do no better than quote from a letter written by Martin Ross to E. Œ. Somerville after the appearance of their first book, 'To write with you doubles the triumph and the enjoyment, having first halved the trouble and anxiety.'

Genealogical note

EDITH Œnone Somerville (1858–1949) was the eldest child of Colonel Thomas Somerville of Drishane, Castletownshend, Co. Cork. Her mother was Adelaide Coghill, daughter of Admiral Sir Josiah Coghill, 3rd Bart, by his wife, Anna Maria, daughter of Charles Kendal Bushe (1767–1843) Lord Chief Justice of Ireland.

Violet Martin, 'Martin Ross' (1852–1915), was the youngest child of James Martin of Ross, Co. Galway. Her mother was Anna Selina Fox, daughter of Charles Fox of New Park, Co. Longford, by his wife Katherine, daughter of Charles Kendal Bushe (1767–1843) Lord Chief Justice of Ireland.

Consequently E. Œ. Somerville and Martin Ross were second cousins.

I
How they began

'YESTERDAY was four weeks since the infant was born,' Colonel Thomas Somerville wrote from Corfu to his father in Co. Cork, 'and now she is a fine fat, jolly little animal and is to be made a Christian of next Thursday . . . [the nurse] is stopped almost every day by ladies to look at and admire the blessed Baby.' This baby was the eldest child of Thomas Somerville of the Buffs, promoted brevet colonel for his service in the Crimea. He wrote on May 31st, 1858, at which date the island, where shipwrecked Ulysses, sheltering behind a modest leafy branch, had approached Nausicaa, was administered by the British. The garrison chapel, a nineteenth-century Doric Temple, where presumably the fat jolly little animal was made a Christian, though closed, still stands at the foot of the Old Fortress. It can be seen clearly from the dusty esplanade where cricket, another relic of British administration, is played on Sunday evenings. The Somervilles lived in hired lodgings in the town of Corfu, Italian in architectural style and, in its turn, monument to the Venetian domination of the island.

Neglecting a legitimate opportunity to call their first-born Nausicaa, the name Edith was chosen, with the addition of Œnone as a tribute to the classical background of her birth. As a painter it was with the initials E. Œ. S. that she signed her work, but it was as a writer that the name of E. Œ. Somerville became linked with that of Martin Ross in a partnership whose success was unique in the history of fiction written in English. This collaboration was an exception to the rule that, while plays and librettos can bubble from a joint spring, novels do not lend themselves to production by dual control. A pair of writers may decide that they have gifts that will be complementary, but only too often the issue of these unions meet a Spartan death on barrows stocked with literary rejects. Writing with one pen the sympathy between Somerville and

Ross became so close that, after Martin Ross's death, her surviving partner and second cousin refused to accept that the link had been broken. For more than thirty years E. Œ. Somerville was left to run a widowed race, but, assured in her own mind that her collaborator, though unseen, was near at hand, she continued to send forth her books as the joint work of Martin Ross and herself.

Soon after Edith's birth Corfu passed from the British sphere of influence, as a result of a report by Mr Gladstone on his mission to the Ionian Islands, a curious foretaste of his relationship with Ireland which was to earn him later much execration from Edith's family. Before the island's legislature had voted for union with Greece, there is a legend that Gladstone had offered self-government in a speech of such classical purity as to be incomprehensible to his demotic-speaking audience. By then Colonel Somerville had retired to Drishane House, Co. Cork, perched on its cliff like a sea-gull's nest, with nothing except the wastes of the Atlantic between its windows and the rain-washed peaks of the Azores. Always his daughter remained proud of the circumstances of her birth by which she had not only been entered on the roll of the Buffs, but, like Ulysses, had been shipwrecked on the voyage home.

This daughter's birth was followed by that of six brothers and one sister, all except one of the family (a son who died as an infant) growing up to full age and in many cases honours. Edith, however, never yielded her seniority, crowning herself with mayflower on each birthday, like Napoleon in her determination that her hand alone should perform her own coronation. Throughout her life she held, undisputed, the position which she recognized among her own dynasties of fox terriers as that of Head Dog. As a child, during family prayers, she stood between her father and grandfather, a hand held by each, while her mother, a string of little brothers, and the servants occupied a lowlier position. Above the worshippers there hung the oval trophy, carved in the village with the battle roll of the Crimea, which had decorated the gate of Drishane on her father's return. He brought with him the Crimean Medal with all four clasps. Wrought with delicacy in silver, the clasps looked more like jewellery than a reminder that wounds and sickness, particularly the latter, had disqualified most soldiers from fighting in the four engagements.

Family prayers began 'The Lord abroad is safe to the beginning of this day', or so Edith thought, suffering from a common childish misapprehension. To pray thus she knelt, with her father, against a canopied chair. The chair had been carved from the black Cork mahogany, said to come from groves reserved for merchants of that city, and extinct after the groves had been cut down. It was a relic of a dissolved Freemasons' Lodge, given to the master of Drishane as some return for unrepaid financial support. The Lodge had failed when the emancipated Catholic priesthood increased their grip on the private lives of their parishioners, driving the Freemasons out of business in the West of Ireland.

Originally it had been persecution by Covenanters that had sent a Somerville, a clergyman of the Anglican Church, to seek religious freedom by rowing his family across the narrow sea between Scotland and Ulster. One of his sons became rector of Castlehaven, where a gable of the church still stands, in the old graveyard to the west of the harbour. With this ancestor began that intermarrying among the local gentry by which was created a pattern of kinship at whose intricacies of cross-fertilization Bourbons and Hapsburgs might have flinched. Castlehaven itself was important to the coastal trade, in the days when the West Carbery roads were tracks unfit for wheels. The Somerville who built Drishane made money in shipping, but later generations entered either the Church or the services of the Crown. The family tendency to marry Townsends in each generation makes it seem slightly unreasonable for E. Œ. Somerville and Martin Ross to have expressed such astonishment when, on a journalistic assignment in Denmark, they discovered the Danish custom of nieces marrying their uncles. Naturally the numerous clergymen in the Somerville family, if nothing else, would have prevented such an infringement of The Table of Kindred and Affinity from taking place, but every permissible permutation of inter-marriage appears to have occurred. Even those who happened to marry outside the frontiers of West Carbery chose their mates from among the landed gentry of Ireland. In the neighbourhood itself the isolation gave idiosyncrasies an opportunity to develop with tropical luxuriance. Feuds could last for half a century, one at least remaining active when one of the feuders had gone to her grave. It was of no account that the cause of the quarrel, the youthful rivalry of two sisters wishing to marry the same young man, had long ceased to be relevant.

Slowly the nineteenth century advanced into the West of Ireland, bringing improved roads and, in due course, the Great Southern and Western Railway, whose vagaries later supplied Somerville and Ross with material for poignant anecdotes of travel. In bad years of blight the young Somervilles rode round the country to spread the news that there was relief at Drishane for those whose potato crop had failed. The relief was distributed by Adelaide Somerville, Edith's mother, the tenth daughter of Admiral Sir Josiah Coghill. Later her daughter wrote that her mother and her aunts deserved to belong to John Davidson's tribe of 'splendid and puissant Alanoths'. Splendid and puissant, Mrs Somerville dominated both the women who had come for relief, and the sub-committee of her two daughters and the kitchen maid. The sub-committee's screening of the most destitute from the merely needy was overthrown by Mrs Somerville's sudden bestowal of food and clothing on families suffering from nothing worse than bad colds in the head and new-born babies. Black shawls pulled half across their faces in the manner of yashmaks, the women waiting for the dole squatted in the yard, short of everything except topics of conversation. When their turn came they politely accepted Mrs Somerville's injunctions that the seed potatoes should be planted to grow next year's dinner, and not boiled for that evening's supper, which they inevitably were.

In these hungry days, a pale reflection of the horrors of the earlier Famine, Edith had already begun to spread her wings. The schoolroom, in her childhood, had been of less importance than the stableyard and the horses who inhabited it. Frequent orders to be quiet and look at *Punch* had led her to much copying of Leech's hunting illustrations, a stylistic influence never entirely shaken off. Her passion for drawing led to the spreading of wings, in a manner permissible for gently born girls with artistic ambitions. At the South Kensington School of Art, first step on the road to emancipation, Edith Somerville's hand was manacled by the insistence that plaster casts should be drawn with infinite care before shading by stippling, both time-wasting and soul destroying. The casts were of fruit, architectural scrolls and the more respectable out-lying portions of the human body. By the time that a batch of her sketches was sent to the School's director with the inquiry if Miss Somerville might be judged proficient 'to pass for the antique', the student only wished to pass out of the school. After this initiation into the current tradition of English drawing schools, which dictated that imitation was the sincerest form of art, Edith escaped for two seasons to Düsseldorf. Paris was obviously the next target, but her family, who had yet to learn that no river in spate is more unstoppable than a daughter with a paint brush in her hand, began to put up a barrage of objections. Many voices said that Paris was no place for a girl, however dedicated to her art. Mrs Somerville became ever more shaken by the perils to which her daughter insisted on being exposed. A single chaperone seemed an inadequate precaution, and, as she afterwards wrote, Edith arrived in Paris with a bodyguard of her mother, her eldest brother, and a cousin, in addition to the friend who was to be her fellow student. While the art students worked from 8 a.m. until supper time, the bodyguard, with no sacred flame to warm their drooping spirits, toiled through a round of sight-seeing, made ever more unenjoyable by the foul discomforts of the *pension* in which they stayed. After three weeks Mrs Somerville turned for home, presumably feeling that nothing that might befall her daughter could be worse than what she herself was suffering, in a land where the endlessness of the repellent meals only emphasized the absence of afternoon tea. Her daughter was left in possession of the field and subsequently, though she found it necessary to supply an edited account of her circumstances to her parents, her studies in Paris were only regulated by the amount of money they were prepared to advance for the purpose.

No one writing of Edith Somerville has failed to mention that she was generous in her dealings, with an open-handedness that sometimes left her as straitened as the objects of her benevolence. In Paris, however, she learnt to count sous with the keenness of a French housewife, for twenty sous made a franc, and her lodging *avec service* cost seven francs a week. Each sou saved by bargaining represented a slowing-up of the process by which her capital diminished, and with it the number of days to be spent at Colarossi's studio in la rue de la Grande Chaumière. With two friends she had abandoned the more ladylike studio, founded by Colarossi '*près l'Etoile*', for what might be called the carriage trade, and had moved to the establishment where the atmosphere was fiercely professional. Light-fingered for anything that could be scrounged from the unguarded belongings of their fellows, the students from many lands struggled on pittances to achieve the magic which Paris alone could give their art. If Edith, in the women's studio, had come from the extreme west of Europe, downstairs, *parmis les hommes*, Alphonse Mucha, from Bohemia, was beginning the career that was to turn his style of Art Nouveau into an American industry. Mucha does not seem to have crossed Edith's path, but even the toughest among the girls quailed when silence fell in the men's studio below. This quiet meant that the professors were making their rounds with '. . . as it were, scythe blades on their chariot wheels and flaming swords in their hands'. Afterwards three sous worth of black coffee, brewed by the concierge, was an extravagant necessity before the professor's corrections could be welded on to the student's slaughtered drawing.

In January, 1886, Edith Somerville, back at home, was working on a commission from *The Graphic* to illustrate three serials. This was an advance professionally, but required models sometimes hard to find in winter in West Carbery. The adventures of a Clergyman—a subject nowadays seldom artistically exploited—merely required the surreptitious borrowing of the Sunday coat and hat of a clerical visitor, but the brother who posed only in a straw hat and bathing drawers, for illustrations to *A Mule Ride in Trinidad*, retired to bed with a heavy cold. Studio stoves invariably operate by extremes, and in the studio at Drishane there was a particularly stubborn example, described by Mrs Martin of Ross as having solved the problem of producing smoke without fire. In this inclement atmosphere Edith worked on the third serial, the adventures of a student of the violin in Paris. In her diary Edith wrote, 'Compelled H. (her sister, then about sixteen years old) to pose as a Paris tram horse, in white stockings with a chowrie for a tail.' This sentence followed one of the greatest personal importance,

'Crucified Martin head downwards, as the fiddle girl practising her music on the floor.' On January 17th, Edith Somerville had first seen her second cousin, Violet Martin, in the church at Castletownshend, and from that moment the revolution had begun, that was to change their lives and turn two people into one writer.

At Ross there can still be seen slabs of slate bearing the names of seventeenth-century Martins and their arms. The first Robert Martin recorded in the 1963 edition of the *Landed Gentry of Ireland* held estates in Galway and its neighbourhood in 1590, being High Sheriff in 1609. In the Civil War the Martins, Royalist and Roman Catholic, were deprived of their property in Galway itself, this being bestowed on the Judge Advocate of the invading Cromwellian army. The army, however, faltered at the prospect of pressing further west, into the territory of the Norman-Irish Tribes. Consequently, though never regaining their property in Galway Town, the Martins spread themselves unhindered from there to the Atlantic, so that at the height of their fortunes they counted four family strongholds. Of these the proudest was Ballanahinch, from whence the countryside was ruled as its owner saw fit. From a nearby mountain Mary Martin, Princess of Connemara and last heiress of Ballanahinch, could point to all the land within sight as her inheritance, together with fifty miles of Atlantic coast. Hardly had she made this triumphant boast when every acre was swallowed by the calamitous economic collapse that was a sequel to the Famine.

The senior branch, the Martins of Ross, had a less spectacular domain, but they prospered. A change of religion in the eighteenth century, following marriage with a Protestant, did not affect the amicable terms on which they lived with their tenants. The tenants themselves multiplied on a diet of potatoes, a crop requiring the simplest cultivation, needing only to be tended in fine weather. With nothing more elaborate than a spade, a man could work the land from which he might, in a good year, feed his family. In bad weather the country people, huddled inside their rain-swept cabins, were protected at least from the worst perils of exposure. When hunger forced them to seek food and work in all weathers, resistance to the diseases of famine was undermined by the disturbance of a pattern

of life which at least allowed for the exercise of an animal
instinct for taking shelter.

The grandfather of Violet Martin, himself brought up as a
Protestant, married a Roman Catholic. However the family did
not again change its faith, though the children were usually
given a second, supplementary, baptism by the parish priest,
at the request of their wet-nurses. At Ross the two religions
dwelt in friendship under the same roof. Robert Martin, Violet's
eldest brother, remembered listening outside the drawing-room
door while Mass was said within for the benefit of his grandmother and her co-religionists among the retainers. The grandfather was, in his way, as patriarchal as old Mr Somerville of
Drishane. Besides ruling his family, he had such financial skill
that, though relapsing into a rather premature senility he
passed on the estate free of debt, in spite of the relentless pressure of the famine years. Unfortunately James, his son, lacked
this acumen, and not long afterwards had to give evidence
before the Land Commission that the Ross estate was burdened
with a debt for Poor Rate of £11,000. James Martin was
further burdened by a family of fourteen children, of whom
Violet was the youngest child and eleventh daughter. Her
mother, Anna Selina Fox, James Martin's second wife, shared
with the mother of Edith Somerville a descent from Charles
Kendal Bushe (1767–1843), a famous Lord Chief Justice of
Ireland; by which descent a strain of artistic and intellectual
brilliance entered both their families.

Anna Selina Fox had grown up in the kind shadow of her
grand-parents, her mother being a widow returned to her
father's house. Maria Edgeworth wrote of Mrs Bushe, 'whenever I meet her she is my delight for her wit, humour and
elegance of conversation'. In this atmosphere of cultivation,
lightened by gaiety, Nannie Fox was educated in the manner
of the eighteenth century. At the age of seven she wrote to
her mother a penitent letter for touching 'that stinking little
cat', modified by indignation that Satan had so tempted her.
Dawnay, the cat, was described sardonically by Nannie's grandfather, the Lord Chief Justice, as a 'well-behaved cat, except for
the murder of birds, stealing of Milk and Polygamy on a large
scale'. Nannie's natural gift for writing fluent verse developed
by the age of eight. Lessons in Latin from a tutor made her

capable, at seventeen, of translating into iambic pentameters a poem written by Lord Wellesley, the Viceroy of Ireland.

On her arrival at Ross, after her marriage to James Martin, the tenants dragged the bride's carriage for two miles up to the house, against a background of screaming bagpipes and blazing bonfires. According to an account of the Martin family written by her daughter Violet, she brought with her much energy, a kicking pony and a profound ignorance of household affairs, the study of domestic science having been overlooked among the elegances of her education. Her eldest child was a daughter, the fifth or sixth to be born in that generation, but this was only a family disappointment compared to the threat that 1845 brought to the land. That summer James Martin shared an experience, sickening in its foretaste of doom, with many who travelled the Irish countryside. He drove to Galway Assizes on a day in July, admiring the rich crop of potatoes on each side of the road. He drove home next day and the smell of the potato blight was heavy in the air, a new and poisonous reek which hung over the West like smoke from the fires of Tanit, persisting until half the population could be counted among its victims.

The following summer, when the more hopeful held that the blight might not strike again, a son, Robert, was born to the Martins, amid wild rejoicings at the first male heir to be born to Ross for forty-two years. The baby's hand was kissed by the men in the yard, while old women down from the mountains spat on him for luck. With her scrupulous respect for her husband and son's religion the child's grandmother asked if a little holy water might be sprinkled on the infant. 'If you heat it first you may give him a bath in it,' said Robert Martin's mother. The tale of his welcome must have been often told, for in his last illness Robert cast back to it in farewell, saying, 'Mother, the little boy you brought to Ross is going away.'

These rejoicings must have been the last at Ross for a long time, for it soon became clear that the repeated failure of the potato crop would bring starvation and fever upon the neighbourhood. Relief was made more complicated by ignorance of dietetic principles on the one hand, and unfamiliarity with any food but potatoes on the other. At Ross there was a soup kitchen to which people came from great distances, sometimes falling dead to be buried at the gates. James Martin's sister caught the famine fever at a school she had organized for little girls on the estate, where, as they learnt to read and write, they were kept alive by breakfasts of oatmeal porridge. Miss Martin survived because, according to family legend, her father did not hesitate to open a vein and bleed her. In the history of the Famine, the landlords who struggled to relieve their tenants have been overshadowed by those who fled, looking on from afar and sanctioning evictions on the doctrinaire principle that the land must be cleared of inhabitants it could no longer support. The landlords who stuck by their estates died among those they were attempting to succour. Thomas Martin of Ballanahinch, a kinsman of the Martins of Ross, died from typhus, caught in the courthouse where he served as a magistrate. His steadfastness was recognized by his tenants, who followed his funeral in a procession which took two hours to pass the gates of Ross on its way to Galway.

At the time of Violet Martin's birth—as an eleventh daughter her welcome was lukewarm—the Famine was still a tale of recent horror, which had undermined the solvency of the estate of Ross. There was a long family of daughters to be clothed and fed, though the aunt, who owed her life to her father's confidence in his medical skill, had married. This match was typical of the family's matrimonial habits, for she had married a son of Lord Chief Justice Bushe. The results were less labyrinthine than the Somerville–Coghill–Bushe alliances, which Edith Somerville recommended only seekers after lunacy to unravel, but had the effect of turning a sister-in-law into a niece, and a brother into the nephew of his brother-in-law. The money-losing combination of James Martin's unbusiness-like habits with a kind heart was in no way balanced by his wife's qualities. She was charmingly irresponsible, light-heartedly facing an ever increasing financial tightness. Though less extreme in extravagance than the Sitwell family of Renishaw, who found themselves obliged to retrench abroad partly because they had mutton cutlets for breakfast every morning, without realizing that for this daily a sheep must die, Mrs Martin held, unshaken, the belief that the weekly sheep killed at Ross should yield four legs of mutton. 'Life at Ross,' her daughter wrote, 'was of the traditional Irish kind, with many retainers at low wages, which works out as a costly establishment with nothing to show for it.'

The patriarch died, in a kind of second childhood, and his youngest grand-daughter, at the age of six, listened in dread when the shriek of a countrywoman's keening pierced the house. James Martin, who had struggled to make money by political writing, was now an Auditor of the Poor Law, an occupation taking him much from home to the further detriment of his own affairs. Gladstone's Land Act of 1870 made little difference to an estate where the tenants never suffered from eviction, and where their own improvements, decreed to become their property under the Act, were illusory. The end of the era came at the election of 1872, when the tenants of Ross deserted their landlord, and, on the orders of a ferociously Nationalist priest, voted for the Home Rule candidate. Struck by this disaffection as by a physical blow, James Martin sank under his difficulties, dying two months later. The staircase at Ross had come from a wrecked ship and, watching over its fine mahogany banisters, Violet saw her brother, supported by one of the tenants, go up to the room where their father lay dead. The son whose birth had given such joy had little left by way of inheritance, and the old days of Ross lay dead with his father.

The front door of the house was barred, the demesne left to the rabbits, and Robert Martin went to London to seek his fortune as a journalist. His mother retreated to Dublin, with the rest of the long family. When Ross was opened again as the home of the Martins the long-lingering twilight of the eighteenth century had at last faded. With it had gone the plenteousness of game, fruit, butter and cream, but the same problems of little ready money, and tenants still largely dependent on the vagaries of the potato crop, had remained behind.

Sixteen years later Mrs Martin returned to Ross in a gallant attempt to salvage the estate. By this time her daughter had begun a career of her own as a writer, drawing material from her childhood at Ross as from a spring in a Lost Paradise. It was, however, the years of growing up in Dublin which had given the youngest Miss Martin experience of a world different in its robust coarseness from the circles usually frequented by the great-grand-daughters of Lord Chief Justice Bushe.

2

Parce que c'était moi, parce que c'était elle

GROWING up, as they did, in a tangled jungle of cousin-hood it appears a surprising accident that the meeting between Edith Somerville and Violet Martin was so long delayed. It was, perhaps, a fortunate accident, for a meeting in childhood might well have been blighted by the gap of four years which separated them in age. Neither did they need to waste time in learning to recognize hereditary influences in each other, for the strongest of these they already shared. The habit of admiring veneration for 'the Chief' and his wife, Nancy Crampton, was, to their myriad descendants, almost a religious practice. Mrs Martin had had the benefit of being brought up in 'the Chief's' own house, Kilmurry, but the Bushe influence was strong also in Castlehaven, of which his son, Charles, was rector for forty years. This civilizing influx from a wider world was resented by the more aboriginal of the Townsend great-aunts, who complained that the parish was being 'be-Bushed, be-Coghilled and bedevilled'.

In addition to his reputation for humanity as a judge, and his oratory, which had won him the nickname of 'Silver-Tongue', Charles Kendal Bushe was famous for the incorruptibility of his character. He had resisted stoutly the attempts of Pitt's creatures to buy his support for the Act of Union of Ireland with England. He might have been particularly vulnerable to bribery, having, on his twenty-first birthday, been tricked by his own father, the Reverend Thomas Bushe, into responsibility for the crippling debts which that dashing clergyman had managed to amass. The offer, from Pitt, of £30,000, with an earldom thrown in, left Bushe gasping, but he told the devil to get behind him. To his wife's family was attributed a quality known to her descendants as 'Crampton dash', which consisted of seeing events slightly larger than life, and adding rococo details in describing them.

Violet Martin was ten years old when her mother, widowed and financially embarrassed, moved to Dublin. This youngest child had already become a gifted pianist, and, beginning as a precocious reader, had absorbed an amount of classical literature which was afterwards to be the envy of her collaborator. Mrs Martin, though enjoying such perils as the carriage horses bolting, or a sudden squall which could buffet a rowing boat on Lough Corrib, had, after the birth of nine children, become statuesque, if not monumental. Her children said that her movements could only be detected by relating her person to a fixed object. Once she was even thought to be approaching when a short-sighted daughter had observed a distant tram-car. Mrs Martin's small and elegant feet had escaped the general expansion of her person, and she was considered to be highly conscious of their grace, for her shoe laces were abnormally given to coming unfastened. She was sailing slowly away, having thanked a cabman for re-tying the trailing lace, when she heard him say to his fellow, 'That's a dam' pleasant old heifer,' and his companion replied, 'Ah, Shakespeare says you'll know a real lady when you see her.'

The change from the wild freedom of Ross, and the devotion of such people as her foster-mother 'Nurse' Barrett, cut Violet Martin's childhood in half. Nurse Barrett belonged to a dynasty of wet-nurses who had suckled infant Martins, retaining 'Nurse' ever after as an honorary title. She cherished her nurseling, and when she caught the nursery-maid Kit Sal 'an' she bating and kicking yerself on the avenue' she described how she had not only torn out Kit Sal's hair but had stuck her teeth into the girl. Later she mentioned the incident to Mrs Martin, who reproved Kit Sal, according to Nurse Barrett in the following terms, 'What call had ye to bate Miss Wilet?' says she, 'Ye big shtump.' 'She wouldn't folly me,' says Kit. 'Well indeed,' says the Mistress, 'I believe ye got a bigger batin' yerself from nurse...I declare to God,' says she, 'I wish she drank yer blood.'

In reality Mrs Martin possessed a graceful distinction of speech and manner, which made it the more surprising that she should have exposed her youngest child to the hazards, social and vocal, of a Dublin Sunday School. This was another fortunate accident, for Violet Martin gained more than a familiarity with the Scriptures which was rewarded by a pile of handsomely

bound, unreadable, prize books. It was at the Sunday School
that she absorbed a knowledge of the lives and feelings of a
world different from her own, which was to blossom in the
brilliant opening chapter of *The Real Charlotte*. It is possible
to speculate that Mrs Martin may have shared with Mrs Fitzpatrick, as there described, the habit of mountainous repose on
a Sunday afternoon, assured that her child's religious training
was in hand. Also she must have shared with Mrs Fitzpatrick
the opinion that it was no indignity that this should take place
in the company of the children of her grocer and her chemist.
Meanwhile in the Sunday School, with its tedious lessons, and
boisterous outings, her daughter escaped from the towering
personalities of her brothers and sisters. Edith Somerville,
Head Dog in her family, had little need for such relief from the
pressures around her, but for Violet Martin to be admired by
her teachers as a prodigy, and revered by her fellows as an
oracle, must have been a stimulating change from her bob-tail
position at home. The best prize she brought away with her
was the reward of having lived among free-booting Dublin
children at an age when she was receptive to the characteristics
of their speech and behaviour.

When Montaigne wished to explain the affinity between
himself and his dead, much-loved friend Etienne de la Boétie
he summed up the matter in the words, '*parce que c'était moi,
parce que c'était lui*'. Left alone, also by an untimely cutting-off,
Edith Somerville tried to crystallize the day when she and
Violet Martin found a deep response in each other. She called
the moment of their meeting 'the hinge of my life', but she
might well have said, with Montaigne, '*parce que c'était moi,
parce que c'était elle*'. The encounter, as has been said, took place
in Castletownshend Church, where Edith, delegated as organist
by her mother from the day her legs were long enough to
reach the pedals, at once conscripted her second cousin Violet
to sing in the choir. Barracking by Mrs Somerville, on the subject of her successor's efforts to keep the choir in tune, was
only one of the hazards faced by those who praised the Lord
in the church, dedicated to a local saint called Barrahane. Later
Edith, herself, had a liking for what she called 'taking the choir
across country', which must have added a new terror to the
words 'o'er moor and fen, o'er crag and torrent'.

Knowing only of the Martins by hearsay, as cousins whose home in Dublin was a family clearing house, Edith Somerville was not particularly prepossessed in their favour, praise from one of her brothers having inspired her with a contrary prejudice. The meeting in January was followed by a complete capitulation. By the time she returned to Paris for further work at Colarossi's she had already begun to despair of making a satisfactory portrait of Violet Martin's fresh and delicate looks. It was in the summer months which followed that the devotion, binding them to each other for the next thirty years, grew in strength with the fine weather, and with its growth came the beginning of their literary partnership.

Among the Martins the composition of prose, verse and music was a natural element, giving a sparkle to the everyday air of family life. Robert Martin took theatrical advantage of his horde of siblings from the age of eight, when he directed a performance of 'Bluebeard'. He was assisted by Tucker, an eccentric hedge-schoolmaster, first employed at Ross to teach in the little school started during the Famine, and remaining as tutor to the children, assistant secretary to their father and poet-laureate to the whole family. Although commanding a company of players who could, if necessary, be controlled by force, Robert Martin had such a contempt for his sisters' histrionic abilities that, in one production, he took the part of the heroine himself, borrowing a dress from the largest among them. The big scene, his elopement with Tucker, was wrecked by the dress splitting from neck to hem.

In her unfinished memoir of her brother Robert, Violet gave an outline of his career in the years when Ross had fallen into strange and despoiling hands. She described his success as a journalist and song-writer in London, where he earned the nickname of 'Ballyhooly', the title of his greatest hit. She remembered the fascination of London with Robert as a host, producing theatre tickets and literary introductions to entertain his visiting kinswomen. She balanced this against the neglect of Ross. This neglect further loosened the bonds of affection, which had seemed, in Violet's childhood, to encircle the Martins and their tenants. When Robert returned to Ireland he undertook the dangerous work of going out as an 'Emergency man', to bring labour and goods to boycotted landlords. Sinking in his last illness (he died at Oughterard, the village nearest to Ross) Robert reflected on these past days, when economic chaos had led to a brutal sequence of outrage and reprisal, believing that murder as a political weapon had been introduced into Northern Connemara by tradesmen imported to work on Kylemore Castle.

The Phoenix Park murders in 1882 may be considered as a manifestation of the same philosophy. Violet Martin wrote of the trial that followed in a mood close to mysticism, struggling to weigh the tender age of the youngest conspirator and the agony of his mother, against the ruthlessness with which the victims had been slaughtered. As an epitaph on the murders she quoted words from a mission sermon, preached in Irish, long before, on a hill behind Ross. The words had been translated for Violet Martin as she kept a death watch in a cottage on a winter's night. 'Oh, black seas of Eternity, without height or depth, bay, brink or shore. How can anyone look into your depths and neglect the salvation of his soul?'

The administration of relief to sufferers in the 'Bad Times' gave Violet Martin a subject for her first article, sold to *The Irish Times*. This was followed by a series in *The World*, signed 'Martin Ross'. As it was the name by which her cousin and collaborator invariably spoke and wrote of her it seems suitable, from now on, to use this style. Edith had published a short story in *The Argosy*, dismissed by herself as replete with faults of conventionality and sensationalism, and with this experience behind them she suggested to Martin that a book, written in collaboration and with Edith's illustrations, might be a profitable speculation.

In Martin's childhood at Ross the family had been held enthralled by hair-raising stories told by a cousin, Willie Wills, a great nephew of Charles Kendal Bushe. Terence de Vere White considers it probable that some employment with the Wills family, rather than kinship, was the reason for the name to be found in Oscar Wilde's pedigree, given to both his brother and Oscar. William Gorman Wills was successful as a dramatist and a portrait painter, but he lived a life of wildest Bohemian squalor, in a studio where the bad habits of his pets were only equalled by the parasitism of his human hangers-on. Mr de Vere White has also remarked 'that everything [in Ireland] however unrelated at first, eventually connects with everything else'. W. G. Wills may well have had an influence on Wilde—one of his early serials was called by the evocative title of *The Love that Kills*—but there is a hint that he may also have set Somerville and Ross on their joint path. Edith records that the rumour that Willie Wills and another cousin were said to be collaborating in a new popular style of cheap novels, the 'Shilling Shocker'. To Martin and herself this seemed to be a promising field of literary opportunity.

A summer of wonderful weather helped the new friends to discover the depths of their sympathy. Their minds began to weave together, so that later their style had the quality of shot-silk, where the colour changes but the texture remains constant. Endlessly exploring each other's thought, they lay on the cliffs above Castlehaven, with a paint-box as an excuse for deserting the bathers, squealing gull-like in the cove below. The following summer, Queen Victoria's Golden Jubilee Year, brought another succession of brilliant days, with evenings so calm that boatloads could row out to the mouth of the harbour under an August moon, paddling into what seemed to be 'a sea of opal oil'. In the October of that year they were encouraged by a local fortune-teller, who, in addition to promising the two young ladies at least three husbands between them, foretold literary success in a strong Co. Cork accent. Buoyed up by this prophecy they began to plan a book.

First obstacle in their path was a fusillade of surprisingly derisive objection fired from the family circle. Neither of them had been brought up in the physical bonds which had imprisoned an earlier generation of Victorian young ladies. They had not had their lives circumscribed by a round of occupations so futile that, according to Florence Nightingale, many healthy and intelligent young women went to bed at night physically ill from pent-up interior fires. Mrs Somerville, nervously mistrustful of horses, had not attempted to control her daughter's exploits on the backs of these dangerous beasts. Neither had this town-bred mother estimated the dangers of the rocks, celebrated by Swift in a Latin poem 'Carberiae Rupes', across which her children bounded, goat-footed. The mother of Martin Ross had a disregard for danger and relish for adventure already mentioned. Nevertheless the nineteenth-century law,

that parents of talented daughters should obstruct any attempt
to make professional use of these talents, now came into operation. Publishing, it was felt, rubbed off some of the maiden
bloom, a delicate commodity, mostly appreciated by those who
had forgotten the handicaps inevitable to its possession.
Charlotte M. Yonge, who wrote ceaselessly until the age of
seventy-eight, never ceased to remember John Keble's warning
that a successful book might well be the worst temptation of
her life. At about the time that the cousins were working
on their first book, Miss Yonge could still describe a female
writer whose parents did not object to her profitable literary
career, so long as it did not obtrude unduly on their notice.

Consequently the climate was unfavourable when it became
apparent that, under the roof of Drishane, there were two strays
from the flock, renegades evading tennis and picnics. Resent-
ment was felt by all at this defection, but it took different forms
and expressions. A staunch upholder of the fourth command-
ment, Charlotte Yonge would, in principle, have supported
Mrs Somerville's objections, though she might have been
shaken by that mother's habit of putting down restlessness in
her children by a blanketing reference to 'your-own-good-
home-and-what-more-do-you-want'. It is also unlikely that
Miss Yonge would have allowed a mother of her creation to
copy Mrs Somerville and call the aspiring writers the 'Hugger-
Muggers'. The rest of the family varied their abuse from talking of 'that nonsense of the girls' to mockingly christening
them 'The Geniuses'. They were said to be arrogant in their
project, wasteful of their time in pursuing it, and selfish in
detaching themselves as playmates from the young crowd
around them. As they were both in their twenties this attitude
does, in fact, recall the family tyranny exerted over Florence
Nightingale, who only gained her freedom of action by agreeing to submit totally to the whims of her sister for months
beforehand. The Somerville circle, affectionately extrovert,
differed as high noon does from twilight when compared with
the neurotic tensions of the Nightingale home, but the tradition that exacted from unmarried daughters a devotion to
everyone's interests except their own still obtained.

The workings of this tradition were sufficiently strong to
produce opposition that gave the collaborators a feeling of

persecution, irritating but essentially stimulating. It must have been an additional grievance that the family were also deprived of the refuge of a studio, where a painter at work possesses what is described in *Dan Russel the Fox* as 'the restful quality of something at anchor'. The practice of literature, on the other hand, could be followed in any hiding place with elbow room. Edith wrote later that they were treated with the 'disapproving suffrance that is shown to an outside dog that sneaks into the house on a wet day'. With some reason they compared themselves to the Waldenses and Albigenses.

Between themselves The Geniuses at first referred to the book they had planned as The Shocker, or The Shaughram, the latter being synonymous with sentimental language and artificial situations. They wanted to make their fortunes, and fancied that they could do so by concocting excitement for the reader, while keeping themselves detached from both emotion and art. While their project was in this embryonic state they had an encounter which changed their point of view, raising their ambitions and their talents to a higher literary endeavour.

When, in 1917, Edith wrote *Irish Memories* she had still a raw wound from the loss of Martin, dead two years before. The book was partly a memorial to their first meeting and the beginning of their collaboration, but when she recalled the day that transformed 'The Shocker', she forgot, for a while her grief in the interest of the event. Martin, in an interview they both gave in 1896, had referred to this slightly blood-chilling episode as marking a change in their point of view when they were in the early stages of their novel. It was Edith, left alone, who gave the details.

They had ridden more than ten miles to a lonely house near Cape Clear, the home of an old spinster kinswoman. Outside there was a ruined castle on the cliff, and an immense hedge of juniper, protecting the flower garden from the Atlantic, and shading also the tomb of a pet dog, with the epitaph:

'Lily, a violet-shrouded tomb of woe.'

Inside the house the past was already dying, their hostess herself belonging to an earlier age. Her great-grandfather, 'Splendid Ned', had been a dashing officer in the County of Cork Militia Dragoons. Her grandfather had raised a troop of

Yeomanry against the Whiteboys, the militant Nationalists of his day. Disbanded by the English government, the yeomen, in a fury, had pitched their arms over the cliffs, redressing the balance of this defiance by drinking the King's health in smuggled claret. The descendant of these rakish forebears was charmingly frail and gentle, with an accent at once well-bred and Irish of an older fashion. She called her cousin 'Eddith', a pronunciation entirely her own. She addressed her manservant, half butler, half coachman, as 'Dinnis', and asked her guests to take a glass of wine with her. The need to eat a tea as vast as their luncheon delayed their start for home until nearly evening, but apparently throughout the day they had felt no more than an amused interest at a visit to a house left behind by the rush of life as they knew it.

'The sunset was red in the west when our horses were brought round to the door, and it was at that precise moment that into *An Irish Cousin* some thrill of genuineness was breathed. In the darkened façade of the long grey house, a window, just over the hall door, caught our attention. In it, for an instant, was a white face. Trails of ivy hung over the panes, but we saw the face glimmer there for a minute and vanish.

'As we rode home along the side of the hills and watched the fires of the sunset sink into the sea, and met the crescent moon coming with faint light to light us home, we could talk and think only of that presence at the window. We had been warned of certain subjects not to be approached, and knew enough of the history of that old house to realize what we had seen. An old stock, isolated from the world at large, wearing itself out in those excesses that are a protest of human nature against unnatural conditions, dies at last with its victims round its death-bed. Half-acknowledged, half-witted, wholly horrifying; living ghosts, haunting the house that gave them but half their share of life, yet withheld from them, with half-hearted guardianship, the boon of death.'

Surviving photographs give an idea of how Edith and Martin looked as they rode home through the October evening, talking of the apparition at the window. Safety skirts had eliminated some of the worst perils facing side-saddle riders, but decency required that the ankle in the stirrup should be covered, and this meant that the leg over the pommel was still heavily draped. Martin sat lightly in the saddle, but, according to Edith, this casual air concealed an absolute firmness in control of the horse. Her chestnut hair was less in control, and, though she rode fearlessly, her progress was made perilous by the short-sight, so endemic among the Martins that it was said in their own country to be 'a sign of their nobility'. Edith wore her side-saddle habit with an elegance not even diminished by the common-place *chapeau melon*. 'Springing through the country', as their hostess had assured them that they would, they rode home, their health and talent in brilliant contrast with the tragically rotting household left behind them.

3
The Irish cousins at work

THE novel, *An Irish Cousin*, as worked out by the collaborators, was certainly no shocker, its more menacing
aspects being somewhat played down. An orphan of about
twenty, Theo Sarsfield arrives from Canada to stay with her
father's brother Dominick and his son Willie. It is not exactly
clear who is the Irish Cousin of the title, for Theo may be
considered to be Canadian, and Willie, though a leading character, can hardly be intended to give the story its name.
Possibly in the fascination of their new-made relationship the
title represented a reflection of themselves to the authors.
Durrus, in Co. Cork, the home of the Sarsfields, has an air
both haphazard and sinister, baffling to Theo from the evening
of her arrival. As a character she is not entirely convincing, her
reflections being often more suitable for a sophisticated woman
than for a young girl in a world unknown to her. However,
as one of the family, she receives hints from the tenants of past
wrongs and present hauntings, while her relations with the
Sarsfields, father and son, become ever more tangled.

Indoors at Durrus, Theo is conscious of a Brontë-esque
threat from Mollie Hourihane, who haunts the house where
she has once been nurse, a speechless haunting, for the woman
is dumb from a past shock. She lives in the gate-lodge with a
daughter, a cast-off sweetheart of Willie's, and a husband
who is prepared to make profitable trouble from this situation.

The local gentry are headed by The O'Neill, descended from
a Sept, and so indigenous, compared with Norman or later
English settlers such as the Sarsfields. The Miss O'Neills are
barely sketched in. Nugent, their brother, a musical bore, is
obviously destined to marry Theo, but The O'Neill himself
bounces off the page. ' "Mind you," said Willie, "He's a great
old buck and expects every girl who goes to Clashmore to
make love to him." ' The great old buck, an unsuitable parent

for the refined Nugent, flaunts a loud suit topped by a scarlet countenance. With what attention he can spare from carving two muscular duck, he makes advances to Theo, which she parries before her prim hostess, Madam O'Neill, can take offence. Willie, jealous of Nugent's wealth and education, becomes exasperated by Theo's tendency to sneak off to play duets with the heir of The O'Neill. Willie makes matters worse by proposing to Theo at a dance in the house of a local squireen. A conservatory is available, but he chooses instead to press his suit, knowing intuitively that it will fail, in a den where bills hang on the wall beside the host's old coat in a fog of whiskey fumes, turf smoke and tobacco. These surroundings are symbolical of Willie's handicaps, but the story comes to life whenever he is present. Even Theo is always more interested in him than in the blameless Nugent, who lacks any characteristic beyond an unattractive tendency to make fun of his neighbours' primitive habits.

As the original of Durrus was the old house which Edith and Martin had visited, so the original of the graveyard where Theo thinks over her problems must have been the old burying ground at Castlehaven. Theo watches a funeral party arriving in a small fleet of boats, and listens chilled to the heart as the Irish cry is raised. Mollie Hourihane is miming the gestures which accompany keening, when another country woman tells Theo that the dumb Mollie and her Uncle Dominick are linked by a hideous secret in the past. Dominick's addiction to drink might well be the refuge of a guilty conscience. The crisis boils over, with Willie marrying the girl from the Lodge and sailing to Australia. Mollie, it appears, had always claimed illegitimate first cousin-hood with the Sarsfields, and in that capacity had helped Uncle Dominick in the inheritance of Durrus by manipulating the death of Theo's father in a manner close to murder.

Dominick, after an attack of *delirium tremens* augmented by guilt, apologizes to Theo for the traffic in the avenue, ' "... these hackney car men, who make it a practice to drive past the house at all hours of the night . . . I have told them several times to go away, but they simply laugh at me. And the strange thing is that," he continued . . . "though I gave orders that the lodge gates should always be locked at night, it does not stop them in the least—they simply drive through them." ' Phantom

B

coaches were omens of death in the Sarsfield family, and
Dominick meets a violent end, keened by Moll Hourihane, who
is shocked back into the power of speech. Theo and Nugent
are left in possession of each other and presumably of Durrus,
a house of their own being a necessity, considering Madam
O'Neill's disapproval of her husband's fancy for young ladies.

Like the ghostly hackney car, Somerville and Ross drove the
plot of *An Irish Cousin* without paying much heed to obstacles
in their path. Theo's background gets little attention; she
appears from Canada after a voyage spent in a vacuum of sea-
sickness which seems to have obliterated her early life. Uncle
Dominick seems to have had an affair with Moll Hourihane, so
might he have been the father of Anstey who marries Willie?
His drinking concealed, perhaps, a horror of incest as well
as remorse for a possible murder. Tragic villains, such as
Dominick, do not appear in any of the subsequent novels, but
Willie is the first, and by no means the least skilfully drawn, of
a long line of buckeen portraits. These young men have an
ability to fascinate girls with experience of wider worlds.
Dazzled by skill in equitation, always beguiling from its aura
of the dangerous and difficult easily performed, inequalities of
education are overlooked. A more attractive suitor prevents
Theo from falling in love with a semi-literate horseman, but
later heroines, such as Kathleen Rowan and Peggy Weldon,
suffer cruelly when the bleak dawn of disillusion breaks over
the landscape of their infatuation. Only in the case of Sally
Knox, who has moments of being the heroine of *Some Experiences of An Irish R.M.*, does the affair end with a happy
elopement, Flurry Knox's expectations from the magpie hoards
of his grandmother reconciling Sally's parents to Flurry's
variable position on the slippery middle slopes of their clan.

Convoluted as the plot of *An Irish Cousin* sometimes becomes, the writers had already developed the power of putting
down what things look like that was to be the essence of their
style. In the ancient graveyard Theo watches the mourners,
'black figures dotted about among the grey stones with their
background of pale blue sky'. These are painter's notes, composition, tone and colour being almost a plan for a picture.
The painter's eye of Edith, and the sense of artistic discipline
fortunately possessed by Martin, working together produced

descriptions of landscape and physical appearances which
convey to the reader a pleasure almost sensuous in its intensity.
If characters occasionally appear who may seem no more than
mouthpieces for witticisms, or vehicles to assist the plot, their
clothes, their houses, and the country around them never
fail to carry conviction. The graveyard with the scattered
mourners is heavy with the dignity of death and grief, but
the dusty study where Willie proposes to Theo leaves as deep
an impression, though it is one of squalor and decay.

The finished book was given to Edith's mother to read. 'She
loathes it', her daughter wrote in her diary. No one in their
families was willing to take the book seriously, somehow combining a wish that the enterprise should be secret with, in Mrs
Somerville's case, 'blazoning it to the end of the earth *and*
Aunt X'.

Martin's life now took a dramatic turn. *An Irish Cousin* had
been refused, without comment, by one publisher and left with
a friend to deal with as he thought fit, when Mrs Martin
decided to return to Ross. It was a brave decision on her part,
but its consequences fell heavily on her youngest daughter.
However, the change also gave Martin the opportunity to look
back at her childhood with the eyes of her grown-up imagination. When Mrs Hewson, an elder sister, arrived on a visit a
welcoming bonfire was built at the gate as Martin had seen it
as a child. She wrote to Edith that their account of such a
scene in 'The Shocker' had been truthful, 'the circle of faces lit
by the glow from the sticks on top of the turf,' the old steward
taking off his hat in courtly welcome, and refreshment with
porter for the company. She made a writer's note that it was
different from her father's time '. . . to see Geraldine walk in
front of us through the wide open gates, between the tall
pillars, with her white face and her black clothes'.

Other scenes were comic as well as touching, encouraging
Martin in her struggle to repair not only the house and garden,
but the confidence of the tenants in the family of Martin. On a
Sunday evening an active old man came to pay a call of welcome, kissing hands, invoking saints, and finally rushing into
the hall.

' "Dance, Paddy!" screamed Nurse Barrett (my foster-
mother and now our maid of all work).

'And he did dance, and awfully well too, to his own singing. Mama, who was attired in a flowing pink dressing-gown, and a black hat trimmed with lilac, became emulous, and, with her spade under her arm, joined in the jig. This lasted for about a minute and was a never to be forgotten sight. They skipped round the hall, they changed sides, they swept up to each other and back again, and finished with deepest curtseys . . .' As an additional stage direction, it should be mentioned that, in her family, a comment on Mrs Martin's size was a comparison of her adhesiveness to an outside car to that of a poached egg to a piece of toast. Although no explanation for her costume, surprisingly informal for a Sunday evening, is given, it is delightful to find that Mrs Martin was still so light on her elegant feet, and that the hall of Ross, with its staircase rising to the roof three floors above, had gay moments to compensate for the dark hours when keening had pierced the heart of the house.

Later, a younger generation brought its own gaiety to Ross. Lionel Dawson, the child of Martin's sister Edith and her husband, a colonel of Dragoons, remembered beginning his remarkable equestrian career on the donkeys and Connemara ponies, both grown fat and wicked on the Ross grazing. Captain Dawson's parents had joined in the family's attempt to salvage the estate, and a flock of little cousins pattered to church on donkeys without saddles to their backs or bridles on their heads.

In the earlier days of the restoration, Martin, as one who coaxes a return of confidence in a frightened animal, set herself to lure the friends of her childhood back to her. A tea-party for local children was nearly wrecked by the nervousness of parents and teachers. Both feared reprisals from the Land League should they allow their children to accept tea and slices of barm brack (a spiced currant loaf essential to Irish school treats) from those who might be subject to a sudden boycott. The position of Ross was awkward beyond the ordinary, the parish priest being a fanatical Land Leaguer with a contempt for the hierarchy of his church which would, in an earlier age, have led him to the stake and faggots. Reprimanded by his bishop for his political extremism, he took his appeal to Rome in person, but lost his case, returning to

Galway dispossessed of his parish. He was met by a brass band, which, leading his parishioners in procession, accompanied him to his home fifteen miles away.

His parishioners' loyalty did not end with this demonstration. For many months afterwards, Martin Ross wrote, the majority shunned the chapel of the newly accredited priest, setting out in the opposite direction to hear the Mass of the rebel, in the green and white Land League Hut, for which he had collected the funds. At least one tragedy was caused by this bitter religious dissension. In January 1892 Martin wrote that one might wish for oneself for the passion for death that was in a young fellow, weak-minded, but steady and very devout, who had disappeared on Saint Stephen's Day. He had been cutting a rope of ferns with his brother, and slipped away at a moment when his brother's attention was distracted. Those seeking him found his scapular and Agnus Dei lying on a stone beside 'an awful pond' called Poulleen-a-férla. It was believed that no one could drown with those round their neck.

'They hooked him up from among the sunken branches of trees, and found him by getting a boat on to the pool and staring down in all lights. Finally they wrapped a stone in a white flannel "bauneen" and dropped it in. They were just able to see where it lay, and it placed things for them, so that they at last recognized some dim companion shadow as what they were searching for, and got it out.' The latter went on to explain that he had been deluded into shortening the chain of the Chapel bell, by people too cowardly to meddle with it themselves, but determined that the bell should not ring for the new priest's Mass. The trick had sent the boy into a state of brooding misery, which finally drove him to cast himself, and his remorse for the innocent sacrilege, into the black shadows of Poulleen-a-férla, the little pool of the pearl. Martin dealt with the story almost as if she was writing a ballad, contrasting the violence of the tragedy of the drowned 'sacred fool', against the slowness of the actions necessary for the recovery of his body.

Six months after the return to Ross, the firm of R. Bentley and Sons offered £25 as an advance with £25 on the first five hundred copies of *An Irish Cousin*. Martin wrote in her diary: 'Wrote a dizzy letter of acceptance to Bentley, and went to church, twice, in a glorified trance.' An elated double church-going, compared by Edith to the sudden appearance of her huntsman at the priest's night school, after he had brought off the feat, rare in West Carbery, of killing two foxes in one morning.

In the interval between the acceptance and publication of *An Irish Cousin* Martin began a series of articles for *The World* on conditions in Galway as she had found them on her return. The editor, Edith wrote, had an enthusiasm for Martin's writing which more than counterbalanced the minuteness of the cheque which came from his cashier. Martin's family, on the other hand, already burdened by the necessity of absorbing *Robert Elsmere*, Mrs Humphrey Ward's best-seller, resented having to give serious attention to articles written by 'one of the girls'. Martin analysed the articles: 'I heap together descriptions with a few carefully constructed moralities interspersed, and hide behind them, so that no one shall discern my ignorance and hesitation.' This pitiless estimate of her own powers was an example of the fastidiousness of Martin's literary standards. Her diary at the age of thirteen, as quoted by Maurice Collis in *Somerville and Ross*, shows that she wrote, even at that age with a clear perception of human behaviour and a strong natural authority.

Largely from the work of its youngest daughter, Ross had been restored from a derelict Castle of Sleeping Beauty to a habitable house, but these exertions and journalism had cut down the time Martin could spend on work with Edith. The latter, still regarding herself as primarily a painter, had become entangled in commitments to illustrate a children's book, and an Irish song of the Crimean War, *The Kerry Recruit*. It was not until the success of *An Irish Cousin* had been followed by that of *Naboth's Vineyard*, their second novel, that they decided to shun distracting side-lines and concentrate on a longer novel. The germ had been for some time alive in their minds, and, as *The Real Charlotte*, the book was to grow into their master-piece.

Looking back, Edith Somerville considered that the success of *An Irish Cousin* was partly due to the lack of competitors in its particular field. A generation earlier Charles Lever's novels had been immensely popular, bequeathing the all-too-immortal figure of the 'rollicking' stage-Irishman to avid English readers, but this writer had been an expatriate, working mostly from notes. Since the appearance of *Castle Rackrent* eighty-eight years earlier there had been few, if any, novels about the Irish countryside and its people, written from the point of view of someone who, like Maria Edgeworth, had this as the background of their everyday life.

Firmly partisan, Mrs Martin was greatly incensed by a letter criticizing an article of Martin's. The writer she had regarded as her oldest ally, and she went about saying indignantly, at intervals, 'Knee-buckles to a Highlander' as her opinion of the use of this old friend's comments. However another letter from a Galway neighbour, Sir William Gregory of Coole Park, was more encouraging, for, with his wife Augusta, he was known to have many 'literary friends'. Sir William promised that they would both do their utmost to help *An Irish Cousin*, and trusted that conscience would permit him to praise it with 'trumpets and shawms'. To fix the relationship in time of Somerville and Ross to the Irish literary movement of the nineties, it should be mentioned that Lady Gregory had not yet become the friend and patron of W. B. Yeats. In 1889 she was under forty, with the Dublin Abbey Theatre below the horizon. (There she became, eventually, a veteran autocrat, her mere refusal giving a title to Denis Johnston's play, *The Old Lady Says 'No!'*) That same year Yeats, a poor young man in London, wrote the imperishable 'Down by the Salley Gardens.' In due course he helped Martin to carve her initials on the tree at Coole, dedicated to the Muses by Lady Gregory.

Each comfortably convinced that their own child had done all the work, Mrs Somerville and Mrs Martin found that only together could they do justice to the prowess of their daughters, and excoriate the unconverted who passed over their achievements in silence. The reviews of *An Irish Cousin* were good, *The Spectator* being particularly kind, but there were critics who questioned the possibility, or even the wisdom, of continuing to write in collaboration. Martin disposed of this objection by writing to Edith that, as they had proved it could be done, they would do it again, adding that for her writing together halved the toil and doubled the pleasure. Edith shared this opinion, but they found a reverse law operated when, their

fame having grown, one or the other happened to be revealed
as half of a literary team. To the imbecility of the usual questions asked of writers, 'Do you write in the morning/in the
afternoon/with a pen/with a pencil?' could be added an
examination as to 'Whose hand held the pen/who did the
words/who did the story?' Edith was, however, somewhat dis-
armed by a lady who, after satisfying herself as to how the
actual writing was done, found on further inquiry that people
were sometimes 'put in' whom the collaborators had never met.
' "Well! I declare, (said she) that's like direct inspiration." '

Their two families might be reconciled to their daughters
becoming professional writers, but they were themselves hope-
lessly unprofessional in their dealings with publishers. Arrangements for *Naboth's Vineyard* were left in the hands of a clerical
acquaintance, who sold the copyright outright. This led to the
book first appearing with a frontispiece that must have irked
Edith by the neatness of the shoes and stockings worn by a farm
girl putting linen out to bleach. It then appeared as a 'yellow-
back', passed through Tauchnitz, and was finally issued for 4d.,
bound like a devotional manual with silver edges to the leaves,
its Biblical title presumably having deluded some religious, if
piratical, publishing house.

Naboth's Vineyard, a sombre book, full of dark wooded paths,
and darker plots in sordid back rooms, has a love story of a
pattern favoured by Trollope. A wilful Beauty, Harriet, jilts a
handsome young man, O'Grady, for a rich Beast, Donovan,
and finds, when she has second thoughts, that O'Grady has
fallen in love with Ellen, a kindlier, truer girl. Donovan uses
the Land League (of which all the characters are subscribing
members) to organize a boycott against the Widow Leonard,
mother of Ellen. It should be explained that the Land League,
in theory, operated to prevent landlords, who had evicted
tenants in arrears, from letting their farms to others for higher
rents. In *Naboth's Vineyard* there is no such neighbourly motive
for the boycott, Donovan, a gombeen man or usurer, being
intent on ousting the Widow Leonard from grazing land
coveted by himself.

O'Grady has a fishpacking business, and most of the population are at work on a bumper catch of mackerel when the
dramatic climax of the book begins.

'The lamps shone fantastically on the double row of intent faces, on the quickly moving arms of the women, crimsoned to the elbows, on the tables, varnished with the same colour, and on the cold silvery heaps of fish. The dark hollow of the night seemed impenetrable beyond this island of light; the frail young moon that had just shown above the trees of Traharta woods . . . had set long before, and the only stars that had not been blotted out by the clouds were those that twinkled at the mastheads of the fishing boats in the middle of the harbour.'

Above the groups of 'wild Rembrandtish women' a strange glow rises in the sky over the dark woods. O'Grady and Donovan set out with a boatload to investigate, but in mid-channel discover that the flames come from the house of the boycotted Widow Leonard. Donovan, again misusing the authority of the Land League, orders the rowers to turn back. When his attempt to rally the rowers, by exposing Donovan's machinations, fails, O'Grady plunges overboard and swims ashore, illogically cheered by some of the men. The widow's house, beasts and daughter are saved. The incendiary, an instrument of Donovan's, had broken his leg after only setting fire to a hay-rick. Harriet Donovan has a triumphant moment when she fancies that O'Grady has returned to her, and that it is he who has arranged for her husband to fall through a bridge to his death. This trap turns out to have been the work of a half-crazed farm boy, in love with Ellen, and so hoping to eliminate O'Grady. Disowned by the central committee, the district branch of the Land League ceases to be active. Harriet retreats into a religious order, where she must have been a problem to the Sisters. Suddenly the sun comes out on the last pages of the book, when O'Grady and Ellen are free from their troubles, and the Widow Leonard, whose mouth has previously held nothing but curses for her enemies, gives way to ribald laughter at the ways of lovers.

The authors were almost alarmed at the respect and seriousness with which the political aspects of the story were considered by *The Spectator*, *The Saturday Review* and *The Times*. Accustomed to the Irish mixture of fierce loyalties among families contrasted with harsh dealings with others, they had not expected that the book would be treated as a contribution to the understanding of the Irish Question. Rossbrin, the little fishing town in the novel, was decorated by Edith and Martin with the two trees, tall sycamores, which still stand in the middle of Castletownshend's cliff-like main street, but otherwise there is little from their own life in *Naboth's Vineyard*. It is a story of publicans, small shopkeepers, and struggling farmers, almost ignoring the gentry and the poorer peasantry. Landlords are barely mentioned, except in so far as they defy the Land League from the personal security of the absentee. Peasants, Irish-speaking and retaining the customs of earlier centuries, are treated contemptuously by those who have raised themselves to wearing broadcloth instead of frieze, hats instead of shawls. One of the best scenes in the book shows the boycotted mother and daughter leaving Mass on All Saints' Day, when the sneers of their neighbours are as much for their shawled heads as for their political immorality. Donovan, the gombeen man, carries complete conviction, from his first appearance, making up his accounts with a stack of leases, dirty IOUs, and farm inventories in a tin box beside him, to his final exit, a corpse floating in the river mud, with his dead hand dragging the epileptic farm boy, in his turn, down to death. Treacherous in all his dealings, with a manner oily or bullying as the occasion required, it is still possible to believe that Donovan suffered hideously from his wife's baleful treatment; allowing him to go unwarned across the bridge she knew to be holed is only the climax of a course of marital torture.

Impressed by the praise of *Naboth's Vineyard*, Edith and Martin decided that they must buckle down to write a work in three volumes, as much the standard practice for presenting a novel as it had been in the days of Maria Edgeworth. As it happened this plan was, for the moment, shelved, and they found themselves following in the footsteps of Miss Edgeworth on the journey which had led her to write her *Tour of Connemara*. Conditions had improved since 1833, but Somerville and Ross do not seem to have been acquainted with this book which is a warning against impulsive travel in the West of Ireland.

4

My second cousin and I

THE journey through Connemara was a counter-attack on the chatty vulgarity of a current guide book, whose ultimate insult was a regret that the Martins of Galway, described as a family of 'Cromwellian origin', had ceased to be. Outraged, Edith and Martin wrote the tale of their own tour, which, after appearing, with illustrations, in *The Lady's Pictorial*, was published as *Through Connemara in a Governess Cart*. Like the rest of their travel books, this work was light in manner, but rich in candid observation and comment.

Prospective tourists were left in no doubt as to the rigours that they might expect, particularly if they started to Galway from lodgings in Bayswater, and travelled by way of Milfordhaven to Cork, a voyage involving twelve hours' imprisonment in the ladies' cabin. The next ordeal was to cross Cork on an outside car. The authors remarked that they, unlike other guide books, did not recommend English travellers to hold on to the sides of the car. Claiming to have gone to their christening on an outside car, they said they had not held on then, and had not done so since. There was something of 'Crampton dash' about this statement, as Edith was, indisputably, christened on Corfu, and though Martin may have travelled on an outside car when she was received into the congregation, she was baptized in the drawing-room at Ross, by a cousin, later Archbishop of Dublin, who administered the sacrament from a silver slop basin. A further rap on English knuckles was a warning that the Irish word for the national fuel is turf. It was therefore to be understood that when the writers said 'turf' they meant peat, 'and when, if ever, we say Pete we mean the diminutive of Peter, no matter what the spelling'. This slightly waspish note was made after they had endured the endless railway crawl through Limerick, Ennis and Athenry to Galway, sharing a carriage with children who were fed continuously in a cycle of seed cake, milk and oranges.

During abortive negotiations to hire a vehicle the beggars of Galway recognized Martin, adding personal endearments to their petitions. The narrative runs as if written by Edith, and she recorded that all other beggars were routed by a deep voice from the level of the step of the carriage, 'Sure ye'll give to your own little Judy from Memlo.' The voice belonged to a seventy-year old nightmare of two foot nothing, 'well aware of the compelling power of her appalling presence'.

The pretence that Martin, the native of Co. Galway, was being observed by her cousin from the outside, allowed for an objective glimpse of her character, as well as for selectiveness in giving information. On their way to Oughterard on the mail-car the travellers must have passed Ross, easily seen from the road, but desolate houses and broken demesne walls were only mentioned in general terms. Silence and a protruding lower lip showed that Martin was brooding on the available horseflesh in her native village. Finally, ignoring the warning 'They mules is neither here nor there' given by an aged female onlooker, they hired a governess cart, to be drawn by a jennet called Sibbie. This jennet must have been bred from a distinctive local strain, for, judging from the book's illustrations, collateral descendants can still be seen looking over stone walls outside Oughterard. Swerving out of the town—Sibbie had various gateways she preferred to the open road—Martin's local pride led her to point out that this was the most prosperous village on that side of Galway. Not long ago it had been said of the widows' almshouse, 'sorra widdy in it, but one little owld man', and now, Martin added, it was simply bursting with widows.

Besides a gingham umbrella, the travellers had equipped themselves with a spirit lamp, and what Edith called 'its glittering bride, the tin kettle'. At a pinch this could be used to fill the rubber bath without which they never took the road, the tin baths of hotels being only too often reserved for heavily tipping male travellers. With a vague idea of protection against the perils of the road such as mad dogs, Martin had also secretly imported an old and rusty revolver. The hideous political murders of previous years had caused the district to be 'proclaimed', which meant that all firearms should be handed to the authorities, so that the revolver, and its ammunition, packed in a box of Easy Hair Curlers, was flagrantly illegal. Faced by a menacing bulldog Martin Ross actually fired a shot, when the revolver threw so high that her arm went up in the air as if hailing a cab. The shot went wide, but the report stampeded a herd of cattle, the bulldog hanging grimly to the nose of the leading cow. When *Through Connemara in a Governess Cart* was published as a book, a version of this scene was engraved in purple and yellow on its green cover. It was no more than a version as, without permission, the Editor of *The Lady's Pictorial* had given Edith's sketches to a feebler hand to be toned-down. The drawing of Little Judy from Memlo had been suppressed altogether, as 'calculated to shock delicate ladies'. Other sketches had been so softened and refined that the travellers appeared to have spent their time in a state of lady-like neatness, hardly disturbed when Sibbie, the jennet, bolted. Seated on window seats or grassy banks they yearned, most uncharacteristically, at the landscape. Even the act of firing a revolver at a bulldog became positively decorous.

Although supposedly written for the enlightenment of travellers, the book was far from encouraging to tourists, and less than complimentary about them. There was a mention, in passing, of an accident of the year before, when a young man had rushed unduly fast down a mountain to be found next day, dead and mutilated, at the foot of a precipice. Emphasis was also laid on the more humdrum agonies to be endured from midges, particularly by those stationary targets, fishermen, the eternal boredom of these sportsmen's conversation at the table d'hôte being made even more unpleasing by the crimson spottedness of their faces. Walking in the woods of Ballanahinch the cousins heard splash after splash from the rising salmon, but never throughout their tour did they see the patient figures flogging the water being vouchsafed even an encouraging rise.

The castle at Ballanahinch had been the home of Mary Martin, 'Princess of Connemara' and heiress of two hundred thousand heavily mortgaged acres. Her grandfather 'Humanity Dick' had combined a taste for duelling with a passion for the improvement of the lot of non-human animals. Not only did he impose his principles on Connemara where he ruled the countryside, but he forced the first act for the protection of cattle through the English Parliament. It was his son, Thomas, who had died of famine fever, and whose funeral procession had taken two hours to pass the gates of Ross. Mary Martin, his heiress, struggled to raise yet more money on her estates to keep the tenants from starvation, and in this attempt all mortgages on the property passed to the Law Life Assurance Company. As Burke's *Vicissitudes of Families* remarked with asperity in 1859, 'corporations behave with an inhumanity that a man acting alone would hesitate to employ'. When the failure of rents, a consequence of the Famine, made it impossible for Mary Martin to pay the interest the assurance company took possession. The Princess of Connemara had married a Mr Gonne Bell, presumably for love, as his only characteristic mentioned in reference books is his poverty. Left without an acre, Mary Martin retired to Belgium, where she earned a little money by writing novels. Friends raised a subscription to pay her fare to New York, but this, again, can have been no large sum as she travelled in a sailing ship. She was confined, prematurely, on board, dying a few days after landing in America. She died in 1850, but the shadowy Mr Gonne Bell survived until 1883.

Edith gave only some hints of this pitiful story, perhaps considering it as meat too strong for the delicate readers of *The Lady's Pictorial*. In the garden of Ballanahinch, a house of less charm than is usual for Irish houses built in the eighteen thirties, they were shown a stone slab known as Miss Martin's seat. Here they came upon a countrywoman, smoking a pipe under a hood made by the scarlet petticoat hitched over her head. She groaned out a dirge for Mary Martin, remembered by her as clearly as the ladies she saw before her. 'She was beautiful and white and charitable, only she had one snaggledy tooth in front of her mouth. But what signifies that? Faith, when she was in it the ladies of Connemara might go under the sod.' Martin Ross, as she gave a donation to the tearful beggarwoman, may have been glad to have had it confirmed that snaggledy teeth, such as she herself possessed, signified nothing to admirers of the Martin family.

Charles Lever made the legends of Mary Martin the foundation of his novel *The Martins of Cro-Martin*, but it was Maria
Edgeworth who left an account of everyday life at Ballanahinch.
She had paid an uninvited and awkwardly prolonged visit to
the Castle, when the roads had proved impassable for a carriage, and one of her companions had become acutely ill. She
admired Mary Martin's red-gold hair and blue eyes, which reminded her of a painting by Leonardo, but she recognized that
the family's reign was on the point of collapse. The house was
rotting and sparsely furnished, though Mary Martin never left
it without a tail of country courtiers following her. '*Je sais
mon métier de reine,*' she said, showing her visitors the marble
quarries, whose working was the last, unfulfilled, hope of re-
suscitating the family fortunes. Imprisoned in this marble lie
all the colours of a wave of the Atlantic as it turns over on the
sand. Mary Martin's father used the marble slabs to pave his
stables, a last splendid gesture. Even today ghillies will keep
impatient fishermen waiting, while they direct travellers to this
memorial of the Martins of Ballanahinch, in their graves for a
century, but alive in local memory.

Mr Collis has found no reference in Edith's diary to a night
that the cousins claimed to have spent in the cottage of the
Widow Joyce, mother of eleven children. Although the episode
appears to have been fictitious, the name of Joyce would have
been appropriate, for they were on the edge of Joyce's Country,
a district strong in tribal spirit. Stanislaus Joyce, brother of
James Joyce, has recorded that, in Dublin, a sergeant of police
called naturally, Joyce, came to warn his father that a warrant
for the arrest of a Nationalist friend of the elder Joyce was on
its way, though the sergeant had arranged for a day's postponement. As a Connaught man, the sergeant put loyalty to Joyce's
country before any other.

In *The London Mercury*, in 1920, a reviewer wrote of the vast
gap dividing the writings of James Joyce from those of Somerville and Ross, an opinion many of their contemporaries would
have unhesitatingly accepted. On closer examination, however, the gap begins to narrow, until, to change the metaphor,
it is as if trains with separate destinations run over the same
rails for part of their journey. These resemblances will be considered as they occur in the course of examining Somerville

and Ross's writing, but mention, at this point, of the name of
Joyce gives an opportunity to point out that Martin Ross
and James Joyce had not only a Dublin but a Galway background in common. On the last page of *Dubliners*, when the
snow is falling all over Ireland, it is in Oughterard churchyard
four miles from Ross, that *The Dead* of the story's title lies
under the soft white drifts. Even politically there are evidences
of a like vision. Martin Ross, writing of Parnell and the Irish
Parliamentary Party, described the latter as hounds, following
'a grim disdainful Master, whose pack never dared to get
closer to him than the length of his thong; but he laid them on
the line and they ran it like wolves'. Referring again to *Dubliners* and quoting from *Ivy Day in the Committee Room*, there is
the same opinion of Parnell's discipline. ' "Right you are,
Crofton," said Mr Henchy fiercely. He was the only man who
could keep that bag of cats in order. "Down, ye dogs! Lie
down, ye curs!" That's the way he treated them.'

The night in the Widow Joyce's cabin is described with an
attention to grisly detail that was later to be developed in the
many restless nights endured by the Irish R.M. Attacks by
fleas (Irish fleas are still highly prized by flea circuses) and an
assault by a goose made the night hideous to the guests,
though the Widow and her many children, inured to fleas and
geese, snored peacefully. Next morning the story had a fairy-
tale ending when Pat James, the eldest son of the house, and
his cat, who had usurped the position of household dog, set the
travellers on their way. Pat James Joyce was 'an idyllically picturesque creature of seventeen, with large gentle grey eyes, set
in a golden brown face, several shades darker in value than
they were . . .' He was last seen sitting on a bog rock, 'His
slouched felt hat and creamy flannel "bawneen" looking all
that could be desired against the background of clear blue sky,
while the cat performed unearthly gambols in the heather at
his bare feet.'

After this pastoral interlude, the tour proceeded on more
ordinary lines, Kylemore Castle being described with no mention of Robert Martin's belief that its builders had brought
murderous propaganda to the neighbourhood. The cousins'
diet was mainly small brown trout and small brown hens, fresh
and delicious, but Edith made a rare, if not unique reference,

to the Impressionist school of painting by complaining that the invariably underdone poached eggs, when punctured 'by a diffident knife' made the eater's plate look like a sunrise painted by an impressionist.

Like a giant neighbour of variable moods, the Atlantic was always a presence in the writings and in the lives of both Edith and Martin. It did not curl an arm inland under the windows of Ross as it did at Drishane, but after bad storms the lawn would be white with spray, blown in from the ocean six miles away. This had happened after the great storm of 1839, still called, Martin Ross wrote in 1905, 'The Big Wind', and so mentioned by Buck Mulligan at breakfast in the Martello Tower in the first pages of *Ulysses*. Reaching the ocean at the farthest point of their itinerary, they came to Renvyle, a rare house to find in Ireland, built in the seventeenth century, with low windows set among strangely shaped weather slates, cut from unmalleable local material. Maria Edgeworth had rejoiced in the library panelled, it was said, with wood salvaged from shipwrecks, finding it a haven of comfort after the rigours of Ballanahinch. Edith and Martin, great-grand-daughters of Miss Edgeworth's dear friends, Chief Justice and Mrs Bushe, also admired the books and wallowed in the lobster soup provided by Mrs Blake, who ran the house as an hotel.

The vicissitudes of the Blake family of Renvyle had been even darker than those suffered by the Martins of Ballanahinch, and Mrs Blake's innkeeping was an attempt to make the estate solvent. On bad terms with the Land League, she had survived the consequent boycott, the cousins viewing her with awe as a woman who had, single-handed, driven the cattle of the Land Leaguers from her fields each morning, only to find them driven back again as night fell. Reprisals had been vicious and revolting. The donkey, carrying away the lawn mowings in his panniers, had an unnatural air of deformity, his ears being the shortest of stumps. Explaining that the ears had been cut off at the time of the Agitation, the gardener appeared to accept this method of vexing the boycotted family as some inexplicable act of nature. The vicissitudes of Renvyle did not end in Mrs Blake's time. W. B. Yeats stayed there with Oliver St John Gogarty (the pattern for Buck Mulligan), and, while the poet was reading aloud from his own work, the door swung open, making the company aware of a ghostly presence. Yeats dealt with the situation masterfully by saying, 'Let it alone— it will go away as it came,' in which he rightly interpreted the ghost's intention. On that evening Renvyle was still the same house visited by Miss Edgeworth, and, in their turn, by Edith and Martin, but, during the Civil War which followed the setting up of the Free State, it was destroyed by fire. Although faithfully rebuilt on the original ground plan, the dark panelling and the uneven weather slates were lost for ever.

As the end of their tour came nearer, the travellers were impressed by finding that, wherever they went, they seemed to be the only natives of the country. At that date the Nationalist determination to reject as Irish anyone with English ancestors in past centuries was only one of many arrows in the quiver of the future. Unselfconsciously, Somerville and Ross considered themselves to be Irish, and called themselves so. Surrounded by the voices of English tourists, they came to the conclusion that it was poverty that hampered the Irish from touring, ignoring the possibility that experience of the average rainfall might make the inhabitants unanxious to leave their homes. They were, themselves, even reduced to envying the waiter, dry shod and snugly occupied indoors, on a day when 'The great mountains of Mayo looked like elephants swathed in white muslin'. It is a matter for speculation if Ernest Hemingway ever read *Through Connemara in a Governess Cart* and chose from there the title of his story *'Hills Like White Elephants'*. He would certainly not have approved of the resignation with which Somerville and Ross included the poor connections of the Great Southern and Western Railway, having declared that, until he met Scott Fitzgerald, he had never known of a grown man missing a train. Edith and Martin regained Galway, and the railway system, on the Bianconi mail car, after Sibbie, the jennet, had thrown a final fit of temper by swerving into her own stable at Oughterard and shaking her passengers on to the floor of the governess cart.

It seems appropriate to follow the principle adopted by Edith in *Irish Memories* and consider the four tours that she made with Martin in one chapter, although the first two were taken in 1891 and the later two in 1893. They welcomed these opportunities to travel and earn at the same time, but the professional discipline was, perhaps unconsciously, a valuable influence on their writing.

In the autumn that followed the visit to Connemara, *The Lady's Pictorial* sent the team to Bordeaux, to cover the *vendange* with articles and sketches. The sketches, before they appeared, were worked over by F. H. Townsend, for many years responsible for political and other drawings in *Punch*. Whether or not he belonged to the clan from Castletownshend, the marriage of his style with Edith's was not entirely happy, as he could not resist the temptation to smarten the travellers' appearance. Martin suggested that the articles, as a book, should be called from Cork to Claret, but the publishers, thinking this too subtle a title, preferred *In the Vine Country*. On their way to Dublin they passed through stations where windblown trees and wailing emigrants waiting for the down train to Cork and a ship to the New World, combined to augur a rough crossing.

The novelist Christine Longford has pointed out that the so-called Anglo-Irish have been deeply influenced by the necessity of facing the horrors of sea-sickness several times a year. The heroine of *An Irish Cousin* makes a first queasy appearance with the remark that sea-sickness has, for her, two aspects, the pathetic in herself and the revolting in other people. This ambivalent opinion, contributed by Martin Ross, became sufficiently celebrated to be quoted, with acknowledgement to 'a gifted Irish authoress', by the 5th Lord Lansdowne, in the course of a debate in the House of Lords on the desirability of a Channel Tunnel. The apprehension of sea-sickness, and the habit of trying to gauge the probable roughness of the crossing, is so deeply ingrained, that an Anglo-Irish traveller has been known to gain reassurance from the motionless pine trees of central Europe as a promise of calm on a Channel hundreds of miles away. Martin also insisted, that, though few things in the world were as bad as might be expected, a bad crossing was worse than the combined efforts of memory and imagination could suggest. On the outset of the journey to Bordeaux the auguries were fulfilled, even the stewardess remarking that it had been a rough passage. It was gratifying, Edith wrote, to have this obvious fact put on an official basis, though as the journey

from Paris took eleven hours they had time to pass from dis-
composure to the paralysis of numb fatigue.

Once the journey was over they blossomed as observers.
Connemara may have been too near home, geographically and
spiritually, for their literary mood was far gayer in the vine
country. Driven indoors by the fierce autumn sun, regarded at
that date as unhealthy, they sheltered in the church of Saint
Michael, repository of a company of mummified corpses. The
custodian used her only English word 'Moshrhume', as she
pointed out *la famille empoisonnée*, a morsel of the deadly fungus
being still in the mouth of one of the children. There was also
a General, so frequently wounded in battle that of his person
little remained, and a fat woman shrivelled to a dreadful dwarf.
It was only the show-woman's affection for her charges that
softened this cruel immortality. 'They [the mummies] might
have been little damaged terracotta figures, had it not been
for the dusty grins that showed unmistakable teeth, and
some indefinable sentiment of genuineness and absence of
effort.'

Throughout the book there is perceptible tightening of
style, an increase of genuineness and absence of effort. In an
unfamiliarly steady steamer they chugged up the Gironde,
enchanted by the unindustrial, country-house air of the wine-
making installations, passing a minor Petra, where houses with
porches and balconies had been blasted and carved out of a
range of tawny cliffs. At Pauillac they became immersed in the
life of the *vendange*, after a nerve-shaking meeting with Black,
the hotel boarhound, to whose collar was chained Bamboo,
the hotel monkey. Bamboo bounced like an india-rubber ball
from the end of his chain, and when briefly liberated, swung
like a trapeze artist on to Martin's skirts, while she fled shrieking up the stairs.

Next day, amid sunlight and gaiety, Pauillac celebrated a
church festival. As Martin and Edith watched a man on stilts,
'stalking with the grave composure of a heron' through the
crowd, they reflected on the commonsense superiority of
French religious custom over the Irish habit of abandoning all
effort after Mass on a Feast day. In Pauillac everyone carried on
with their work, and, if they had none, walked about enjoying
themselves. These last included the proprietor of a small local

vineyard. He escorted them to his property mounted on a bicycle with the boarhound (Bamboo up) in attendance, a rabble of children hailing '*des étrangères*' at the tops of their voices.

Passionately as Edith objected to the word 'rollicking', which had been stamped like a postmark on the novels of Charles Lever and tended to rub off on the works of Martin and herself, it is hard to find a substitute to describe their adventures among the *vendangeurs*. Hardly had they reassured each other that the process of fermentation would be also a purification from the bare feet of the treaders of the grapes, when they were urged to drink a tumbler of *moût*, the heady, unfermented juice that is the first stage between the wine-press and the bottle. Fleeing this offer, Martin blundered into the vintagers' sleeping quarters, nearly treading on one of them who was sleeping off the effects of too much *moût*. Shocked as she was when a red-faced, white-bearded head reared itself from the straw beneath her feet, her feelings can have been nothing to those of this drowsy Silenus when he saw Bamboo, the monkey, who had escaped from his guardian boarhound, and was following Martin over the straw with demoniac leaps and cries.

Socially the cousins found life was simple when they adopted the Cockney twang with which the Bordelais spoke French. They even spent a night in the loft of a *cuisine de vendange*, reminiscent of the Widow Joyce's cabin in the battalions of its fleas, led, additionally, by spearheads of mosquitoes. Higher social levels were more of a strain, the studios of the Latin Quarter not having supplied them with a vocabulary of small talk suitable for a French drawing-room. Baron de Rothschild's private cellar, where the bottles regarded the visitors 'with cold, uncountable eyes', presented no problem for their guide spoke perfect English, but a day at a local manor house was a struggle of non-communication. The enduring domination of a former French governess had obliged the invitation to be given and accepted. Driving to the house with their frigid and monoglot hostess, Martin alone raised a faint smile by referring to the election posters on the walls as '*des postiches*'. There was a history of such mistakes in the family. In search of an extra pillow for her hotel bed, a particularly godly aunt of

Edith's had asked a baffled shop assistant for '*un sommelier*', adding, '*Je dors toujours avec deux sommeliers.*'

Released from the agonies of polite society they were taken to a dance to celebrate the end of the *vendange* where they whirled deliriously in *contre-danses*. As a final compliment a nearly obsolete square-dance, the Bignou, was performed for their benefit by four agile crones, whose age was no surprise, the steps being of such intricacy that it was obviously a life-time's work to master their ins-and-outs. A feast in Bordeaux prepared them for the long haul back to Co. Cork, whither they had dispatched their well-hated portmanteaus in advance, rejoicing, as they saw these incubi 'squatting sullenly side by side', in the knowledge that their detested faces would be seen no more till the journey's end. This still left Edith and Martin with their White Knight-like assortment of packages for con-veying spirit lamp, kettle, Bovril, ginger biscuits, and a half empty bottle of claret, the gift of a *vigneron*. They were also virtuously conscious of having resisted the temptation to see *La femme à Papa* then playing in Bordeaux. At the ages of twenty-nine and thirty-three this would, they knew, have either laid a guilty secret on their consciences, or have been the final overthrow of whatever confidence their families might still have in their discretion.

By the time the cousins set off on their next trip, a riding tour of North Wales, *The Real Charlotte* was finished, but a lack of enthusiasm among publishers had side-tracked it for a year. *Black and White* had commissioned the riding tour, but owing in some degree to the success of *The Real Charlotte* it was in *Blackwood's* that the articles finally appeared. Reviewers of *Beggars on Horseback* do not seem to have appreciated that it had come from the same stable as the novel. There were complaints about the anglicized spelling of Welsh names and about the writers' determination to make a joke in every sentence. Even the illustrations, though called 'dainty' by one reviewer, were passed over in silence as an act of kindness by another. For the moment the pen was in Martin's hand, drawing occupying Edith.

They started from Welshpool on two hireling ponies, called Tom and Tommy, to whose saddles were strapped, insecurely, holdalls containing those tried favourites, the kettle, the spirit lamp and the india-rubber bath. Beds were less alive with fleas than on previous trips, but Edith's illustrations, for the first time published as they came from the artist's hand, did full justice to the agony of riding at a horse-fly's pace through the Welsh countryside. *The Lady's Pictorial* would never have published her self-portrait, hair-descending and face mottled by her efforts to fight off the flying persecutors. In spite of heart-lifting moments when they rode past chapels where the congregation was in full song, the Welsh were sometimes less than sympathetic, one white-bearded patriarch going so far as to bombard them with pebbles as they rested below a bridge. Ascending Snowdon at the heels of a fast-climbing, Welsh-speaking guide, Edith attempted to slow him down by asking if there were eagles on the mountains. Met by incomprehension, she took to mime and broken English, arching her fingers on her brow for a beak and flapping her arms like wings. 'Big birds,' she reiterated, 'who steal lambs.' At last the guide understood. 'Oh yess,' he said, 'many fahxes.'

Writing of their earlier journeys, Edith had worked up some mock indignation about Martin's maddeningly unfrightened laughter when the jennet bolted, and her unfair evasion of the polite tasting of a glass of *moût*. These compliments were returned in *Beggars on Horseback*. Besides the misunderstanding on Snowdon, Martin, who called her companion Miss O'Flannigan, remarked on the paint-box, made, apparently of lead and filled with stones, a burden on all who travelled with Miss O'Flannigan, and particularly so on an equestrian expedition. She wrote, also, that only when the saddle had slipped so far round the stout flank of one of the Tommies that the rider was standing on her head, did the flow of Miss O'Flannigan's conversation momentarily cease.

On the last Sunday of their tour, they sweltered up the hill from Llangollen to Plâs Newydd, the home of the two Ladies who had brought fame to Llangollen by settling there at the end of the eighteenth century. In theory the Ladies had lived in seclusion, if not in what John Aubrey called 'eremetical solitude', devoted only to each other's society and the collection of antique objects of a kind little valued by their contemporaries. To emphasize their emancipation from feminine fashions, they dressed always in riding habits, with beaver hats

sitting on top of their close-cut powdered curls. As young
women Lady Eleanor Butler and Miss Sarah Ponsonby had
eloped together from their homes in Ireland, repulsing at least
one attempt by their families to break up their ménage and
fetch them away. They had had the good fortune to bring with
them a devoted housekeeper, who saw to their good dinners,
which was important to a hermitage sited with forethought on
the Holyhead coach road. Having escaped from both social
boredom and the tedious duties exacted from unmarried
daughters, they became eventually an illustrious institution. A
black and white lace-work of Gothic beams was added to the
plain Welsh front of Plâs Newydd and in the porch they gave
tea to Wordsworth and Sir Walter Scott. Travellers paused on
the way to and from Ireland and no Welsh tour was considered
a success unless it included an introduction to the Ladies of
Llangollen.

Edith and Martin found Plâs Newydd closed for Sunday and
could only peer with exasperation at the little of the treasures
inside that could be seen through the narrow windows. They
sat outside, reflecting on what they considered to be 'the
grotesque romance' of the Ladies' lives. It appeared to them an
incomprehensible eccentricity to wish to leave families in Ireland to reside on this Welsh mountain. Exclusive devotion was
an idea that had not suggested itself to them, any more than a
conception of a future when their own relationship might be
scrutinized for evidence of perverse affections, as had happened
to the Ladies of Llangollen. They had just spent two weeks in
riding habits, and could only imagine that to endure such life-
long discomfort was a form of penance chosen by the Ladies to
expiate their unfilial behaviour.

Conscientiously travelling with the Tommies, as they returned
by horse-box to their native Welshpool, was only the beginning
of Edith and Martin's journey to their homes. The demon who
presided over so many of their travels arranged that their
luggage should still be rambling round the line from Bettws,
while they stood on the pier at Holyhead, faced with the
agonizing decision of sailing without it or missing the mail-
boat. Like a cardinal bird among blue-black crows, the scarlet
coated porter of the hotel watched them complacently, while
the porters in their blue jerseys laughed unkindly. The hotel

porter, like Sibbie the jennet, one of a dynasty, knew that the decision would run his way. 'We stayed, and the Kingstown boat moved out on an oily sea into a murky west, and the rain began to fall.'

Although on the ascent of Snowdon icy fog had frozen the climbers and veiled the rising sun, it had, in fact, been made at the summer solstice. The autumn equinox of the same year was approaching when the cousins were sent to Denmark, once again on behalf of *The Lady's Pictorial*. Their spirits were even lower than usual before a journey, for their route to the Danish frontier lay through Hamburg where cases of cholera had been reported. In a London lodging house they sat, hatted and veiled for the journey, fortifying themselves with underdone chops, washed down with overdone tea. The apprehension of cholera, the hats and veils, the tea and chops, give an unusually dated air to their situation, the vitality of their writing normally bringing with it the gift of timelessness. After seventy-five years Edith and Martin appear in historical perspective much as the Ladies of Llangollen, divided by the same gap in time, may have appeared to them. Incidentally, tea and chops must have been thought to be a good foundation for a journey, for that was the breakfast they had ordered on their last day in Connemara.

Resolutions to refrain from drinking anything brewed from the cholera-laden waters of the Elbe failed when the plan of travel was disrupted at Hamburg. Edith was busy reclaiming their heavy luggage, always volatile in its determination to go its own way, when the train with Martin on board sneaked out of Hamburg and on to Altona. Before they were reunited the threat of cholera had become incidental. Edith had been obliged to double from station to station in Hamburg with a stout German lady as her guide. It was Martin's opinion that this kind helper must have been returned to her home in the condition of a horse spirited from its stable and ridden all night by a witch. In the meantime Martin, penniless, with a memory rich in the declension of German adjectives but poor in nouns to which they could be harnessed, explained to a fellow-traveller that she had lost 'meine Freund'—my she he-friend—a description produced by the agony of the moment and not to be regarded as a Freudian slip. *The Lady's Pictorial* had ceased to tamper with Edith's illustrations. Her sketches of herself, horror-struck in the custom house at Hamburg and fleeing across its deserted streets, do full justice to the mallard's tail in her hat and the checks of a greatcoat with capes as innumerable and 'becomingly important' as that worn by Henry Tilney driving Catherine Morland to Northanger Abbey.

Back on the right rails, they reached the station restaurant at Fredericia, a junction lying on the neck of Denmark, which in the great days of Les Grands Express Européens offered a choice of a *wagon-lit* direct to Rome or a domestic trip into Jutland. Following the latter line Edith and Martin travelled on to Aarhus in a *Damen Koupee*, not having discovered that Danes regarded such exclusiveness as an unwarrantable extravagance. The State Railway of Denmark has a tradition of regarding travel in the guard's van as a reasonable solution when holiday travellers overflow the second-class carriages. The blue Baltic sparkled between the trunks of the beech trees, but though the Danes accepted the sunshine at its face value, hotel stoves presenting cold, black faces, the Irish cousins found themselves thankful for their winter stockings.

The Danish articles remained as such until 1920, when Edith gathered together the uncollected writings of Martin Ross and, adding some essays of her own, published the collection as *Strayaways*. In her first book of memoirs, *Irish Memories*, she had written that those who might feel their hospitality had been abused by Somerville and Ross little knew the restraint that had been exercised. Introductions to Danish families brought invitations of equal social awkwardness equal to the hospitality of the country-houses of the Médoc. Except for those to whom Kierkegaard and Hans Andersen in their native tongue are familiar friends, travellers in Denmark can experience a repose which is only bestowed by the incomprehensibility of the surrounding conversation, increased by the muted tone of voice which makes Harwich sound like Bedlam after the hush of Esbjerg. From tourists enjoying this peace, the cousins were obliged to transform themselves into country house visitors, dining in *demi-toilette*, at about the hour when, in the lackadaisical West, they would have been struggling to put up the tennis net. Wagonette rides through the forests of North Jutland, where even today deer hardly bother to make

way and even foxes pause for a good stare, were little strain.
Conversation indoors was a crueller matter, to quote from their
story *Sharper than a Ferret's Tooth* they were entertained within
an inch of their lives. Questions on politics and contemporary literature were only abated when the company sat
down to whist, revoking at least proving to be a form of inter-
national communication.

Dutifully they inspected a dairy farm, fleeing from the aroma
of pigs in their parlour, only to be led into the overpowering
reek of cheeses ripening on their grey stone shelves. Finally
they came to Copenhagen, their summer clothes still inadequate
in the bright chill of the Danish autumn. In the harbour the
royal yacht of the Princess of Wales (Queen Alexandra) floated
beside the imperial yacht of her brother-in-law, Czar Alexan-
der III. Both were visiting her parents—his parents-in-law—
the Danish King and his Consort. The Danish Queen was, with
reason, called the mother-in-law of Europe. The Czar, shaking
off his detectives, rode about in the trams of Copenhagen,
Danes regarding his drive with an escort of sailors to the Russian Church as part of Sunday's gala.

Before these articles, entitled *In the State of Denmark*, had
appeared the Czar had escaped from his ever-threatened life
into what Martin called 'the impenetrable security of death'.
Edith suggested, in the preface to *Strayaways*, that, as Martin
had been mainly responsible for writing *In the State of Denmark*
the curious might compare this with her other writings and so
'discern something of her individual outlook'. Besides her
reflection on the Czar's precarious existence, Martin had also
speculated if there was not some vital element missing from the
apparently wholesome lives of the Danish peasant women,
when she looked at their pale doomed faces and learnt that they
rarely lived beyond middle-age. These ideas, examples of her
'individual outlook', would seem to be remote from the workings of Edith's imagination.

Three years later, in the studio at Drishane, they gave the
interview already mentioned in connection with the genesis of
An Irish Cousin. In the inevitable discussion as to how their
collaboration worked, Edith told the interviewer that they had
in reality three styles: their joint style, Martin's style and Edith's
style. It was, she said, like blue and yellow, separate colours but

together making green. Even allowing for the simplifications of journalism there is force in the comparison. The green was never deeper nor richer than in *The Real Charlotte*, when Martin's artistic sensibility and powers of philosophical speculation blended with Edith's passionate response to landscape and instinctive appreciation of character.

5

The Real Charlotte

THE skeleton of *The Real Charlotte* was first strung together at Ross, soon after Mrs Martin had returned there with her youngest daughter. Regaining the Lost Paradise may well have brought back to Martin the impressions of her first years in Dublin, when she had been catapulted into a strange, urban world. Life at Ross had had its elements of toughness; losing her hoard of treasures to the turf boys at Spoil Five, a card game favoured by Kipling's *Soldiers Three*, and slow gorging on hot soda bread and hard-boiled eggs, washed down with port, at the tenants' weddings must have taught a clever child of ten that life could be unrefined. At her Dublin Sunday School, however, the toughness and lack of refinement was of a different kind, ornate with vulgarity and pulsing with adolescent precocity.

The book opens at a Sunday School on a hot August afternoon, in the unfashionable North Side of Dublin. In the first few pages the character and dazzling prettiness of Francie Fitzpatrick spring to life. Left without parents, she had been brought up by an uncle and aunt in Mountjoy Square, her only dowry being £25 a year and ravishing good looks. These looks surmount the gawkiness of her fourteen years and her aunt's atrocious taste in hats, to say nothing of her decorated spring boots and her crimson silk gloves. Children, as the writers point out, are as much influenced by prettiness as grown-ups, and her little round-eyed, white-lashed cousins are solidly loyal to their gay princess. Her class-mates are equally in her thrall, until Tommy Whitty, an admirer of sixteen, rebels at being taunted with the adult charms of a stranger who had that day dined with the Fitzpatricks. In the scuffle that follows Tommy Whitty's attempt to snatch back a silver ring he has forced on to Francie's crimson silk finger, Francie bolts down the street, until the stitching on her new boots checks her

flight. Always enterprising she boards a stationary milk-cart
and trots off in triumph, only dashed when she finds she has
lost control of the horse.

The milk cart is halted by Roderick Lambert, the young man
about whom Francie has boasted to her friends. He has already
begun a condescending flirtation, promising to come on the
Sunday School excursion if she would agree to stay beside him
throughout the day. ' "So now, how grand I'll be! And he has
a long black mustash!" ' she had teased Tommy Whitty, goad-
ing him to reprisals. Francie's accent and mode of expression
would, wrote Somerville and Ross, be impossible to convey to
a reader who had no 'slight previous notion of how dreadful a
thing is a pure-bred Dublin accent'. Lambert, wondering how
Nosey Fitzpatrick could have had such a pretty daughter, teases
Francie about keeping her goings-on from the authorities. She
has relapsed into the red-faced embarrassment of a child in a
scrape, fatuously mistaken by Lambert for interest in his own
handsome appearance. They stand on the doorstep in the dusty
August sunlight, Francie attempting nonchalance, Lambert
promising patronizingly that he won't tell on her and that they
will be friends. That is the meeting of two who suffer bitterly
from each other, and at the hands of a third, until catastrophe
ends the tragedy.

In this first chapter the reader learns all that needs to be
known about Francie, her knowledge of the power of her
beauty, the dashing gaiety which carries off gaudy finery, her
sudden sensitiveness. Lambert's character, common, vain, with
a suggestion of a flashy crook, is made almost equally clear.
With the appearance of Charlotte Mullen, the dark force which
is to wreck both their lives takes its place beside them. Charlotte Mullen, a squat plain woman of forty, comes into the
story at a moment when she is said never to have looked
plainer. With one of her hair-pins she is scraping the ash off a
candle she has just lighted in the sick-room of her dying aunt.
Outside the sobbing wind is rising, to blow a gale across the
lake on whose shore stands the small town of Lismoyle. Indoors at Tally Ho Lodge the ugly bedroom is shabby but not
poverty-stricken. Miss Mullen's face above her magenta flannel
dressing-gown is yellow from watching by the death-bed.
Presently the cook, Norry the Boat, daughter of Shaunapickeen

the ferryman, struggles in with a savage Tom cat, called Susan, wrapped in her apron. Old Mrs Mullen wants to say good-bye to him and Norry has retrieved him from the ash-pit. In a last rally the patient has qualms about her will, which leaves her possessions to Charlotte, ignoring the closer claim by blood of Francie Fitzpatrick. Charlotte, even at this late hour, 'would not brook the revolt of a slave'. With a rough tongue she scouts the idea that Francie needs compassion, forcing Mrs Mullen to turn her thoughts to Susan, and holding the cat in her arms with soothing gentle words, in contrast to her tyranny over her aunt and her harsh abuse of Norry the Boat. The low moans from Mrs Mullen cease and the cat leaps from the bed. The cook gives a howl and begins to pray loudly. Miss Mullen, 'with some preliminary heavings of her shoulders, bursts into noisy transports of grief'. Already on this wintry night of death there are indications of Charlotte's strong passions and potentialities for evil.

Summer comes and Charlotte, now in possession of Tally Ho Lodge, attends a pay-off tennis party given at Bruff, the big house of the neighbourhood. Sir Benjamin Dysart, the owner, is not present, a stroke brought on by a fury of jealousy at the celebrations of his son's coming of age having immobilized him in a bath chair. Christopher, the son, a victim of paternal bullying, has grown up into a diffident dilettante, finding an outlet in photography for his self-admitted creative inadequacy. With less obvious charm, and ultimately more moral fibre, he has some resemblance to those cultivated but forceless heroes of Edith Wharton, incidentally, an exact contemporary of Martin Ross. Christopher Dysart shares with his sister Pamela an instinctive distaste for Miss Mullen. Her brother speculates how anyone could be as good as Pamela and live, and it is this goodness, and his own sensitivity, that quiver like geiger-counter needles in awareness of the sinister twist in Charlotte's nature. Lady Dysart, their English mother, accepts Miss Mullen as a comic Irish good sort, and a cultural oasis in a vulgar desert, where no one else has skill in acrostics or ability to discuss the prophetic dimensions of the Pyramids.

Miss Mullen's father had been the Dysarts' agent, Roddy Lambert, his pupil, having succeeded him in the agency. He is in the tiny group of gentlemen to whom Charlotte attaches herself, her character as a robustly humorous eccentric giving her brevet rank as masculine, and allowing her to escape from the rows of superfluous ladies awaiting tea in midge-bitten agony. Emotional stirrings below the surface begin to send up bubbles. Irritated by the general assumption that Francie, whose impending visit she has announced, is her niece, Charlotte is further exasperated by Lambert's facetious jokes about 'Welsh aunts' and his air of knowing familiarity with Francie's tastes and character. Charlotte has no trust in Lambert's wife, a dowdy hypochondriac with a helpful income, as a brake on his interest in Francie, whose acquaintance he has obviously cultivated since their meeting outside the Sunday School six years earlier. Displeasure at Lambert's complacency over Francie makes Charlotte display a bad temper so ludicrous that a spectator cocks an eyebrow at Pamela Dysart, who is on the edge of nervous laughter.

This is the first appearance of Gerald Hawkins, an officer on detachment, stationed at Lismoyle, who is to be the instrument that brings ruin to Francie. Under the cheerful appearance of a hearty, red-faced, yellow-haired, young Englishman, Hawkins hides a ruthlessness in his love affairs worthy of greater mental powers, his stupidity handicapping him from gaining full advantage of his callous behaviour as a Lothario.

The world of the Dysarts of Bruff, Protestant, with English affiliations, shades off through the middle reaches of Lismoyle society until, in their turn, the level of the Catholic tenants and servants gives way to the *bas-fonds*, the doers of odd jobs and, ultimately, the beggars, each world overlapping the one below it. Miss Mullen may be Lady Dysart's jester, but the fact is made bearable to the ladies of Lismoyle by the knowledge that her mother was a National school-teacher and her grandmother a bare-footed country girl. From them she has inherited an accent she can hardly broaden when she is telling comic stories, and a peasant habit of wearing thick clothes throughout the year. She lives on terms of smouldering warfare with Norry the Boat, her cook, whose unclean habits combine with her employer's penny-pinching ways to make co-existence possible. Supported by a white cockatoo, like herself a relic from an earlier dynasty at Tally Ho, Norry conducts a running battle with Miss Mullen's tribe of cats, the cockatoo going to the extreme of murder when chance arises. Charlotte also has her dark schemes, and prepares in an affable mood to greet Francie. However, when, unexpectedly, Lambert drives Francie to the door the familiarity of their behaviour to each other, and Francie's beauty, with raindrops shining on her golden head, freeze the smile of welcome on Charlotte's face.

Lambert's wife, 'the Turkey Hen', is a poor, good-natured creature, her only pleasures a row of patent medicine bottles and a Yorkshire terrier. Relapsed into unresentful middle-age she makes no objection to her husband taking Francie out riding, both of them on horses for which the Turkey Hen's money has paid. Squeezed into a tight-waisted green habit, bought on credit, Francie's riding is less neat than her waist. She bumps along beside Lambert, exasperating him by her frivolity, and coaxing back his good temper by her knowledge of his character. In this style they reach Gurthnamuckle, a good farm decaying in the hands of Julia Duffy. Old Miss Duffy is the daughter of a drunken Protestant farmer, who had married his Catholic dairywoman. By this means she is a cousin of Norry the Boat, but she has abandoned church and chapel. Consulted by the neighbourhood as one wise in herbal remedies, she lives in filth that makes her cousin Norry's domestic habits appear positively salubrious, her only companion being Billy Grainy, a red-eyed beggar. Francie is greeted ceremonially, both by Miss Duffy and Billy Grainy, for her grandparents' sake, but these civilities get Lambert no farther in his attempts to persuade Miss Duffy to give up the farm, which would be in Lambert's own interests as well as his employer's. There are, in fact, indications that duns and betting losses have begun to erode Lambert's financial probity in handling the estate accounts.

It is Charlotte who comes to Lambert's rescue with the loan of a few hundred pounds. They meet as Charlotte is, in her turn, on the way home from Gurthnamuckle. There she has dealt a body blow to Miss Duffy with the news that her grazing tenant is bankrupt, a bankruptcy engineered secretly by Charlotte herself. Lambert is on the prowl after Francie, but her weakness for him makes Charlotte blind on this one point. Callow embraces in their younger days have given Lambert a sexual power over the unattractive woman, which, between satisfaction and disgust, he can still exploit for his own purposes. Their mood is broken, symbolically, by Francie, who erupts on to the road and into the ditch, on a tricycle belonging to the curate, latest fly round this honey-pot.

Gerald Hawkins is an admirer far more dangerous to Francie. In her world the conquest of an English officer is a tall feather in any girl's cap, and this additional excitement upsets the balance of airy flirtation which is Francie's amiable approach to all men. Lambert, wracked by jealousy, brings about an accident to his yacht, and Francie is only kept from drowning by the efforts of Christopher Dysart, who, in defiance of his own standards, is beginning to fall in love with Francie. After Lambert has made an embarrassing exhibition of himself over the half-drowned Francie, the party are rescued by Captain Cursiter's steam-launch. Hawkins has been sent on detachment to Lismoyle by his commanding officer, in the unfulfilled hope that Captain Cursiter's disillusion with women will curb Hawkins' amorous propensities. Not only is this hope unfulfilled, but Hawkins continually contrives to involve his senior in social gatherings. Cursiter shows a faint interest in the kind-hearted Pamela Dysart, but suffers martyrdom from Miss Hope-Drummond, an English visitor, who has been imported as a possible wife for Christopher. Miss Hope-Drummond has found Ireland a disappointment. Not only does she observe that every man neglects her for 'that Miss Fitzpatrick', but she is persecuted by the bathchair-ridden Sir Benjamin, who screams at her for picking a rose and hooks his walking stick round her ankle as she passes his door. Miss Hope-Drummond's mind is an intellectual blank under her beautifully curled hair, but she gets her own back by subtly insulting Francie, and by grilling the misanthropic Captain on the subject of the Lincolnshire Cursiters.

Charlotte has, of course, noticed that Christopher is drawn towards Francie, which possibility had been her reason for inviting the girl to Tally Ho. She is increasingly anxious to keep Hawkins at bay, having found a bracelet, belonging to Francie and inscribed with the date of the sailing accident. In reality the bracelet is a gift from Lambert, bought with the money Charlotte has lent him to pay his debts. Among the skilful subtleties of *The Real Charlotte* is the frequency by which Miss Mullen's passion for Roddy Lambert leads her to false conclusions. On this point alone she is vulnerable, her genius for intriguing for her own ends availing her nothing. Setting a snare for Christopher, she engineers that Francie shall spend a few days at Bruff.

As Francie arrives at Bruff her honey-pot quality even warms mad Sir Benjamin's old heart, and he is profuse with compliments and offers of rides in his carriage. Both wearing tall hats, he and his keeper, James Canavan, progress through the woods, one wheeling, the other wheeled, like a couple by Daumier strayed into a painting by Corot. James Canavan, a character based on the hedge-schoolmaster at Ross, plays the same role as theatrical producer for the Dysart family. The play performed in the coach house is an insane version of Kenilworth. James Canavan plays Queen Elizabeth, strikingly dressed in the cook's skirt, a gold-paper crown on his iron-grey locks, a ham-frill concealing his whiskers, and Sir Benjamin's deputy-lieutenant's coat, with long tails and silver epaulettes. The play ends with Queen Elizabeth's dance of triumph on the old ottoman used as Amy Robsart's tomb, that heroine, played by a young cousin, only being rescued when Canavan's weight has broken the lid and he is dancing on the body. Francie has suffered social agonies among the refinements of Bruff, but only after she has spent the period of the play closeted with Hawkins in a brougham at the back of the coach house does she begin to have doubts as to her handling of her admirers. Lady Dysart, already disapproving, is further appalled when Hawkins runs the steam-launch aground and Francie is stuck with him for hours on a shoal. By now Francie is far gone in love. Far gone in jealousy, Lambert with savage pleasure reveals that Hawkins is engaged to a rich girl in Yorkshire. Discreditable as is its source—Hawkins's soldier-servant has read the letters and told Lambert's groom—Francie has to believe the news. They are all together at a rough-and-tumble party at the lower reaches of Lismoyle society. Shaken by his treachery, she snubs Hawkins, who is congenitally incapable of supporting a moment's frustration. His revenge is to make a vulgar exhibition of himself, dancing with two partners at once, and, after they have let him fall flat

on his back, chasing them with boxes on the ear as they polka
round the room.

Charlotte, preparing to make a scene about the misadventure
in the steam-launch, is placated by the news that the detrimental Hawkins is already booked for marriage. Unknown to
her, a meeting takes place when Francie, in her anger and her
beauty, excites Hawkins to the pitch of promising he will marry
no one but herself. Their careless, sunny idyll is, however,
over, and thunderclouds of trouble roll towards them. Mrs
Lambert begins, at last, to be aware of her husband's infatuation with Francie, and her choice of Charlotte as a confidante
is a factor in bringing about her own death. Charlotte, herself,
winds her snares with increasing success round Christopher
Dysart. He can see the trap set for him, but Francie's attraction
makes him unable to resist, quieting the criticism of his intellect
by endeavouring to awaken a spiritual response in this Undine,
a nymph without a soul.

Miss Duffy of Gurthnamuckle, ill and barely sane, struggles
as far as Tally Ho on her way to Bruff, in the desperate hope
that an appeal to Sir Benjamin may avert the action threatened
by Lambert. From her cousin Norry the Boat, a hovering
vulture for gossip, she learns that it is Charlotte who is behind
the intrigues to get possession of Gurthnamuckle. Reaching
Bruff, Miss Duffy makes her appeal to Sir Benjamin, apparently
a benign patriarch in his bath-chair. A mention of young
Mr Christopher brings forth a flood of madman's curses. Miss
Duffy staggers back to Tally-Ho, to find Christopher in the
garden reading poetry aloud to Francie. In a last effort before
madness closes in on her, she taunts them with being the
puppets in Charlotte's matrimonial schemes.

Mrs Lambert's confidences have bred a worm of jealousy to
eat Charlotte's heart and she bullies the poor Turkey Hen into
the belief that it is her duty to go through Lambert's private
letters. Self-righteously she refuses her physical assistance in a
search only permissible, she says, for a wife. The heavy box of
papers brings on a heart attack under which Mrs Lambert collapses. Charlotte has a moment of decision when she can read
the letters or revive her friend. Choosing to read the letters, she
finds that Mrs Lambert has passed beyond hearing her noisy
lamentations. The day of the funeral precipitates a proposal

from Christopher, but Francie regretting, with objectivity, that she cannot respond, brushes the offer aside. Her distressed state is obvious, and Norry the Boat, loyal only to her own tribe, betrays what has happened to Charlotte. In a scene where Lambert's name is torn between them as dogs tear a bone, Charlotte drives Francie from the house, back to her Fitzpatrick kindred.

Come down in the world, the Fitzpatricks are living at Bray in an Irish version of Jane Austen's Price family's life at Portsmouth. Suffering already from the cramped discomfort and bad food, Hawkins' brief and wounding letter in which he makes it clear that he has been lured back to his betrothed by the prospect of an escape from his debts, reduces Francie to the lowest spirits. When the widower Lambert appears at Christmas he is particularly welcome as someone from the happy past. Together on the pier at Kingstown they watch the passengers disembarking from the mail-boat, among them not only Lady Dysart and Pamela but also Hawkins. In this confrontation Hawkins offers an uneasy apology for his perfidy but, though Francie keeps up a brave front, she is aware that the train that bears him away in a first-class carriage is carrying him finally out of her life.

The tenancy of Gurthnamuckle has now been passed to Charlotte, and, though her scheme for Francie has failed, she feels that Lambert's young horses, grazing outside her windows, are hostages, showing that he is securely in her power. Lambert's letter telling her that he is marrying Francie brings on a fit of passion so terrible that even the mother of all the cats flees from her. Below in the kitchen, Norry hears the news, and the look of wild hilarity which crosses her face shows that she has seen further than others into Charlotte's dark mind. The days of Miss Mullen's blindness are over, and with them Lambert's security, built on the belief that he can rely on her infatuation.

A jovial letter of congratulation from Charlotte is the first crooked step on the path of her revenge. It is so successful in lulling Lambert into unsuspicious confidence that, when he and Francie are summoned home by Sir Benjamin's death, he writes to ask Charlotte to see that his house is ready for his bride. This gives her the opportunity to go through his letters, and, after some quick work with a hair-pin has shown her that the bills which were the excuse for her loan are still unpaid, she goes for bigger game. Ordering a kettle on the pretext of warming her chilled frame with some punch, she steams open the passbooks belonging to Lambert and to the Bruff estate. Their content gives her the evidence to effect his material destruction, but she needs to tear his heart to cauterize her own wounds.

Hawkins, returned to Lismoyle, begins to show renewed interest in Francie, no longer a cast-off sweetheart, but a well-dressed married woman of increased good looks. Lambert, too obtuse to conceive that Charlotte may be plotting against him, leaves her as chaperone to his wife when he goes rent-collecting. Charlotte makes Hawkins's way so easy that Francie, struggling with the revival of her old love, begins to weaken. Apprehending that Francie is on the point of agreeing to elope, Charlotte strikes, laying her evidence of Lambert's peculations before Christopher Dysart. The collapse of the prosperous appearance of a life built upon fraud shatters Lambert. His piteous state gives Francie a revulsion from the idea of deserting him to go with Hawkins to Australia. Reassured that at least Francie will stand by him, Lambert rides to Gurthnamuckle to raise a further loan from Charlotte, still unconscious that she is the instigator of his downfall. Christopher Dysart, finding that he cannot bear to sack Francie's husband, calls to tell her that Lambert may keep the agency. Francie is back in her quandary, but feeling that here, at least, is some good news for Lambert she also rides towards Gurthnamuckle, with the object of finding her husband and evading a call from Hawkins. However she is overtaken by her lover, in the state of aggrievement into which any thwarting of his appetites invariably puts him. Beside the road Billy Grainy, the red-eyed beggar, is drooling drunkenly, ' "Ould bones is wake." ' Miss Duffy is being brought home for burial, while Billy curses those who drove her to die, mad, in the Union. Francie and Hawkins find themselves riding level with the funeral, Francie begging Hawkins to wait for her answer until the procession of carts, with the long yellow coffin in the midmost, is past. Crouched round the coffin, a group of women prepare to raise the *caoine*, the Irish cry. Norry the Boat, still vulture like, rises from the straw, the black wing of her cloak flapping across the face of Francie's mare. The mare, with a succession of bucks, unseats Francie, whose hat is shaken off as she falls on her head into the road.

When Lambert arrives at Gurthnamuckle, Charlotte is mending rat holes in the potato loft. The dank, hot loft, and the obscenely sprouting potatoes, make a suitably sinister background for the revelation of Charlotte's real nature. Relishing the slow torture, she allows Lambert to piece together the stages by which she has ruined him. Then she moves in for the kill, with the news that Francie will be leaving him for Hawkins. Replete with revenge, she watches him wither at the blow, only to be interrupted by wild cries from Norry that Francie is lying dead on the road with a broken neck. Seeing Lambert, Norry the Boat covers her face with the cloak which has precipitated the final tragic accident.

6

Shoneen games

IT will be clear from the previous chapter that the texture of *The Real Charlotte* is tightly woven. Also, though the stage is full, it is never overcrowded, each character having a function in the plot that could be fulfilled by no other. In this book weather plays the part of a character, appearing in different costumes, as the hot Dublin streets, rancid with the smells of urban summer, change to the blazing blue skies and sudden storms that come rustling across the lake at Lismoyle.

'Late that afternoon, when the sun was beginning to stoop to the west, a wind came creeping down from somewhere back of the mountains, and began to stretch tentative cat's paws over the lake. It had pushed before it across the Atlantic a soft mass of orange-coloured cloud, that caught the sun's lowered rays, and spread them in a yellow glare over everything. The lake turned to a coarse and furious blue; all the rocks and tree stems became like red gold, and the polished brasstop of the funnel of the steam-launch looked as if it was on fire as Captain Cursiter turned the *Serpolette's* sharp snout to the wind, and steamed at full speed round Ochery point. The yacht had started half an hour before on her tedious journey home, . . . her sails all aglow as she leant aslant like a skater, swooping and bending under the threatening breeze.'

It is in this storm that Lambert, distracted by Francie's presence, capsizes the yacht, and, in his furious reaction to Christopher holding Francie out of the water, betrays how strongly jealousy has already gripped him. The scene when Charlotte turns Francie out of the house has for a background a heavy damp day, 'both close and chilly', the foggy dew hanging on the fuchsias as Francie edges into the window, in retreat from Charlotte's brutal inquisition. The meeting at Kingstown, when Hawkins makes a casual apology for jilting Francie, takes place when a frosty December evening has already chilled her. Undernourished, thinly dressed, and abandoned by her lover, she finds an escape in her surrender to Lambert.

An essential quality in *The Real Charlotte* is the fairness with which the authors treat the three principal characters. Although, Edith wrote, they felt that they had killed a trusting bird when they 'finished Francie', they did not lose objectivity. Francie regrets sincerely that love for another hinders her from marrying Christopher Dysart. Stranded at Bray among the Fitzpatricks, she even dreams of summoning Christopher to her rescue. It is only a dream, for Francie shares the distaste of a very different Frances, Fanny Price in *Mansfield Park*, for the idea that the inferiority of her connections might be a more powerful deterrent to an unwanted suitor than her own unwavering resistance. Through all his vanity and lack of scruple, Lambert's passion for Francie is so strong that he becomes a genuinely tragic figure. Charlotte is endowed by her creators with a variety of physically repellent traits, including bubbles of rage which appear like snail's horns at the corners of her mouth, but she is allowed a moment of sardonic enjoyment when Christopher Dysart, deluded fool of love, lends Rossetti's poems to flutter-brained Francie. Charlotte has to suffer acute sexual jealousy, both of Mrs Lambert and of Francie, when the Turkey Hen, helpless before the passions that are disrupting her life, reveals that Lambert talks about Francie in his sleep. Even after Charlotte has begun her system of revenge she can still admire Lambert's swaggering seat on horseback. Systematically she undermines Francie's confidence in her husband, but gives the girl moral support by briefing her with the scandals of the neighbourhood when they pay calls together.

Balancing between biographical fiction and creative fantasy, Somerville and Ross fitted together, with extreme smoothness, the creations of imagination, and characters acknowledged to have been based, to a certain extent, on real people. James Canavan, who unfortunately leaves the story at Sir Benjamin's death, is, as has been said, a recollection of Tucker, the hedge-schoolmaster, employed as a kind of steward at Ross. Sir Benjamin has a possible genesis in Martin's childhood memories of her grandfather in his dotage. In the novel he lures Francie towards his bath-chair with senile ogling, while James Canavan executes a young rat, bolted by a ferret, with a sadistic flourish of a stick, in keeping with his behaviour when impersonating Queen Elizabeth. These figures came from Martin's background. Edith contributed Lady Dysart, a portrait of her own mother, someone who 'habitually said what other people were half afraid to think', but who could be easily gulled to behave as it suited such smooth operators as Lambert and Charlotte. Edith must also be considered responsible for the closest acquaintance with the unhappy woman some of whose characteristics were reproduced in Charlotte Mullen. Other characteristics were the work of creative fantasy, but among them, as often happens to novelists, the imaginary turned out to be the real. After the book had appeared it was revealed to the authors that they had reproduced, in Charlotte's relationship with Lambert and his wife, a love affair, thought by Edith and Martin to have been impossible. Dealings with the psychic were much practised at Castletownshend. It was hardly surprising that a message should have been mediumistically received through Edith's sister Hildegarde, breathing bitter hatred, and supposedly emanating from the deceased original of Charlotte.

The lake, like the weather, almost an actor in the plot, would seem to be Lough Corrib, but Lismoyle is filled with more middle-class Protestants than Oughterard is likely to have housed. In a book rich in *tours de force*, the party at Mrs Beattie's is set before the reader with the kind of brilliance that brings to life those awkward social occasions by which Dostoievski furthers the plot of *The Devils*. Mrs Beattie gave two parties every year, one at Christmas for the mistletoe, a wise step for the mother of six daughters, and one for the raspberries in their season. It is at the raspberry party, where the hostess had 'trawled Lismoyle and its environs with the purest impartiality', that Lambert breaks the news of Hawkins's engagement to Francie, and Hawkins riots with two partners at once. The spirit of the occasion is further illuminated by one of the young lady guests. ' "Well, I suppose I might as well confess," said Miss Baker, with a frivolous laugh, "that there's nothing I care for like flirting, but p'pa's awful particular! Wasn't he for turning Dr. M'Call out of the house last summer because he caught me curling his moustache with my curling tongs; 'I don't care what you do with officers,' says p'pa, 'but I'll not have you going on with that Rathgar bounder of a fellow!' " ' Reasons for this poor opinion of Rathgar are not given. (Curiously enough, it was the Church of the Three Patrons, Rathgar, that Joyce selected for the baptism both of L. Bloom and S. Dedalus.) Mr Hawkins, the only officer available at Mrs Beattie's, does his best to come up to the company's expectations. His deviousness, a contrast to his cheerful red face and yellow curls, comes into play when, repulsed by Francie, he enjoys himself uninhibitedly without her. This gives him the opportunity to assure Captain Cursiter that he has hardly said a word to Miss Fitzpatrick.

The Real Charlotte was received by the family circle with the usual volley of abuse, and its first reviews were equally disapproving. Mrs Somerville spoke for her familiars when she wrote to her daughter, 'All here loathe Charlotte,' modifying her own opinion, as was her custom, when that of the public improved. Eventually, as the book's fame increased, only the die-hards in their families held out against its fascination. Among these was a cousin, who repudiated it as holding nothing but 'curses and dirty kitchens', and a younger brother who wrote that 'such a combination of bodily and mental hideosity as Charlotte could never have existed outside of your and Martin's diseased imaginations'. Unintentionally, this harsh criticism contains an element of truth regarding the part that imagination plays in a novelist's creation of character. Even for the writers themselves some months passed before they realized that they had hit a jack-pot.

A visit paid by Martin to St Andrews in January, 1895, first brought them to a knowledge of the extent of their success. Martin found herself to be a literary lioness, to whom people were introduced at their own request. *The Real Charlotte* was represented to her, more than once, as resembling *La Cousine Bette*, obliging her to admit that neither writer had read Balzac. Her letters to Edith, describing this triumphant progress, brought out an aspect of her personality that was usually in the background. At her first dinner party she sat on the left of Andrew Lang, her host. He opened the conversation with the conventionally banal, 'I suppose you're the one who did the writing?', but he accepted Martin's exposition of their method

of work, and they settled down to a long talk about Oscar
Wilde. The Wilde family were famous, and indeed sometimes
scandalous, figures in Martin's Dublin life. Edith had had
an interview with Oscar some years before when he was editing
The Woman's World. The interview had not gone well. She had
been repelled by his physical appearance, and by his editorial
unwillingness to buy the goods that she and Martin had to
offer. Edith had also complained about his oily praises of
Martin's sisters, in which Edith Dawson was singled out for
particular commendation. With these prejudices, had Edith
Somerville been in Martin's place, it is improbable that Oscar
Wilde would have been her subject of conversation with
Andrew Lang. As it happened, shortly after this dinner party,
Wilde became a subject undiscussible in mixed society.

Through fog and snow, Andrew Lang took Martin sight-
seeing in St Andrews, where, shown some ruins, she acquitted
herself well by quoting Lang's sonnet which begins;

> 'The sacred keep of Ilion is rent
> With shaft and pit;'

Indeed the only awkward moment in their association came
when Martin gave her famous imitation of a dog whose tail
has been shut in a door. Perturbed and unamused by this parlour trick, Lang asked in an unhappy way how she did it. 'I
said by main strength,' Martin wrote, 'the way the Irishman
played the fiddle.'

A tour of Edinburgh, also conducted by Lang, happened to
end at the house of an Irish professor of Greek. Here Martin
was pinned down by her hostess and Mrs Andrew Lang, and
cross-examined on the question as to whether there had been
an original of Charlotte Mullen. In her extremity, she found
herself obliged to admit that Miss Mullen had been a portrait
of a particular person, far better known to Edith than to herself. This disclaimer was a comfort to her when, having let slip
the name of the original, it turned out to be that of a cousin of
her host. The professor of Greek was, however, delighted. *The
Real Charlotte's* popularity as a book seems, almost, to have
been equalled by its original's unpopularity as a person.

In an album of press cuttings and odd photographs, Martin
preserved a collection of views of St Andrews, memorials of

this visit. Andrew Lang, the resident Scotch lion, had treated the visiting lioness from Ireland with respect, finding her company intellectually stimulating. Considering this encounter with Andrew Lang, and her later meeting with Yeats, it is impossible to believe that, even had she belonged to a less talented tribe, Martin would not have made for herself a literary reputation. She found her complement in Edith, but contemporary writers and their writings were to Edith like a Foreign Affairs department, for which she was happy that Martin should act as Secretary. Lang saw Martin off from Edinburgh station, bundling himself out of the carriage in the middle of a description of Buddha dying from a surfeit of roast pork.

From St Andrews to Edith in Paris, Martin wrote that, in the *Weekly Sun*, there was a long and favourable review of *The Real Charlotte*, headed *The Shoneens*, 'whatever they may be'. The review was by T. P. O'Connor, who had founded the paper a few years before. Originally elected to Parliament for Galway as a supporter of Parnell, in this year, 1895, he was returned for the Scotland division of Liverpool, a staunchly Irish constituency which he represented for the next forty years. O'Connor took the opportunity, in his review, to release some of his own feelings about Ireland. These make strange reading to those accustomed to the uncritical adulation of their country habitual to Irish politicians of a later vintage.

O'Connor wrote that he found the depression of a visit to Ireland so weighty that, on his return, it took him several days to recover his tone. Much as he had admired *The Real Charlotte*, its effect on his spirits had been to put him into an equal state of gloom. Analysing the reason, he came to the conclusion that it was the pitiless exposure of the Shoneens which made him feel so low. Shoneen, he explained, was a Gaelic word, more derogatory than the English hybrid 'squireen', and much favoured as a term of political abuse. It implied a lower middle-class struggler, trying to raise himself by hanging on to the English-dominated class above him. O'Connor thought that to be a complete Shoneen it would be necessary to be a Catholic, so that religion, race and class would, all three, be betrayed.

Although the principal characters of *The Real Charlotte* were

Protestants, O'Connor recognized the book as a faithful mirror
of the world of the Shoneens. He considered the writers to be
so savagely truthful that they must be born Shoneen, casti-
gating the corruption of their own class. Carried along by this
basic misapprehension, he reproached Somerville and Ross for
giving nothing but virtues to the 'English' characters, while
heaping vices on the Irish. He overlooked the sinister goings-
on of mad Sir Benjamin, the exquisite boringness of Miss
Hope-Drummond, and, even less excusably, the selfish vil-
lainies of Hawkins. Although in love with Francie, he deplored
her vulgar obsession with officers. Equally he was repelled by
the squalor of Miss Mullen's action in scraping ashes off a
candle with her own hair-pin, though admitting that the gesture
was fascinatingly familiar to him, typical of a land where, if a
live coal or sod of turf was available, to strike a match would
be sinful waste.

The smallness of Ireland's population, stabilized at about
four-and-a-half million, has meant that certain experiences have
been shared by all levels of society. For example, the expression
'to take the boat' used, as it still is, by those emigrating to
work in England, would mean that mail boat which Stephen
Dedalus saw cutting through the sea between the Bailey and
Kish lights. The same boat brought the Dysarts and Hawkins
back to Kingstown Pier, where, had it not been Sunday, Davy
Stephens 'ringletted . . . with a bevy of barefoot newsboys'
(*Ulysses*) might well have been shouting 'Irish Times'. James
Joyce's own family, when in financial straits, left Bray, to live
in Fitzgibbon Street, near Mountjoy Square. Conversely, it was
to Bray that the Fitzpatricks retreated to economize, leaving
Mountjoy Square, in whose garden Francie had played what
Joyce called 'Shoneen games, the like of lawn tennis'. Her
uncle, Robert Fitzpatrick, settling a greasy satin tie under his
beard before catching the 8.30 train into Dublin, and her father
'Nosey' Fitzpatrick would have been suitable familiars of
Leopold Bloom. Francie, throwing pebbles on the shore with
her medical student admirers, under the shadow of the martello tower, is as evocative of the same Dublin background as
the creations of James Joyce with whom she shares it. Like a
repertory company, with all the plays in the world to choose
from but with few other resources, the actors and scenery

constantly reappear. Somerville and Ross never again made a sustained effort to write of such a world as Francie Fitzpatrick's, but they used the same skill to build other worlds in which the ghost of Francie sometimes walked.

7

Poulleen-a-Férla

UNTIL they wrote *The Silver Fox* in 1897, hunting had not been in the foreground of any of Edith and Martin's books. The few hunting scenes in *An Irish Cousin* are not essential to the movement of the story. If *In the Vine Country* begins with a disastrous morning's cub-hunting it is only as a contrast to the pleasures of the *vendange*, and in *The Real Charlotte* fox-hunting is barely mentioned, except as a past glory of Gurthnamuckle. A new element, both inspiring and intrusive, entered the cousins' work when Aylmer Somerville, supported by Edith, restarted the West Carbery Hounds. There had been no history of hounds at Ross, except for a ghostly white pack described in Martin's story *The Dog from Doone*. These manifested themselves from 'a drift of white mist clinging to the grass . . . They went on into the wood, over a wall, and they were blurred and cloudy as they went over the wall.'

Ghostly the revived West Carbery were not, but they were almost as unorthodox as the country over which they hunted. Except for far-off days when, flouting the commands of her parents, Edith's grandfather would sneak away with her to find the hounds, the only hunting in the neighbourhood had been arranged by contractors engaged on building the local railway. In the year in which Edith and Martin met, these enterprising sportsmen had persuaded the master of a private pack to hunt the country one day a week. The master, Dick Beamish, came from a huge clan, of whom it was said in Cork, 'If a gentleman unknown to you should pass you the time of day you will be safe if you respond, "Why then, Captain Beamish, it is a soft day indeed!" ' This would cover the probable identity of the stranger and the prevailing state of the weather in Cork. In the middle reaches of the clan, the name would change in its bearer's mouth from 'Beamish' to 'Baimish'. Dick Beamish moved at this half-way mark, his position being

analogous to that created for Flurry Knox when Somerville
and Ross brought a clan of their own to birth. The resemblance
went no further, for Dick Beamish was an ebullient, red-
bearded figure, remote from the guilefully calm Flurry. He
went through a covert cheering his hounds, 'Thatsy-atsy-atsy
my darlin's! Find him for me Thruelove and Naygress, good
bitchies!'

Edith wrote an ecstatic letter to Martin telling her of a day
with Mr Beamish's Hounds, when 'besides old friends, Wood-
boine and Waurrior and Saulaman and Jaally' there were newcomers, 'a couple and a half of long-legged black things, with
long ears, and melancholy faces, that Dick calls Kerry Beagles
(I mean Baigles), and look like harriers in deep mourning.' By
luck and valour, Edith and Aylmer found themselves alone
with hounds. 'An adorable Kerry baigle (Naygress, I think)
was leading them, and her yowls were enough to tear the very
heart out of you—like the most piercing old woman at a
funeral!'

When, four years after the run with Mr Beamish's Hounds,
Aylmer began to hunt the revived West Carbery, Edith took
the hounds to her heart. She wrote in her diary, 'Christened the
new draft, seven and a half couple of puppies . . . The instant
they were coupled they went stark mad and fought, mostly in
the air; it looked like a battle of German heraldic eagles.'

These hounds had been built by loving and judicious care
into a useful pack when they were struck by hydrophobia.
Rarely encountered today, the story of the terrors of this
disease reads like an eye-witness account of the Black Death.
For humans, bitten by rabid dogs, there was the hope that a
swift journey to Pasteur's clinic in Paris might save their lives.
Subsequently Edith, by the kindness of Pasteur, was allowed
to make drawings of the consultation and treatment of the
patients at his surgery. Pasteur's reputation was already so
great that Lionel Dawson, only child of Martin's sister Edith,
was rushed to Paris from India, after being bitten by a dog, to
be inoculated by the wizard himself. For the hounds death
was the only solution, but the poison, that should have been
given them before the onset of the raving phase, was delayed.
The kennelman saw the symptoms of raging madness beginning to appear and, with wild courage, dragged out and shot

every one of the twenty couple. He loved the hounds, Edith wrote, and, after this holocaust, he had the white face and glaring eyes of a man who had seen hell.

Gifts from other hunts rebuilt the West Carbery, which was hunted by Aylmer Somerville for twelve years, until a crisis induced Edith to buy the hounds. With one interval they remained hers for nearly twenty years, during which time 'Master' was an inadequate word for her position. More appropriate was the title bestowed by a petitioner to the Fowl Fund. The letter merely set forth the familiar list of casualties among hens and ducks, but the envelope was addressed with poetical splendour.

> Miss Sommerville,
> Castle Thousand
> Commander of
> Hounds.
> In haste.

Away from the rough and tumble of her own hunt, Edith took her young mare, Novelty, to Leicestershire, where cousins were willing to take her out with the Quorn, in the hope of attracting a buyer. Novelty took to hunting High Life, jumping her fences flippantly. Edith was almost equally flippant about human High Life, writing to tell Martin that Lord Lonsdale had laughed when she rode down Prince Pless. She was hardly more repentant at having cut in, at a nasty place, on Tom Firr, most famous of Quorn huntsmen. Firr's lugubrious appearance made Edith think of a stage butler, and gave her a pang of home-sickness for her own unorthodox huntsman, cheering the West Carbery into a shaggy hillside. She did not realize that Tom Firr's air of decorum was superficial, concealing his longing for a bit of fun. When the wilder followers of the Quorn secretly organized a moonlight steeplechase, Firr was furious that his neck had been considered to be too valuable to be risked on such an enterprise. Edith's day ended in a spectacle of violence, such as she had never seen in her own country. Against a frosty sunset sky, two figures, as she said, by Charles Lever out of Randolph Caldecott, suddenly laid into each other with their hunting crops.

A portrait of Novelty, the young mare, survives in a delicate study, photographed on the strand at Castlehaven. Sir Joscelyn Coghill, brother of Mrs Somerville, had been a pioneer of photography and his family maintained his high technical standard. In *Wheel-tracks* Edith reproduced a 'fancy study', taken by Sir Joscelyn, her uncle, of her father Colonel Somerville, a cowled monk in prayer, with a skull at his elbow. He holds a small cross before his eyes, and a rosary depends from his fingers. Although Church of Ireland principles probably required that both crosses should be bare, rather than crucifixes, there is a zeal in the model's attitude which suggests that Colonel Somerville might have felt such a vocation a relief from the strain of family life.

Whether taken by Sir Joscelyn or not, the group on the strand is composed with an originality that recalls Degas. Hildegarde Somerville, who must have married her cousin Egerton Coghill at about this time, stands on the shingle holding a fox terrier. Other dogs lounge on the pebbles with that consciousness of the camera's presence born in all domesticated canines. In the shallow water Edith gently walks her mare, Novelty. The repose of the moment is complete, girls, horse and dogs, caught motionless, but intensely alive against the long arm of water that shimmers between the headlands on its way inland from the Atlantic.

Professor Guy Fehlmann, of the University of Caen in his study *L'Irlande disparue de Somerville and Ross*, makes the following comment. '*Le lecteur a l'impression d'assister à un dialogue entre deux races, deux sociétés, deux conceptions de la vie qui s'opposent en tous points.*' This opinion, unusually objective in coming from a source neither English nor Irish, applies particularly to *The Silver Fox*, the novel which followed *The Real Charlotte*. Edith considered, with some justice, that the book had suffered from forced dramatic curtains, made necessary by its original appearance as a serial. The division between the two societies is clearly marked. On the one hand stand Hugh French of French's Court, and his cousin Slaney Morris. This girl has 'the intolerance of the clever provincial' for Hugh's wife, Lady Susan, and the bantering screech of inanities which pass for conversation in the brassy Englishwoman's world. Slaney can, however, admire Lady Susan's elegance, while deploring the black pencilled eyelids and the hair dyed fox-red in Paris. Opposed to the Frenches, stand the family of Quin, who have sold land of ill-omen to a railway contractor, Wilfred Glasgow. The local legend says that if the hill of Cahirdreen is thrown into the lake of Tully, which Glasgow's new railway line has brought about, evil fortune will follow. Naturally everyone assumes that this outrage is responsible for the appearance of a silver fox in the neighbourhood, obviously either a fairy or a witch.

Danny Quin, first victim in the chain of disaster, breaks his neck, his funeral owing its vividness to Martin's experience of Galway wakes. The steadfast presence of the corpse in the open coffin mutely rebukes the living, who, soaked in cheap whiskey and gossip, take a gambling interest in the size of 'the altar', moneys contributed for Masses by the condolers. Tom Quin, Danny's son, after a series of violent scenes, disappears and his body is dragged by boat-hooks from a pond that glimmers darkly in a pale setting of sedge grass, as Poulleen-a-Férla must have glimmered in the Wood of Annagh at Ross. Like the poor mad boy of Martin's letter, Tom Quin had left his scapular lying beside the Little Pool of the Pearl, to make sure that his drowning should not be hampered by a sacred object.

In Wilfred Glasgow, the railway contractor, Professor Fehlmann considers that Somerville and Ross created a 'stage Englishman'. Insensitive to the point of stupidity, his mishandling of the local labour force lands him in financial troubles. Slaney Morris, who has been courted by Glasgow, has the luck to discover that he is already married to a wife he conceals. Rebuffed, Glasgow begins a flirtation with Lady Susan. A kind of railway picnic is arranged, which involves Slaney in a melodramatic race on a light engine, to intercept what appears to be the elopement of Lady Susan with Glasgow, on the only other engine working the line. The elopement remains a matter of speculation, as a landslide stops both engines and wrecks Glasgow's contract. The silver fox's malign influence follows Glasgow to the Argentine, and sends him to his death in a fall down a mine shaft. At home the ghost of Old Quin, and the silver fox itself, contrive a run with the hounds in which Hugh French, tortured by an anonymous letter about his wife and Glasgow, regains his nerve, which he had lost, and survives a nasty fall. Payment being complete, the rest of the characters settle down, Lady Susan with renewed affection, and Slaney with an admirable friend of the family, Major Bunbury, as a husband.

Among a caste of characters, thin in comparison with the richness of *The Real Charlotte*, Lady Susan is the most success-fully achieved. Her incomprehension of the country into which she has married is made plain when she picks up a letter, addressed to her husband and pushed under the hall door. To any native of Ireland such a letter would suggest either a threat or a warning, needing immediate attention in the in-terests of personal safety. To Lady Susan the straggling writing suggests only a washerwoman's bill to be dealt with at leisure. *The Silver Fox* opens with a skating party at Hurlingham, when Lady Susan has to be placated with champagne for having to make her luncheon from a share of the waiter's under-boiled leg of mutton. Throughout the book there is an atmosphere of seedy smartness at home, and high courage in the chase. The fast indulgences of hock-and-seltzer, and endless games of bézique, were far from the hard-working, unluxurious lives of the authors, but, essentially fair-minded, they allowed Slaney, 'the clever provincial', to feel that Lady Susan had her own fascination.

The only contrast to the hunting set is the Quin family, bound by a bargain gone sour, whose ill effects persist until Tom Quin lies dead, his face torn by the boat-hook that has dragged him from the pool. In their struggle against their 'Shocker' tendency, Edith and Martin do not appear to have considered death by drowning as excessively sensational. It was familiar to them both, Lough Corrib being as avid for victims as the Atlantic, and is a recurrent climax in their novels, from the grisly end of *Naboth's Vineyard* to the near murder in *The Big House of Inver*. About the time that *The Silver Fox* appeared the West Carbery hunted a silver grey prototype, which only obliged once with a run, but confirmed that such a creature, magical or material, could exist. Reviews were good, though there were complaints about the vulgarity of Lady Susan. The Nationalist *Irish Independent*, on the other hand, objected that a wake was observed without sympathy, but, as a compensation, found the devices for getting a fox out of a drain extremely amusing.

8

An assortment of angles

CHRONOLOGICALLY *The Silver Fox* was followed by *Some Experiences of An Irish R.M.*, but it is obviously desirable to treat the three volumes of R.M. stories as one book with a strong backbone of its own. It seems suitable, therefore, in this chapter, to consider the two volumes of collected writings, *All on the Irish Shore* (1903) and *Some Irish Yesterdays* (1906). The former was composed mostly of hunting stories, and the latter of reminiscent sketches from the early life of both cousins. *Some Irish Yesterdays* did, however, include two hunting items, both in their way worthy to be considered separately, as they were thus originally published, *A Patrick Day's Hunt* in 1902 and *Slipper's ABC of Fox-Hunting* in the following year.

A Patrick Day's Hunt was written by Martin, and, as a *tour de force*, may be compared with her trick of imitating a dog's squeal. Its opening, 'I wash myself every Sathurday morning whether I want it or no,' sets the tone for this tale of spoofs worked on one neighbour by another. From dislike of Anne Roche, the narrator beguiles her husband William Sheehan to come out with the hounds on Patrick's Day. William had been sent by his wife to borrow harness from Conny, the narrator, but finds himself instead at the meet at Kyleranny, on the back of his Shan Bui, the Irish name for a butter yellow horse with a black stripe down his back. Following a drag laid by Conny's two sons, the Shan Bui, after jumping into a line of washing and draping his head with a widow's petticoat, ends in his master's own yard. The hounds are in full cry and the Shan Bui 'wheeled into the gate as neat as a bicycle and every hound in the pack was in it before him'.

Conny was blasted by Anne Roche, when she met him a week later on his way to a funeral. He added, 'I'm told she gave William the Seven Shows of Cork on the head of it, but

indeed poor William had great courage the same day.' Edith
illustrated this story and *Slipper's ABC of Fox-Hunting*, for
which she wrote the rhymes. Late in her life she said that she
could still not draw a horse as she would wish, but she had
often a less ambitious and more merciless approach to her
human subjects. The final scene of the Patrick's Day hunt,
when every hound in the pack is harrying Anne Roche, her
children, her fowls and her livestock, is conceived with a
brutality approaching the Hogarthian, from Anne Roche beating off the hounds with a frying pan from a cart where she, an
infant and a goat have taken refuge, to the cat escaping from a
bedroom window, out of which a hound's face peers in frustration. The animals are all beautiful in their various states of
blood-lust and terror, but the human faces, contorted by
similar emotions, are generally repellent. In *Slipper's ABC of
Fox-Hunting* the verses jog along at a hound's pace, but their
point is made by the content of the drawings. For instance, the
four gaiters worn by the clever, plain mount of 'V is for Vet'
with their air of neat efficiency give a glimpse into the history
of both horse and rider. Even more masterly is the illustration
to the quatrain:

> 'Here's the Wrecker and earth-stopper,
> Bowld Willy Roche,
> They say a fried egg's
> The one thing he can't poach.'

The saturnine face of Willy Roche under his slouch hat is only
surpassed in villainy by the calculating wickedness in the eye
of his mongrel dog. In this drawing Edith got her effect by
economy of line, together with a bold, yet subtle, juxtaposition
of dark and light. It was when she combined the lessons she had
learnt in Paris with her deep observation of her own country
that her talent came nearest to genius. She makes the sad pictorial comment that pleasure must often be paid for in pain in
'J for Jog home', where two tired riders and a few limping
hounds recede into invisibility through a heavy sea-mist. It can
be compared in feeling to Leech's engraving 'A Wreck of a
Belle' from *Ask Mama*, in which the Earl of Ladythorne and
Miss de Glancy make their bedraggled way home through a
thunderstorm.

To return to *All On The Irish Shore* (1903), the theme of the first story is again the founding of a new pack of hounds, but the tone is one of cheerful brutality, lacking the melancholy which permeates *The Silver Fox*. A handsome tinker insinuates himself into the new M.F.H.'s establishment, fascinating also the Master's mother. This enthusiastic woman was 'one of those persons who may or may not be heroes to their valets, but whose valets are almost invariably heroes to them'. *The Tinker's Dog* of the story's title is surreptitiously hung by the tinker, who brings a claim that his dog has been slaughtered by the new draft of hounds. Rescued by the tinker's deaf and dumb sister, both the dog and woman develop ghostly habits. Eventually, after the tinker has been discovered to be making potheen in an illicit still in the gate-lodge, the dog and his rescuer replace their master and brother, to the culinary benefit of the hounds. 'Miss Fennessy, being deaf and dumb, is not perhaps a paragon lodge-keeper, but having . . . been brought up in a work-house kitchen, she has taught Patsey Crimmeen [the kennel-man] to boil stir-about *à merveille*.'

The tinker reappears as a crooked manipulator of horses in the next two stories, *Fanny Fitz's Gamble* and *The Connemara Mare*. Fanny Fitz is a pale, upper-class reflection of Francie Fitzpatrick, lacking the vulgar zest which made Francie so beguiling, but sharing the impecuniousness, which leads to buying a mare as a speculation. When the tinker has reissued the mare as a cob, she bolts with Fanny and a faithful admirer, bringing them to a happy ending. This climax is reached after a performance by the Green Coon Concert Party, given to raise funds for the hounds. The show opens when the amateur company with blackened faces under green turbans, sing 'While we were marching through Georgia', as they run out on to the stage of the local town hall. The audience, mostly farmers and country people, accept the entertainment in the spirit in which it is offered, only adhering to the rule, familiar to all who try to enliven their patter with local jokes, by which audience reaction to a mention of anything familiar is blankly negative, while supposedly esoteric witticisms from distant worlds promote the wildest laughter and stampings of applause. Edith's experience in raising money for the West Carbery by means of concerts enabled her to describe the antics of the Green Coons on the stage, and their painful struggles, after the show, to remove the burnt cork from their faces.

A Grand Filly sets out to describe a mixture of Mr Beamish's Hounds and the West Carbery, from the point of view of an Englishman in search of a horse. Having described the M.F.H.'s house as a square yellow box, that had been made a fool of by being promiscuously trimmed with battlements, the Englishman abandons his detachment. Acidulated horror is conveyed by Edith's picture of 'Robert's Aunt', an aged harridan who dines in bonnet and kid gloves, terrorizing her nephew the M.F.H. Less oracular than 'Mr. F's Aunt', she is more active physically. At the end of the story the Englishman has become so assimilated that he finds himself gripping a 'tink an', into which a hound puppy has wedged his greedy head, while Robert's Aunt tugs at the puppy's neck.

A Nineteenth Century Miracle gives the authors an opportunity to describe how a blind Blood Healer stops the flow from a cut artery, so that a horse, wounded on a stake, is saved from bleeding to death. The mysterious magic of the charm, half Christian, half pagan, by which the wound's edges are held together, is a moving contrast to the ungenerous vulgarity of the woman whose horse is healed. On the other hand, *High Tea at McKeown's* is a romp, having something in common with the gayer scenes in a much later novel, *Mount Music*. It is concerned with a vast family of Miss Purcells, who make a lightning reappearance in *A Horse! A Horse! (Further Experiences of An Irish R.M.*) when, mounted 'on an assortment of astute crocks' . . . 'apparently each was telling the others to get out of her way'. *High Tea at McKeown's* is served by 'a grey-haired kitchen maid, who . . . at a distance in the backyard was scarcely distinguishable from the surrounding heaps of manure'.

It was this description that roused a reviewer on *The Times* (and therefore anonymous) to accuse Somerville and Ross of unsavouriness. This unusual reaction shows a point of view it is hard to consider as anything but effete. On occasion Irish reviewers complained that readers might suppose the island to be inhabited solely by workshy drunkards, staggering from cattle market to wake, but most English reviewers handed out praise. The praise was, occasionally, misconceived, *The Bookseller* referring to G. Œ. Somerville [*sic*] as 'Mr. Somerville'

whose 'illustrations are at the top of his form'. (It is pleasant
to reflect that 'Mr. Somerville's' second initial might have
stood for Œdipus.) *The Times* reviewer was, however, under
no such misconception. Praising the vigour and delicacy of the
writing, and its feeling of out-of-door liveliness, he protested
at the details of cow-house and muck heap which, deplorably,
these two women writers were in the habit of including in their
stories. Particularly his stomach turned at a turkey, rescued
from the jaws of a hound, being served up for dinner with half
of its breast shaved off and a drumstick missing. This critic
was unable to face the uncomfortable fact that the gifts he
admired in Somerville and Ross grew not only from a knowledge of out-of-door life, but also from a knowledge of the
importance of muck heaps in the world of which they wrote.

Martin achieved another *tour de force* in *The Bagman's Pony*,
which is a reproduction of an Indian reminiscence as it was
told by Colonel Kendal Coghill, the most violently extrovert
of Edith's uncles. The story is strongly Kiplingesque, with its
atmosphere of absconding bagman, gibbering *sais* and tem-
peramental memsahib, but though the personality of the narrator comes roaring across to the reader, the Indian background, at second-hand, has none of the brilliance of observed
detail, colours, sounds and smells, which lifts the slightest of
Somerville and Ross stories above the commonplace.

The Times critic, previously quoted, praised the story *Match-
box*, only complaining that a man could not have ridden across
country on a lady's side-saddle without any practice. This was
the predicament of a Cork buckeen, riding across country to
head hounds from a drag line leading to a poisoned carcase,
laid down from spite as the result of local 'troubles'. Matchbox
goes well with her side-saddle male rider, but a countryman
slashing with a spade brings her down and she breaks her neck.
While the hounds are being whipped back from the poisoned
kill, the countryman and his confederates disappear, not, however, neglecting to steal the dead pony's bridle. Attacks on
riders by aggrieved countrymen are not rare in Somerville and
Ross, but this particular scene recalls the operations of the
pickpockets at the death of Jack Spraggon in *Mr. Sponge's
Sporting Tour*. The realism is maintained by mentioning that, in
due course, the hounds she has saved eat Matchbox.

As a story *The Dane's Brechin*' is a far more knockabout
affair. It should be explained that the brechin' is a piece of
harness and not an ecclesiastical garment. The only macabre
presence in the story is that of the Dean of Glengad's elderly
sister, 'not all there', and 'with a monstrous appetite and a
marked penchant for young men'. The philosophy of horse
dealing is examined in a sketch called '*As I was going to Bandon
Fair*'. Although only a slight knowledge of horses is needed
to recognize the air of solemn innocence which dealing in
them bestows, Edith and Martin point out that 'in the highest
walks of horsiness the desire to appear horsey has been left behind'. At Bandon Fair one dealer, at the summit of his profession, carries nothing more horsey than a matronly umbrella.
At the end of the day mysterious bargains are consummated in
the local hotel, where dirty pound notes are transferred among
the inevitably tough mutton chops and glasses of whiskey and
soda. 'On the wall above . . . a print in which Ananias and
Sapphira were the central figures gave a simple and suitable
finish to the scene.'

The most serious of the stories in *All on The Irish Shore* is
also the liveliest. Two travellers beguile a wait between mail-
cars, those Leviathans of the Irish roads, by listening to a case
in a small court-house in West Galway. The chairman of the
bench is the keeper of the local shop and public house. In fact
the imminence of the case is announced by his young son, red-
haired and dressed in a madder-dyed flannel frock. The child
summons his father's porter-drinking customers in between
spasms of whooping-cough, and, before they flock out to the
halls of justice, a kind drinker pours the dregs from his glass
down the messenger's throat as medical treatment. In the cottage court-house the visitors are given seats inside a kind of
abbreviated rood screen, while the chairman, supported by the
local doctor, sorts out a case against Sweeny brought by Darcy,
a neighbour, for the loss of a sheep supposedly driven into the
lake by Sweeny's dog. Darcy speaks only Irish, and the law
requires that the case should be heard in English, which allows
the magistrates to produce some bi-lingual wisecracks. The
two visitors are a 'general public' more in need of an interpreter
than anyone in court. The lost sheep is said to have been driven
into the lake by Sweeny's 'gorsoons' and the discussion as to

whether this Irish word means boys only, or children of both
sexes, reaches such a state of confusion that the doctor scores by
pointing out that children are usually of one sex or the other.
The chairman makes a hit when, on the question of the sheep's
identity, the interpreter is unable to translate the 'ullan' that
was on the animal's back except to suggest that some might
call it the 'rebugh'. Blasting the interpreter's incompetence,
the chairman asks the schoolmaster, considered to have more
command of the two languages, for his rendering. No one
appears surprised when the schoolmaster explains that the
expression is locally applied 'to what I may call a plume or a
feather, that is worn on various parts of the sheep's back, for a
mark, as I might say, of distinction'. When the increasingly
angry defendant invokes the Lord Almighty, he is cut short by
the chairman, who states firmly, 'The Lord's not interferin' in
this case at all, it's me an' Doctor Lydon has it to settle'.

Like an audience leaving at the end of a play, the observers
climb on to yet another mail-car, joining again the company of
tourists, whose generalizations on the Irish scene seem in-
finitely remote from the pattern of family quarrels that had
erupted in the cottage court-house. The story was called *An
Irish Problem*, the writers believing that near the heart of this
problem lay the fact 'that a virtuous, God-fearing man [such
as Sweeny] could enmesh himself in a tissue of sworn lies for
the sake of half-a-sovereign and a family feud, and that his
fellows would think none the worse of him for it'.

Some Irish Yesterdays, apart from *A Patrick Day's Hunt* and
Slipper's ABC of Fox-Hunting, was composed from articles
which cast light on Edith and Martin from their wild childhood
days to the middle of their careers. Muriel Currey, the daughter
of Martin's sister Katie, has analysed these pieces, much as an
expert on woodwork can indicate joins so imperceptible to a
less knowledgeable eye that they do not appear to interrupt the
surface. *An Outpost of Ireland*, the history of a holiday on the
Aran Islands, sprang from the chance remark of a landlady in
Galway town. She had repulsed the fore-quarter of mutton
offered by an Aran islander with the contemptuous words that
the islanders had 'a way of their own and a sense of their own like
the Indians'. Not as yet crowded by those seeking the remote
purity of a primitive society, Edith and Martin found that

neither the sense nor the way peculiar to Aran led to ease in housekeeping. When a subscription list was opened for a sheep it was only to be slaughtered if all possible physical options had been taken up, and, as the market was slack, the sheep continued to live as it could on the thin grass among the boulders. Failing a share of the sheep, Edith and Martin also lived as they could, the doom which seemed to hang over their domestic arrangements forcing them to exist on underdone potatoes, American bacon, and eggs, tasting, they insisted, of fish.

From their windows, however, the view was wide 'across a plain of sea to where the Connemara Mountains have pitched their tents in a jagged line'. Edith, the artist, was in her gentlest mood when she painted the summer daylight fading behind the Twelve Pins. Even a sketch of the bastion of Cromwell's castle, built with stones torn from the nearby Round Tower, has, with its figure of a rider retreating up the hill, a serenity which she sometimes failed to find in more familiar scenes. This serenity hardly came from a sympathy with the men of Aran, who were to the cousins hard-bargaining enigmas, 'motionless on the edges of Europe with the dust of the saints beneath their feet'.

Although veterans of many picnics, none of the elementary principles of cookery seem to have adhered to either Edith or Martin. Edith's sister Hildegarde, on the other hand, cooked successfully for some days on board a yacht in Youghal Harbour, only failing when she attempted to hash a tough duck in a sauce of flour, onions and sugar, 'a kind of onion jam', Edith wrote. *Picnics* begins with Martin's description, both lyrical and gruesome, of a secret meal in a disused lime-kiln, when knives were wiped on such spots on the deer-hound's back as were thought to be beyond the reach of his tongue. It was on this occasion that the turf boys, having shared the meal, skinned the children of their employers at Spoil Five as completely as any of the Soldiers Three could have wished. The rest of the picnics seem to have belonged to Castletownshend, a rosary of luncheon baskets forgotten, or becalmed in yachts, while hungry bicyclists watched from the shore. The Little God Pan who, according to E. M. Forster, presides over unsuccessful picnics, was apparently a regular guest at those attended by Edith and Martin.

Some Irish Yesterdays, a valuable book for disentangling the threads of Somerville and Ross material, owes, on the whole, more to Ross than to Castletownshend, though due to Edith's illustrations her presence makes itself felt in writing which can be attributed solely to Martin. Into this category comes *In Sickness and in Health,* words first heard by Martin at Ross, when, at an early age, the Irish marriage question came to her notice. Dressed in what she called 'a holland waggoner' she gaped from under a brother's elbow, while the couple made their uncompromising vows, and a few drops of brackish holy water found their way into Martin's open mouth. Afterwards the bridegroom mounted his shaggy horse, 'much as a man would climb a tree', and, hauling the bride up behind him, set off home at a lumbering gallop, pursued by cheering friends. Martin spent the afternoon gorging on soda bread, port and a boiled egg. 'At no subsequent wedding breakfast', she wrote, 'have I been as enjoyably dressed, and as a natural consequence at none have I eaten so much.'

Years later, a grown-up young lady in pince-nez, she went to a funeral at the same chapel. The priest was delayed, and burial took place by amateur hands. Earth, blessed by some vague agency, was shaken from a newspaper into the grave, followed by holy water from a soda-water bottle, which was itself thrown into the coffin. Walking away, Martin was hailed by the woman who had been the bride of twenty-five years before. Miss Violet, she said, would be known as belonging to the Martins ' "by the two eyes and the snout" '. These features, it may be mentioned, were said sometimes to be seen on the countenances of tenants on the estate.

That March Shrove Tuesday, with its jovial gallop, double-banked on the bridegroom's stout horse, seemed to Martin a sad contrast to the wet autumn evening and the long home-ward trudge. The wife would be walking behind a husband who 'would complete, at the always convenient shebeen, the glorious fabric of intoxication, of which the foundation had been well and truly laid at the funeral'. Martin's old acquaint-ance had a special reason for attracting her attention, wishing to pass on the news of the birth of triplets to a niece, 'daughters, unfortunately, but still a matter reflecting much lustre on the parish'. Towards this attraction the neighbourhood swarmed, but no feudal deference greeted Martin when she joined the crowd at the cabin where the triplets held their levée. A five-year-old boy, 'with tough, tight curls of amber, and an appallingly dirty face, regarded me from the doorstep with brazen sang-froid as I approached, and said in a loud and whining drawl: "What have ye on yer noase?" ' Taking this as a hint to remove her pince-nez, Martin squeezed into the room where the triplets, rocked in a cradle by the fire, received visitors. One had already, Martin wrote, 'retraced her way so far into the white trance of the unknown' that all had been made ready for her washing and laying out. After one day more 'the weak and lonely struggle ended in defeat'.

Contemplating the leisurely squalor of the life which this fleeting passer-by was not to share, Martin edged out from the mother's bedroom, making way for the Wise Woman who had come to give luck to the triplets by spitting on their heads. 'The evening . . . held like a headache the question whether it is useful to be sorry for those who are not sorry for themselves, and, unrepining, grope out their lives in the dark house of ignorance.' She speculated that, in her experience, the arranged marriages of Co. Galway seemed to carry their happy ending within themselves. Sordid family bargaining over the couple concerned, probably almost strangers to each other, was the natural prologue to a life as lived in the triplets' cottage, ending with such feelings as were once described to Martin in the words ' "their hearts were within in each other" '.

Except for *Children of the Captivity*, which considers the Irish imagination and its expression, the remaining pieces in *Some Irish Yesterdays* do not probe philosophical questions. *Boon Companions* was written mostly by Martin, beginning with the history of various ill-fated dogs at Ross, and ending with the Reign of Terror which two successive monkeys had inflicted on Drishane. Both equally repulsive and vicious in their habits, one had the additionally horrid trick of stealing matches and burning the hair off its arms, 'Thus invalidating the vaunt that man is the only animal that cooks.' The other monkey was subject to fits. They left little behind them, except the name of Mary the Monkey, attached to the much-bitten but devoted kitchen maid who had provided their meals.

The Biography of a Pump, also by Martin, would be worthy of a place in any History of Plumbing, particularly of that section which might deal with the unhappy marriages between the pumps of the eighteen-twenties and the bath-rooms of the eighteen-eighties. A lesser strain on the pump than supplying baths was the small quantity of water required for making punch on New Year's Eve. This was added to a jar of John Jameson poured into a hip bath, the last drops being lapped up by the ubiquitous turf boys, who lay round the bath in a ring and licked the enamel dry. In the background, Pete-een Bawn, the albino fiddler, scraped out a reel tune, 'The hare was in the corn', to the nodding of his lint-white head. On the floor maenad dancing went on until it was time to adjourn for the early Mass on New Year's Day.

Martin turned from the primitive, but touchingly spontaneous, gaiety of this occasion to consider an embryonic revolt which did not come to birth. The election of 1872 had always been to her the moment when the priest-led Nationalism of the new Galway had vanquished the feudalism of earlier days. Twenty years later, she wrote in *Out of Hand*, it was all that even an old and popular priest could do to shield an anti-Parnell candidate from a village mob. The moment when rival supporters might have got out of hand passed, and the *bona fide* travellers reached their journey's end in the shuttered public house. Edith underlined the story with a picture of a haunted-looking countryman, giving it as his opinion, 'A man must wote as his priest and bishop'll tell him.'

Horticultural is Edith's version of the relationship between a gardener and his employer, who has elements of Kendal Coghill, her uncle, in his character. Choosing only to cultivate three flowers, red geraniums, blue lobelias and yellow calceolarias, the gardener conceals them from his employer until he is able to plant them, fully grown, in the herbaceous border, 'uttering a note of colour only comparable to the shriek of a macaw'.

A Record of Holiday is more truthfully a record of shared holidays, ending with a declaration of loyalty to West Carbery on Edith's part, loyalty which did not include admiration for the Latin poem to the Rocks of Carbery composed by Dean Swift. The translation of this poem, which is appended to *A Record of Holiday*, was made by the Reverend Doctor Donkin,

a contemporary of Swift's, and it had been quoted in Doctor Smith's *History of the County Cork*, published in 1749. Lord Orrery wrote of Swift that 'he could not or would not distinguish between low flattery and just applause'. Edith was prepared to bestow neither flattery nor applause on Doctor Donkin's rendering. For a native of the Rocks such lines as 'And sea-calves stable in the oozey lake' could arouse nothing but derision.

Martin's childhood, as set out in *Boon Companions*, can be compared with Edith's as she described it in *Alsatia*, which is also a good example of the difficulties of deciding whose hand had held the pen. Maurice Collis has concluded that *Alsatia* is by Martin, judging that Edith had not the solemnity of style to achieve the opening sentence of the second paragraph, 'I look back and see a procession advancing from the most ancient places of memory.' In fact internal evidence, confirmed by Muriel Currey, shows that its background belongs to Drishane. Besides references to cliffs and tides, neither of which lay in the neighbourhood of Ross, there is mention of the village at the gates which can only be Castletownshend. There is also a family pattern, strictly Somerville in its shape, of a ruling patriarch and a young family of children close together in age, unlike the Martins, whose patriarch became senile before the youngest of the straggling family had reached the age of two. Edith's persistent persecutors were the savage turkey cock, and the almost more malignant stable helper, Old Michael. A mad dog had bitten Old Michael, but though he had obtained the recognized antidote by killing the dog and eating its liver, the vileness of his temper caused speculation as to the efficacy of the cure.

Hunting Mahatmas deals with those whose devotion to following hounds is combined with such an ability to avoid undue danger that they operate almost entirely in the Fifth Dimension, materializing at the end of a run to confound those who have merely ridden as hounds ran. This essay was Edith's, but, with Martin, the theme was fully developed in *Dan Russel the Fox*. Both hands were at work in *Lost, Stolen or Strayed*, but it is the relationship of the family of Sweeny to the Big House (of Ross) which animates the story. The surprise of seeing a copy of Byron's *Marino Falieri*, bound in green morocco and

D

reposing between a salt-herring and a hairbrush, when sheltering from the rain in the Sweenys' cabin, is scarcely dispersed
on learning that Patsy Sweeny, on his death-bed, had asked for
the consolation of a book. By the good will of some agent of
the Sweeny family this slightly unconsoling volume had been
plucked from the drawing-room book-case at Ross. More personally affecting was the occasion when Martin, attending the
confirmation of a Sweeny daughter, realized that the final touch
of whiteness to the child's snowy outfit had been given by
Martin's own new tennis shoes.

Although some of these articles are unpretentious bits of
journalism, and were so regarded by their writers, taken together they reflect life from an assortment of angles. There is
also, always, the sudden sparkle of the unexpected phrase, a
gift shared by both cousins. For example, in *A Record of
Holiday*, there is the discovery, in the public baths in the
Boulevard Montparnasse, that soap and towels are extra. This
involved handing out the needed coins 'through a difficult slit
of doorway, receiving in exchange a small fragment of slightly
scented marble and a gauze veil'.

Children of the Captivity, however, is on a grander scale, starting with the proposition that the country people of West
Galway were not, at that date, aware of their position as court
jesters to the English, aloof from the temptation, ever-
increasing since the days of Tom Moore, to exploit their native
speech and its songs. ' "As for our harps," said the Children of
the Captivity, "we hanged them upon the trees that are there-
in." That was when the songs of Zion were required of them
in a strange land and the strong Euphrates saw their tears. The
sympathy of all the centuries, wrote Martin, has been theirs for
that poignant hour; yet, as far as can be known, they were
spared an extremer pang. It is nowhere recorded that the
people of the strange land made any attempt to sing the songs
of Zion to the Children of Israel.'

Developing this idea, Martin pointed out that the English
conviction of being able to reproduce an Irish accent led not
only to telling Irish stories to Irishmen, but to the habit of
assuming that all classes of the Irish spoke with one tone of
voice and one vocabulary. Thackeray, with Captain Costigan,
she found to have been a particularly gross offender, and Kip-

ling, though admired, had carried on the guilty practice. She gave a shrewd assessment of Kipling's handling of supposedly Irish phraseology in his prose, in the same manner that George Orwell, forty years later, remarked Kipling's verse gained power by being transferred from Cockney spelling to plain English. Having said that the conventions of writing girl as 'gurl' and Queen as 'Quane' were unprofitable, Martin went on to give Kipling a salutary lecture. 'A laborious system of spelling exasperates the reader, jades the eye and fails to convince the ear.' The example she gave, an extract from *Krishna Mulvaney (Soldiers Three)*, proved her argument. Mulvaney, describing the Praying of the Queens at which he successfully impersonates Krishna, does indeed speak of 'the like of any loveliness in heaven', but to ears tuned, as were Martin's, by long hours of Irish conversation this was the only indication that the speech could have been made by an Irishman. She found no hint of 'the wayward and shrewd and sensitive minds that are at the back of the dialect'. Edith illustrated this essay with groups of figures, cutting turf and digging potatoes, that resemble Brueghel's peasants more closely than such figures of Etty-ish prettiness as Sir Frederick Burton's sketch of a Connemara peasant girl to be seen in the National Gallery of Ireland. Martin had the perception to appreciate and the objectivity to write, 'that the women digging the potato lands are talking of things that England does not understand'.

9

The Resident Magistrate

THE book which was to mis-label Somerville and Ross as writers concerned principally with fox-hunting came to birth almost accidentally. It brought them fame on a scale that might be called global, but at the same time pushed them into a category which deprived them of much serious consideration as literary artists. If the collection of the Irish R.M. stories is treated as a consecutive work it will be seen that it is not unworthy of the creators of *The Real Charlotte*.

Étaples, in the Pas-de-Calais, had become famous in the eighteen-eighties, when the painter Jean Charles Cazin won a medal and great acclaim for his painting of Hagar and Ishmael. Brutally driven out by Abraham, they were, as Edith remarked, preparing to spite him by dying on the sand dunes of Étaples, chosen by M. Cazin to represent the desert. Hung in the Luxembourg Gallery, the picture became even more widely known by its reproduction in illustrated editions of the Bible. Essentially a landscape painter, M. Cazin took full advantage of the necessary insignificance of Hagar and Ishmael, concentrating on the vast background of their predicament. His luminous treatment of sand and sky sent coveys of art students fluttering down from Paris in emulation of his genius. Among them was Edith, who met Martin there in 1899, and, with her, settled to life among the dunes.

In the beginning they had been so discouraged by what seemed to be the simple ugliness of Étaples that they made plans to return to London. The rain teemed down on painters who had no dry spot on which to pitch their easels. Martin, engaged on some articles about life in the Latin Quarter, as she had observed it when staying with Edith, found their rooms too cold for work, the northern French sharing the English prejudice against fires in June. Martin wrote in her diary, 'We find the beauties of Étaples rather too esoteric for us and dis-

cuss revolt and flight.' Then the sun came out, and Edith had
a vision of its setting from the long bridge over the mouth of
the River Canche. She was, however, still uninspired, when she
sat down to paint at a spot which recommended itself to her
no more than any other. Presently the magical light of that
north facing countryside and coast caught her, as it had caught
both Bonington and Sickert. In any case Edith stayed to paint
pictures of wide skies reflected in the broad flow of the
river.

In a hollow of the dunes below, Martin lay writing her
studies of the Latin Quarter, springing into activity when
persecution by the children of Étaples passed the bounds that
even hardened landscape painters might be expected to tolerate.
Appeals to the local authorities were parried with the assurance
that these children, undeniably *méchant*, would become entirely
sage after the rite of confirmation. The artists were not prepared to wait for this future reformation by the Holy Ghost.
Not for nothing the youngest of sixteen, Martin, by a mixture
of cunning and blows, cleared away the persecutors, making
herself feared in the process. '*Elle est méchante, celle là,*' said a
particularly obnoxious boy in warning to his fellows. He had
deliberately tortured a calf to terrorize the ladies, only to find
his weapon thrown beyond retrieving into a dyke and his cap
sent spinning after it.

Into this mixture of work and holiday there came an appeal
from the *Badminton Magazine* for a series of hunting stories.
This magazine had already published Somerville and Ross,
jointly and separately, but an engagement for a complete series
had been overlaid by other work. The editor's inquiry was
supported by pressure from their agent, but they still refused
to look this new assignment in the face. Eventually a day of
such wetness that writing indoors seemed the only possible
occupation, descended on Étaples. The technique they had
evolved of discussion and argument created a new circle of
characters, who, in their turn, dictated almost inevitable experiences. It may have been a particularly fortunate moment
for this evolution, for Martin had been clearing her mind by
writing independent essays, and Edith had been painting with
dedicated concentration. Years later, Edith repudiated her
work of that period, writing that to her older eye her sketches

appeared to be devoid of all beauty and indistinguishably alike,
but she retained an affection for the Long Bridge, which she
painted slinging its high legs across the estuary in whose
shallows three grey horses cooled their noses. Across this
bridge Martin had pursued one of the persecuting boys, beating him with Edith's sketching umbrella. This required some
science as a baby rode on the boy's shoulder, sitting, Edith
said, 'as tight as Tod Sloan'. On this bridge also, by a miracle
of happy coincidence, Edith met a young man leading a fox
on a chain, just as she needed a model for the end-drawing of
the first story in the series for which the *Badminton Magazine*
was clamouring.

Great Uncle McCarthy, the story terminated by the portrait of
the fox from Étaples, became the first story in *Some Experiences
of An Irish R.M.*, which was published as a book in November,
1899. The distance between the Pas de Calais and County Cork
may have given an enhanced literary perspective, for in this
story, written against time in two weeks, such a sure foundation was laid that in no subsequent expansion of the theme was
the original outline lost. On to the stage strolled characters
who became dear to a far-flung company of readers, and who
displayed that mixture of familiarity and unpredictability characteristic of all friendship.

These enthusiastic readers have done some disservice to the
book's reputation by praising the more obviously eccentric
characters, at the expense of the less picturesque but delicately
drawn figure of the Resident Magistrate himself. Major Sinclair
Yeates' situation at the opening of *Great Uncle McCarthy* is one
more usually arrived at on the last page of a book of that
period. He has recently become engaged to a young lady called
Philippa, and so is faced with the necessity of finding some
means on which to live happily ever after. It is this which
induces him to canvas for the job of an Irish Resident Magistrate, obtaining the position partly through the instrumentality
of Philippa's godfather, formerly a member of some government. When *Some Experiences of An Irish R.M.* appeared it was
recommended to a French sportsman, who said in surprise that
he did not know such things existed in Ireland. He had mis-
heard the incorrectly given title as *Some Reminiscences of An
Irish Harem*. Additionally an American reviewer complained

that, to his readers, the title would be incomprehensible. It should therefore be explained that a Resident Magistrate was a kind of legal umpire, brought into a neighbourhood from afar to add objectivity to the judgement of local benches. This official's usefulness will be acknowledged if the complications revealed in *An Irish Problem* are considered as reproducing themselves in every courthouse throughout the island.

Florence McCarthy Knox has inherited Shreelane from Great Uncle McCarthy. *The Oxford Dictionary of Christian Names* gives 'the inimitable "Flurry" Knox' as an example of Florence surviving in Ireland as a male Christian name, while in England it had become a purely feminine appellation. Joyce, in Bloom's parlour, opposite the mantelpiece with its timepiece of 'striated Connemara marble', places in the bookcase a copy of 'Denis Florence M'Carthy's Poetical Works (copper beechleaf bookmark at p. 5)'. This was a male Florence who translated Calderon, but on the other hand Aubrey Thomas de Vere, in his heart-twisting poem, *Florence MacCarthy's Farewell to her English Lover*, treated Florence as feminine. To this day the two names survive over a shop in Skibbereen, which seems to show that however the name of McCarthy may be spelt, it has an affinity with Florence regardless of its bearer's gender.

Major Yeates chooses to rent Shreelane from Flurry Knox because, among the many properties to let in the neighbourhood, it possesses the largest proportion of intact roof in ratio to the number of acres of poached shooting. From the moment of his first appearance, Yeates is obviously one of life's victims, frequently indeed the instrument of his own defeats. He is, for example, obliged, in his professional capacity, to impede the dilatory repairs to Shreelane by sending both the plumber and the carpenter to prison, on account of a dispute about stealing piping which comes to blows. Finally he moves in, to find the damp and mildew indoors barely less penetrating than the streaming rain outside. He has inherited Great-Uncle McCarthy's cook, Mrs Cadogan, and her nephew Peter. At that date the Lord Lieutenant of Ireland was Lord Cadogan, so Somerville and Ross explained that the name was made locally possible by being pronounced Caydogawn. Plagued by a cold in the head, Major Yeates is in no state to resist when Flurry Knox calls with a chubby, dappled grey horse for sale. The

Quaker having changed hands, Flurry Knox comes into the house to wet the bargain, and to take up a commanding position in Yeates' life.

Black Protestant descendants of a soldier of Cromwell's, the Knoxes range from Sir Valentine of Castle Knox to the auctioneer Knox, known locally as Larry the Liar. Flurry's position in the middle of the clan is volatile, allowing him to dine at Castle Knox, without inhibiting him from attending an auction of brandy, stolen from a wreck, and put up for sale by Larry the Liar. 'He was a fair, spare young man, who looked like a stable-boy among gentlemen, and a gentleman among stable-boys' . . . 'He seldom laughed, having in unusual perfection the gravity of manner that is bred of horse dealing, probably from the habitual repression of all emotion save disparagement.' His hands red from the cold rain, his covert coat sodden, and his boots steaming, he stands before Major Yeates' fire, telling of the bad time he had had following his Great-Uncle McCarthy through the house. These midnight roamings took place when the great-uncle had been attacked by fits of 'the Horrors', which condition had once incited him to shoot his own donkey, under the impression that the devil, complete with two horns, was coming up the avenue.

Already favourably inclined towards spiritualism, Yeates attributes mysterious nocturnal noises to haunting by Great-Uncle McCarthy. Particularly on Fridays, sleep is interrupted by what seems to be the noise of coffin-hammering, followed by the sound of a ghostly hearse driving away. Simultaneously Major Yeates finds he has been boycotted by his neighbours; when he invites them to shoot woodcock, they refuse and the inevitable anonymous letter tells him that he is suspected of selling foxes. Until then he has failed to understand the remarks of Slipper, who, in his chronic state of semi-intoxication has given Yeates a hint that something queer is on foot instead of the absent foxes. The mystery is cleared up when Flurry's hounds mark a fox to ground in the loft at Shreelane. Yeates' keeper has been trapping and selling foxes, and these transactions, assisted by a couple of Flurry's poor relations, who have been squatting in a back room, have produced the ghostly manifestations attributed by Yeates to Great-Uncle McCarthy. Except for Flurry's mother's first cousins, run to ground by his hounds, a general amnesty is declared, with Mrs Cadogan plucking and roasting ten couple of woodcock 'in one torrid hour' to make a feast for the huntsmen who had boycotted their shooting.

It should be explained that Slipper, who makes his first appearance whipping on Flurry's hounds with a surprising burst of speed for a tippler of fifty, was founded on a famous Skibbereen character. He accepted the notoriety he acquired by way of Somerville and Ross as an excuse for demanding the price of a drink whenever he happened to meet the authors. According to Edith, when Slipper came to pose in her studio he could only rationalize the situation by remarking at the end of the session that they would certainly know each other in future. Edith also wrote that Slipper arrived with a vast bouquet to greet a new draft of hounds at the station, which, as the hounds happened to arrive by the same train as some Friesians bought by Edith and Hildegarde, made a splendid occasion. Slipper's career ended tragically in the streets of Skibbereen, where a stallion he was leading went wild and savaged him.

The mixture of the occult with the farcical, sometimes used in subsequent stories, makes its first appearance in Great-Uncle McCarthy, and the descriptive passages keep a beautiful balance between these extremes. Hunting for ghosts and looking out into the night, Yeates is conscious of how lonely his house stands in 'the dumb and barren country'. In daylight he has a change of mood and from his roof he rejoices at the view over 'a string of little blue lakes running like a turquoise necklet round the base of a firry hill . . . A silvery flash . . . told where the Atlantic lay in immense plains of sunlight.' It will be seen how the strength and delicacy of Somerville and Ross writing has increased since the days of *An Irish Cousin*. As a house, Shreelane continues to have a restless character of its own, until, in one of the later stories, it acquires a sinister anecdote from the past.

Having bought the grey horse from Flurry Knox, Major Yeates is not only beguiled into going out with the hounds, but into joining a foray of Mr Knox's Hounds when they visit a neighbouring hunt. *In the Curranhilty Country* depends for its action on a devious feud between Flurry Knox and Tomsy

Flood, a befuddled follower of the Curranhilty. It is a story
that could not have been written with any other background
than hunting, a point of importance when considering the
R.M. stories. Somerville's and Ross's reputation as writers
about sporting life, particularly hunting in Ireland, has left an
impression that hunting stories formed the bulk of their production. The 1934 edition of *The Oxford Companion to English
Literature*, appearing when Edith herself was still writing
books, bestowed a brief paragraph of cautious praise along
these lines with no mention of *The Real Charlotte*. Equally lukewarm, Harold Williams's *Modern English Writers* refers to
Somerville and Ross as writers of 'a number of sporting tales
. . . which are commendably written and vigorous, if a little
tiresome and laboured in humour'. On examining the R.M.
stories, however, it will be seen that, out of thirty-four, only
ten are directly concerned with days out hunting, and, of
these ten, at least five have their climax in what might be called
a non-hunting situation.

After an inglorious morning leading the off-scourings of the
Curranhilty Hunt, who 'liked to have someone ahead of them
to soften the banks', Yeates finds himself riding home with the
monumental but handsome Miss Bobbie Bennett. Miss Bennett
is courted by Tomsy Flood, but at the moment she is refreshing
herself by a flirtation with Flurry. Tomsy Flood, already in a
foul temper from jealousy, gets even angrier when the hunt
comes upon Yeates frantically attempting to nail Bobbie
Bennett's hair to her head with some iron hair-pins borrowed
from a cottage. At the grisly ball which winds up the day's
sport Bobbie Bennett is able to warn Flurry that Tomsy Flood
has planned to spoil next day's hunting by feeding the hounds
with a barrow load of dead mule. Flurry's revenge is to put the
whole pack of hounds into Tomsy's bedroom to await his
drunken return. Assuming that the hounds chasing him downstairs are symptoms of 'The Horrors', Tomsy goes to ground
in the pantry, leaving his coat-tails as a trophy. Flurry relents
enough to shout through the door that the hounds are real, but
completes his revenge by laying out the most appetizing bits of
dead mule round the breakfast table. Doctor Hickey, a saturnine character with a beard who acts as Flurry's amateur whip,
remarks that the bits of mule 'smelt very nice'.

Yeates is now so completely in Flurry's toils that, when asked to find a four-year-old for an English friend, he applies to Mr Knox with the resigned remark that he would rather be stuck by a friend than a dealer. This leads to an introduction to Flurry's grandmother, Old Mrs Knox of Aussolas, who lives the life of an independent sovereign in a demesne overrun by the descendants of Trinket, a nearly clean-bred mare. Unlike her grandson, Mrs Knox has a cultivated mind, quoting from classical authors in an imperious voice, which is untouched by such a Co. Cork accent as belongs to Flurry. If Edith admitted that Lady Dysart had owed something to the personality of her own mother, there is evidence that at least one reader, Lady Gregory, was strongly reminded of Martin's mother by Mrs Knox's conversation. On the other hand there are those who to this day maintain that the originals, both of Aussolas and its owner, were to be found in the neighbourhood of Youghal. In any case Aussolas is a house where squalor and splendour compete to make a guest's life perilous, both qualities being also displayed in the hostess's appearance. Mrs Knox was said to have worn her purple velvet bonnet since the Famine, the rest of her costume consisting of grimy white shawls kept in place by equally grimy diamond brooches. *Trinket's Colt* sees the first of a series of battles between Flurry and his grandmother, in which Yeates is treated as a pawn by both sides. Insisting that a colt has been promised to him as a birthday present, Flurry involves Yeates in a horse-lifting operation assisted by Slipper. This ends with Yeates hiding from Mrs Knox and her white woolly dog in a patch of gorse in which Flurry has buried the colt up to his withers. Mrs Knox's appreciation of this stratagem is so intense, that she excuses the robbery, and all parties dissolve into 'wild cackles of laughter'.

Incapacitating attacks of laughter are common throughout the R.M. stories. Philippa (Mrs Sinclair Yeates) has a particular difficulty in keeping her countenance. She shared this disability with Martin, who sometimes spent an entire church service in helpless tears of laughter. She may have inherited this tendency from her mother, Mrs Martin being chronically overwhelmed when attempting a verse of the Psalms at family prayers. Tremendous waves of the hysteria of mirth belonged, in the nineteenth century, peculiarly to worship in the home, where opportunities for comic associations proliferated day by day. Martin's aunt, Miss Fox, nicknamed 'Pie', was once reduced to wrapping herself in the window curtains to stifle her laughter at Admiral Coghill's histrionic rendering of the story of Joseph and his brethren. The thunders of Joseph and the squeaks of the brethren affected her so strongly that, finally, she pulled the curtain down upon herself; '. . . the Admiral, in the voice of Joseph, interpolated the command, "PIE FOX, LEAVE THE ROOM," into the Biblical narrative.' When every morning ceased to bring the necessity of keeping a devotionally straight face before a row of solemn domestics, the *fou rire*, as it afflicted the Martin family, declined; but it was still in its heyday when Martin and Edith used it as a literary device to bring about a neat ending to *Trinket's Colt*.

Indomitable but near-sighted, Martin was obliged to accept mounts out hunting who might be trusted to look after her as well as themselves. After three of the R.M. stories had been written, she was out on a hunter whose experience was flawed by laziness. Following Edith over a pole blocking a gap, the horse hit the jump with his knees, rolling on Martin before he got back on to his feet. The fall was a petrifying spectacle to Edith, and Martin's recovery was agonizingly slow. For the rest of her life she was plagued by its after effects, some of her family even believed that her last illness could be traced to this accident fifteen years before. In spite of Martin's state, she struggled with Edith to complete the R.M. stories, and, though she may have found distraction from pain in the work, the effort frequently led to nervous prostration. Their work, however, showed no falling-off. *The Waters of Strife*, written during Martin's painful convalescence, remains the most haunting story in the series.

The expression 'corner-boy' is ignored by the *Shorter Oxford Dictionary*, so it should be explained that it is applied in Ireland to those who spend most of their time leaning against the wall outside shops which combine selling groceries with selling drinks, these premises for business reasons being frequently on corner sites. Bat Callaghan, the principal character in *The Waters of Strife*, and his fellows vary their corner-boy routine by attending the weekly sittings of the bench. It is Callaghan's heavy eyebrows bent in superfluous concentration which first brings his personality to the Resident Magistrate's notice. Sometimes he held the Quaker, the R.M.'s horse, or rather sat on the counter of the nearest public house while the Quaker slumbered in the gutter, and once Yeates sent him to Cork Jail, 'to meditate on the inadvisability of defending a friend from the attentions of the police with the tail board of a cart'.

A regatta on Lough Lonen precipitates tragedy. A race of complicated fouls has nearly ended, when the cox of the leading boat knocks out the bow of the challenger with the unshipped tiller. At this point Yeates is aware of Callaghan, balanced on one foot on the box of the R.M.'s wheel, while, with shining eyes and a face white with excitement, he cheers on the aggressive cox. A supporter of the beaten crew pulls him down off the wheel, but the inevitable fight is averted by the solid bodily intervention of a sergeant of the Royal Irish Constabulary. As Yeates drives away, the competition for winning a pig, slung in a bag at the end of a greased pole, is in progress. 'My final impression of the Lough Lonen Regatta was of Callaghan's lithe figure, sleek and dripping against the yellow sky, as he poised on the swaying pole with the broken gold of the water beneath him.'

After the fight that had only been postponed at the Regatta, Callaghan and Jim Foley, the supporter of the losing crew, both disappear. Yeates, working late before an open window, hears a rustle outside, followed by a hurried whisper that they who wanted Jim Foley should look in the river. In the river Jim Foley's body is found, with the head bashed in, and the hunt is on for the missing Bat Callaghan. Nothing has been cleared up when Yeates goes to visit his old regiment in England, to be given a wedding present and a dinner. The game of whist, often hankered after in exile at Shreelane, is broken up by the sound of two shots. The first report, that a sentry had been shot dead, turns out, typically for an army rumour, to be the reverse of the truth. The shots had been fired by the sentry, who had then collapsed into a series of fits. In a moment of lucidity he tells the doctor that he has seen a face looking at him from an angle of the barrack wall. Having told how he fired two shots, only to see the face still immovably staring at him, the fits come on again, ending in death. Yeates, who had been aware of some puzzling resemblance in the contorted face as the sentry was carried away, is asked to read a letter from the dead man's mother in Ireland. There are clues in the letter and Yeates is taken in to see the body. It is the end of a corner-boy's story.

'I leaned over and looked at it—at the heavy brows, the short nose, the small moustache lying black above the pale mouth, the deep-set eyes sealed in appalling peacefulness. There rose before me the wild dark face of the young man who had hung on my wheel and yelled encouragement to the winning cox-swain at the Lough Lonen Regatta.

' "I know him," I said, "his name is Callaghan." '

This tragedy of senseless violence, wasted human lives and supernatural manifestation, was followed by one of the most remarkable stories ever achieved by Somerville and Ross. *Lisheen Races Second-hand* begins with a sequence of the disasters which only too often attended Major Yeates when bent on pleasure, or indeed on any enterprise. He has been forced to entertain Leigh Kelway, an old Oxford friend. This more than usually fatuous politician has assumed that, on one visit to Yeates, he will easily grasp the complexities of the Irish Question. Flurry Knox has organized an expedition to some irregularly conducted local races, but horses bolt, carts collapse, rain falls. Finally the political guest, his smart race-going suit sodden with rain, is forced to make up for a missed midday meal in a ramshackle public house. By sheer force of character Flurry has induced Mary Kate, the daughter of the house, to give their party tea and bread and butter 'back in the room', when the door is burst open by Slipper, one of a company of intoxicated, homeward-bound race-goers. Delighted with his captive audience he begins to descant on the beauties of the race-meeting at Lisheen, the well-stocked tents for selling porter and whisky 'as pliable as new milk', and the regrets of the assembly at Flurry's absence. 'Divil so pleasant an afternoon ever you seen,' [said Slipper]. 'Does your honour know O'Driscoll? . . . Sure you do. He was in your honour's stable. It's what we were all saying; it was a great pity your honour was not there for the liking you had to Driscoll.'

Slipper's address and personality makes him a forerunner of the story-tellers who stream through the pages of *Ulysses*. He tells of his taunts at Driscoll, felt by Slipper to be getting above himself on account of his jockey's boots. ' "May the divil choke ye!" says he [Driscoll] pleasant enough, but I knew by the blush he had he was vexed.' This is near in feeling to the moment in *Ulysses* when, 'Mr. Dedalus looked after the stumping figure and said mildly: "The devil break the hasp of your back!" '

Edith Somerville had, of course, the advantage of being able to draw a portrait of Slipper, fifty years old, with the face of a profligate pug. Famous as a non-stop reader, Joyce could hardly have missed reading the Irish R.M. with Edith's illustrations, and it is not, perhaps, too fanciful to transfer the drawing of Slipper, that Ancient Mariner of the Whisky tent, into the background of Bloom's visit to Fairyhouse races. It would be also no surprise to read of Slipper happening to remark, 'The bloody mongrel let a grouse out of him would give you the creeps. Be a corporal work of mercy if someone would take the life of that bloody dog. I'm told for a fact he ate part of the breeches off a constabulary man in Santry that came round one time with a blue paper about a licence.' (*Ulysses*)

Slipper proceeds to describe the manœuvres by which he places himself in a position to give a belt with an ash plant to Driscoll's mount, Owld Bocock's mare, as she comes into the third fence from home.

' "Have you any jam, Mary Kate?" interrupted Flurry, whose meal had been in no way interfered with by either the story or the highly scented crowd who had come to listen to it. "We have no jam, only thraycle, sir," replied the invisible Mary Kate.' Slipper sweeps firmly on with his tale of the race, which culminates in Owld Bocock's mare taking the ash plant so much amiss that she stands on her head in the field, before rolling on Driscoll 'as cosy as if he was meadow grass'.

' "The blood was dhruv through his nose and ears," continued Slipper, with a voice that indicated the cream of the narration, "and you'd hear his bones cracking on the ground! You'd have pitied the poor boy."

' "Good heavens!" said Leigh Kelway, sitting up very straight in his chair.

' "Was he hurt, Slipper?" asked Flurry casually.

' "Hurt is it?" echoed Slipper in high scorn; "killed on the spot!" He paused to relish the effect of the *dénoument* on Leigh Kelway. "Oh, divil so pleasant an afthernoon ever you seen; and indeed, Mr. Flurry, it's what we were all saying, it was a great pity your honour was not there for the liking you had for Driscoll." '

Leigh Kelway has hardly had time to begin a protest at Flurry's frivolity, when into the room squeezes a tall young man, with a face like 'a red-hot potato done up in a bandage', crying for vengeance on Slipper. This, of course, is Driscoll, and Slipper fades from the scene.

Aeons later, Flurry, Leigh Kelway and Yeates accept lifts on the outside-cars returning to Skebawn. At the end of this terrible day, Yeates is able to feel some gratification at the sight of Leigh Kelway sharing one side of a car with a roulette wheel and its proprietor. On the other side Driscoll and Slipper, mysteriously reconciled, are locked drunkenly in each other's arms, Owld Bocock's mare being between the shafts. Driscoll strikes up 'The Wearing of the Green' and five discordant voices howling

'When laws can change the blades of grass
From growing as they grow———'

drown Flurry's warning that the vast Bianconi mail-car, with one lamp out, is bearing down on them. The crash that follows puts the party in the ditch, with the roulette wheel on top of the heap. When Kelway is rescued Driscoll is hanging round his neck, still singing 'The Wearing of the Green'. From the top of the mail-car there is an astounded recognition of Leigh Kelway by his political Chief, who is returning from a fishing holiday. 'Meanwhile Slipper, in the ditch, did not cease to announce that "Divil so pleasant an afthernoon ever you seen that was in it!" '

In her biography, *Doctor E. Œ. Somerville*, Miss Geraldine Cummins mentions, in passing, that she once overheard a gallant American lady offering to smuggle a copy of *Ulysses* through the U.S. customs by hiding the banned volume in her knickers. Miss Cummins adds that the book, in its early edition, was about the size of a London telephone directory. In Joyce's vast panorama, irrigated from a myriad sources, the possible influence of Somerville and Ross has not been remarked upon. Joycean exegists have missed the moments when Bloom and his companions sing on the same note as Slipper and the boys at Lisheen Races.

10

Mr Knox's courtship

Philippa's Foxhunt covers both the end of Major Yeates' bachelor discomforts and the beginning of Flurry's courtship of his cousin, Sally Knox. Philippa enters well—as they say of hound puppies—not only accepting gaily the rigours of life at Shreelane, but distinguishing herself on her bicycle at a cubbing meet at Castle Knox. Sally Knox, as near the heroine of the first R.M. volume as circumstances permit, has the nature and appearance of a sensible ginger kitten. Edith's drawing of Sally on Cockatoo fixes the girl's character and the temperament of the impatient horse with a sure economy of line. Philippa, in the course of the morning's sport, finds herself having breakfast with old Mrs Knox, followed, alarmingly, by family prayers. These devotions are, however, brought to a sudden conclusion by Mrs Knox. Having said 'Amen' at an unexpected place, she scrambles up from her knees with the remark, 'They've found,' and joins the chase in her bath-chair.

In the Aussolas woods there is a confrontation between Lady Knox on her 'sedate monster' of a hunter and Mrs Knox in her donkey-drawn conveyance. This chair, throughout the book, is a *motif*, heralding Mrs Knox's appearances when on the lookout for ill-doings among her subjects. 'Blood may be thicker than water, but it is also a great deal nastier,' Lady Knox remarks to Major Yeates, as her opinion of the whole Knox clan, and particularly of Flurry. She is an Englishwoman who 'would have made a very imposing little coachman', and her daughter's fancy for Flurry is, to her, the latest impertinence of the proliferating Knoxes. At the end of the morning's hunt Philippa mobilizes an archidiaconal meeting to assist Mrs Knox, who is hanging on to the legs of her donkey boy, who is hanging on to the tail of a hound, who, in his turn, has his jaws fixed into a cub who has gone to ground in a culvert. It is typical of the skill of Somerville and Ross that one of the clergymen should be the vicar of Mrs Knox's nearest church, to whom she has not spoken for thirty years, after an argument as to the position of the gratings in this particular drain. Edith and Martin were prepared to introduce any number of clergy into a story, but only to heighten drama or increase absurdity. They did not feel the passions which involved an aunt of Edith's and Martin's mother in a slanging match over their competing favourites for the bishopric of Cork.

A rival for Flurry in his pursuit of Sally appears in the shape of Bernard Shute, who has inherited a local estate and quickly tumbled out of the Navy. He possesses a sister, who, unlike Philippa, does not take to Ireland, and is prepared to support any suitable match which will enable her to retire to sophisticated winters in Florence. Bernard himself remains a popular buffoon throughout the R.M. stories, from the moment of his first appearance at the horse fair at which *A Misdeal* takes place. He hoists Sally Knox over a bank with so much force 'that she landed half on her knees and half in the arms of her pioneer. A group of portentously quiet men stood near, their eyes on the ground, their hands in their pockets; they were all dressed so much alike that I did not at first notice that Flurry Knox was among them ... surveying Mr Shute with the measure of disapproval that he habitually bestowed on strange men.'

Philippa burns to abandon her bicycle for a horse, and, to satisfy his wife, Yeates buys a reliable mare from his old acquaintance Bobbie Bennett, who greets him 'with just that touch of Auld Lang Syne in her manner that I could best have dispensed with'. The misdeal of the title confuses Yeates' and Bernard Shute's purchases. Having shocked all onlookers by giving the sum asked for a mare 'whose grandsire was the Mountain Hare', and caused a spasm of anguish to cross the seller's face, 'first pang of a life-long regret that he had not asked twice the money', Shute tries a horse of Flurry's. This horse, Moonlighter, a good hunter with a vicious nature, bolts and throws his rider into a bog, Yeates remarking that early training in climbing the rigging may have helped Bernard to hang on with his hands, and prevented him from leaving the saddle even sooner. Too obtuse to recognize a rival, Bernard insists on buying Moonlighter, but he is, at least, wise enough to set off home with Yeates on the descendant of the Mountain Hare. Miss Bennett's mare becomes more and more of an awkward ride, eventually giving Yeates a nasty fall over a pole. In a world where things are strange shapes, he becomes remotely aware that he is in a cottage, being tended by Miss Bennett, who looks curiously frightened, but makes him understand that he has dealt himself Bernard Shute's horse instead of his own. The grey-haired woman, owner of the cottage, greets Philippa with a welcoming shout. ' "Don't be unhappy, achudth; he's doing grand. Sure I'm telling Miss Binnitt if she was his wife itself, she couldn't give him better care!" The grey-haired woman laughed.'

The background of *The Holy Island*, dealing with the illegal disposal of a wrecked steamer's cargo, belongs to Edith, with her experience of three-day fogs, punctuated by booms from the Fasnet gun, and the sirens of American liners, 'uplifting their monstrous female voices as they felt their way along the coast to Cork'. Throughout her life the Atlantic laid drama before her eyes, from the sight of the proud *Titanic*, racing into the sunset on her last and maiden voyage, to the corpses washed into Castlehaven by many tides after the *Lusitania* had been torpedoed off Kinsale Head. Local fishermen making a poor living, Edith wrote, should be honoured for the respect that left untouched the jewels and money of the victims. At last, when she was nearly seventy, there came a Sunday morning when her family and friends for once deserted service at St Barrahane's to light a bonfire, signal of their farewell to the ship that was carrying Edith across the Atlantic.

After the fog Shreelane is shaken by a frantic storm, which drives a three-masted American barque on to the rocks of Yokahn. 'It was rumoured that the crew had got ashore, but this feature being favourable and uninteresting, was kept as much as possible in the background.' Mrs Cadogan, veteran of a trip to the States, expresses the opinion that anyway sailors would be likely to escape, from their habit of battening the passengers down below, 'the way theirselves'd leg it when we'd be drowning!'

Yeates is summoned to help control the crowd, five hundred strong, which waits on the strand for the ship's break-up, and a chance to loot from the cargo of rum, bacon and butter as it is washed ashore. On the edge of the beach, outside a public-house a bagpiper is droning out 'The Irish Washerwoman', with nodding head and tapping heel. The house itself is crowded with those now extinct figures, 'bona fide' Sunday travellers, entitled to be served with a drink had they come from a certain distance. All are filling in the time until the ship breaks up. 'A hill of water had smothered the wreck, and when it fell from her again nothing was left but the bows, with the bowsprit hanging from them . . . in that greedy pack of waves, with the remorseless rocks above and below her, she seemed the most lonely and tormented of creatures.'

Until nightfall and the effects of unlimited rum drinking bring a respite, Yeates struggles with coastguards and police to capsize the hogsheads that come bobbing in from the wreck. It is only possible to rescue an occasional barrel from the Bacchanal, until, having swilled rum from anything that would hold liquor—hats, boots, filthy buckets—the drinkers begin to collapse on the shingle. At the same time Yeates is aware that sober men are busy in the darkness, loading hogsheads and barrels on to carts. When Doctor Hickey arrives with his stomach pump, the R.M. thankfully withdraws to Mr Canty's farmhouse, stumbling on the way over 'something soft with a squeak in it; it was the piper, with his head and shoulders in an over-turned rum barrel and the bagpipes still under his arm'.

While his soaking, exhausted guests are feasting on Mrs Canty's potato cakes, 'hot and hot from a pot-oven, speckled with caraway seeds and swimming in salt butter', Mr Canty denounces the debauch with pious unction. Put in charge of a previous wreck by the underwriters, Mr Canty had been offered a consideration to release some of the cargo of brandy to the neighbouring publican. Mr Canty assures the company that he had resisted this temptation, but he [the publican] swore 'by the Holy German' an awful curse 'that had he twelve gallons of that brandy in Cork he could make twenty-five out of it'. The police inspector and the coastguard officer take this invocation of St Germanus as a tip to investigate the public-house on the strand, 'handy sort of place for keeping a pub', as one of them remarks. Barrels are found there and in many other potato patches and turf ricks, but everyone is aware that the bulk of the loot has been safely stowed to await a propitious moment for its sale.

A snipe-shooting expedition to the lake on which stands the Holy Island, with its spring of water credited with miraculous powers, introduces Maria, Philippa's water spaniel. Edith insisted that Maria and Slipper were the only two direct portraits in the R.M. stories, so it is appropriate that Slipper should have been sober enough on this occasion to thrash Maria for retrieving a jack-snipe and crunching it, out of reach of rescue, if not of retribution. Later, on Holy Island, Slipper becomes mysteriously intoxicated and between hiccups assures Philippa that snoring sounds she has heard are manifestations of the Little People. It seems by chance that Mrs Canty is met being rowed across the lake to fetch Holy Water for medicinal purposes. Canty is next seen by Yeates boarding the funeral train of the Roman Catholic Bishop of the diocese. Canty says he has passed on information about the 'wreckage' to the police inspector. 'I saw him depart in a first-class carriage and the odour of sanctity; seeing that he was accompanied by seven priests, and that both windows were shut, the latter must have been considerable.'

Canty's latest tip is that hogsheads and barrels will be found on Holy Island, and, sure enough, a good haul is unearthed and brought to the police station. Flurry Knox, with his demon-king-like facility for appearing at dramatic moments, points out that a keg seems to have been tampered with, and when opened it is found to be filled with bog-mould, the rum barrels being filled with water 'with a small indication of sperrits'. Yeates' suggestion that it might be Holy Water is received by the Inspector with only less displeasure than Flurry's news about the destination of the rum and butter. Canty, having covered himself by betraying smaller operators, has made a killing, spurred on by Slipper's warning of the mysterious fairies heard snoring by Philippa on Holy Island. Transferred to fish boxes, the 'wreckage' has been dispatched to Cork in a truck attached to the Bishop's funeral train and labelled 'Fresh Fish—Urgent'.

Somerville and Ross were rightly roused to anger whenever the word rollicking was applied to their work, which was certainly never 'jovial and boisterous', the dictionary definition of the term. *The Policy of The Closed Door*, which returns to the affairs of Sally Knox, although concerned with a day's hunting has no element of rollick in its composition. Sally Knox has been lent the grey, Moonlighter, which Flurry had sold to Bernard Shute. The grey bolts with Sally, and Bernard's mount bolts with him. This second bolting involves riding into Flurry's mare and riding over a hound. Flurry manages to get a back-hander across Bernard's shoulders with his crop, but the gesture is neutralized by Sally's presence of mind.

' "O Mr Shute!" shrieked Miss Sally, as I stared dumb-foundered; "did that branch hurt you?" ' Deprived of the opportunity to work off some jealous aggression, Flurry's temper is further disimproved when the fox goes to ground in the ice-house. 'He (Flurry) had not the least idea of how absurd was his scowling face, draped by the luxuriant hart's-tongues that overhung the doorway.' Sally forces an armistice by letting the fox out of the ice-house and locking Flurry in with a couple of frustrated hounds.

As a counter-attack to Flurry, Lady Knox insists that Sally shall join the Shutes on board a squalid yacht hired by Bernard. Equally reluctant, Yeates is inveigled into the party by his wife. Sally is sea-sick; Yeates is sea-sick; Maria, the water spaniel, who has swum, uninvited, out to the yacht, is sea-sick also, though not enough to prevent her from stealing the ham from the dinner-table. Finally the yacht runs aground on a dark night, while feeling her way into what is said to be a harbour. Taking to the boat, the party steers for what is assumed to be a masthead light, only to find they have grounded on a pebbly beach, guided by the light of someone's bedroom candle. The shipwrecked party reach the house, 'a small two-storeyed building, of that hideous breed of architecture usually dedicated to the rectories of the Irish Church; we felt there was something friendly in the presence of a pair of carpet slippers in the porch, but there was a hint of exclusiveness in the fact that there was no knocker and the bell was broken. The light still burned in the upper window, and with a faltering hand I flung gravel at the glass. This summons was appallingly responded to by a shriek; there was a flutter of white at the panes, and the candle was extinguished.

' "Come away!" exclaimed Miss Shute, "it's a lunatic asylum!" '

She is not far out in her estimation. The door is opened by a little bald-headed man in a short dressing-gown, with a white cockatoo perched on his shoulder, like an unclean spirit. This is the tenant of the Rectory, Doctor Fahy from Cork, who has taken in some patients as paying guests. The cockatoo, 'extremely fierce if annoyed', belongs to old Mrs Buck, most paying of the patient-guests. It has the run of the house, Doctor Fahy says, its owner having a passion for it 'amounting to dementia'. Left to themselves the company collapse into exhausting and painful laughter, culminating in Sally Knox putting her elbow through a pane of glass in the window. Trying to conceal the damage Bernard Shute pulls the blind off its roller. A foray to the horrid depths of the kitchen results in the scullery tap, that had filled Philippa's constant companion the picnic kettle, refusing to be turned off. (Yeates was always convinced that something had been the matter with it before he touched it.) As they return through the hall with a meal filched from Doctor Fahy's stores, Sally's red-gold hair attracts a diving attack from the cockatoo. In the mad rush to escape into the drawing-room chairs are overturned, and at least one broken. Sally, like 'Pie' Fox, takes refuge in the window curtains, while Philippa and Miss Shute go to ground under the table. Bernard drives out the cockatoo with a sofa cushion. 'There was only a chink of the door open, but the cockatoo turned on his side as he flew, and swung through it like a woodcock.' Awaking from an uncomfortable doze, Yeates remembers, uneasily, that he has last seen Maria in the kitchen. In the kitchen, sure enough, he finds her. 'There on the mat regarding me with intelligent affection was Maria; but what— oh what was the white thing that lay between her forepaws?'

Between them, Yeates and Bernard bury the feathered corpse under a bed of stocks, while Maria licks her lips. It is now six o'clock, and they suddenly see that, by an unusual kindness of the sea, the yacht is afloat, lifted off by the tide. Suppressing the latest enormity, they muster the rest of the party and sneak down to the beach, Bernard having left 'a beautiful note' for Doctor Fahy, with half-a-crown as recompense for the broken window. 'No allusion was made to the other casualties. As we

neared the strand [Bernard] found occasion to say to me: "I put
in a postscript that I thought it best to mention that I had seen
the cockatoo in the garden, and hoped it would get back all
right. That's quite true, you know! But look here, whatever
you do you must keep it all dark from the ladies——" At this
juncture Maria overtook us with the cockatoo in her mouth.'

The common quality of the Knox clan is their willingness to
sell a horse at any hour of the day or night. Buying a horse is
accomplished with more deviousness and less spontaneity,
which is demonstrated in the story *Occasional Licences*, next step
in the romance of Sally and Flurry Knox. Largely at the in-
stigation of a publican called Sheehy, the magistrates of the
district agree to grant no one-day licences for the sports to be
held on the Feast of Saint Peter and Saint Paul. With their
laudable object of suppressing drunkenness and fighting, the
bench are unaware that Sheehy has deliberately left a J.P. of
notorious venality uncanvassed, which enables Sheehy to
obtain a licence for himself, and with it a monopoly of selling
porter at the sports. The irritation caused by this fast work is
used by Sally Knox to persuade Yeates to connive at a scheme
to get back at Sheehy. She has, with Flurry, cooked up a plan
which will lower the price of a four-year old for which she is
haggling with the publican. The plan involves Flurry riding
Sultan, one of the Castle Knox carriage horses, with the object
of defeating Sheehy's four-year-old in the highly irregular horse
race that will end the sports. Yeates is horrified, for Sultan, an
aged hunter, has already pulled the omnibus for twelve miles,
but Sally adroitly plays on the pleasure it would be to be
revenged on Sheehy for his manipulation of the magistracy.
Flurry wins the race from Sheehy's four-year-old, who provi-
dentially bolts off the course by way of a gate Slipper has
chanced to leave open. Sultan is, however, in no state to rejoin
his stable mate and pull Lady Knox back to her castle. The
Knoxes' coachman has added a complication by taking too great
an advantage of Sheehy's occasional licence and passing out
under a wall. Luckily rain begins to fall, so that Lady Knox
can be hustled into the bus without the opportunity to observe
that there has been a change under the horse rugs. With a glare
of distrust at Flurry, she insists that no one except Major
Yeates shall touch the reins. Slipper travels on the box as a

kind of grotesque footman, and, replacing the dignified Sultan on one side of the pole, Flurry has harnessed a stocky brown mare, clearly unused to double harness. A difficult situation becomes frightful when 'a pale yellow foal sprinted up beside us with shrill whickerings of joy. Had there been a bog-hole handy, I should have turned the bus into it without hesitation; as there was no accommodation of the kind, I laid the whip severely into everything I could reach, including the foal. The result was that we topped the hill at a gallop three abreast, like a Russian troika; it was like my usual luck that at that identical moment we should meet the police patrol, who saluted respectfully.' In a flood of bad language Slipper reveals that Molony, to whom he had given the foal's halter to keep, was disgruntled by the R.M.'s refusal to grant him an occasional licence. Letting the foal loose is a neat revenge, which doubles itself when Sheehy comes galloping up behind the bus, bellow-ing that the mare and foal are his property. ' "Shtop! Shtop thief!" he was bawling; "give up my mare! How will I get my porter home!" ' The situation is only saved by bribing Sheehy to remove the foal, without Lady Knox, unanxious to risk a new bonnet in the heavy rain, realizing that more than a set-to with a drunken publican has taken place.

It is a tough day, even in Major Yeates' calendar, as during the sports he has had to help Flurry to milk a pair of goats for Philippa's tea-party. Philippa often shows signs of a weakness for Flurry, and her thanks to him show a depressing disregard for the bruises the goats have inflicted on her husband. *Occasional Licences* does not have the poetical sparkle which illuminates, for example, *The Waters of Strife* or *The Holy Island*, but the chain of events develops with a classical in-evitability, from the R.M.'s refusal to grant Molony a one-day licence, to the climax when he has to bribe the double-dealing Sheehy to keep a shut mouth over what is undeniably Yeates' theft of Sheehy's mare and foal.

On the whole the geography of the R.M.'s life derives more from Cork than from Galway, but the drama of *Oh Love! Oh Fire!* owes much to the days of Martin's childhood at Ross. When Yeates walks over to Tory Lodge, Flurry's house, to complain of the evil behaviour of the hound mother Venus and her family, who have been laying waste all around them at

Shreelane, the M.F.H. is in a strange mood. There is 'something chastened in Mr Knox's demeanour, with a touch of remoteness and melancholy with which I was quite unfamiliar; my indictment weakened and my grievances became trivial when laid before this grave and almost religiously gentle young man'. Not only is Flurry's demeanour chastened, his garden, 'a very old garden, with unexpected arbours madly overgrown with flowering climbers', has been tidied up. Inside the house, the drawing-room has a new carpet, new curtains, and a new piano. Off-stage 'the untrammelled voice of a female domestic at large among her fellows' announces that ' "the tay's wet and there's a man over with a message from Aussolas. He was telling me that the owld hairo beyant is giving out invitations——" ' The old hero beyond is Mrs Knox, and her invitations are to a tenants' ball. The effect on local domestic labour of balls at Aussolas is as detrimental, according to Flurry, as getting the influenza into the country, or a mission coming to the chapel. Flurry's inspissated gloom is explained when Yeates meets Sally on the way home. The discovery of Sultan's afternoon as a steeplechaser has caused Lady Knox's objections to Flurry to boil over in insults so offensive that it is unlikely he will ever again enter Castle Knox. Though this is Lady Knox's object, she is making doubly sure by exiling Sally to her own family in England.

Yeates is Mrs Knox's escort at the tenants' ball, where he notices that there is an added element of hysteria amid the ordinary chaos of Aussolas. As the fiddle and concertina are wailing their way through a polka, Flurry arrives, apparently more drunk than Yeates has ever seen him, and, dismissing the polka as effete, calls on Yeates to name a jig. 'Haste to the Wedding' is the only name that comes to mind, which puts Flurry into such a state of euphoria that he snatches his grandmother from her donkey-chair, and they stand up to each other for three repeats of the tune, amid wild applause. The ball brings Ross alive out of the past, with the punch made in the copper for want of a bath, and the coach-house shaking with the relentless stamp and shuffle of hob-nailed boots. The night's entertainment is disrupted by fire in a chimney stack, which threatens to incinerate Aussolas, until brought under by a chain of buckets from the lake. At six-o'clock in the morning

Flurry drives off at a gallop, whirling his whip over his head at the young horses. Yeates finds that he himself looks like the ghost of a waiter who has been drowned in a bog-hole, but Mrs Knox, though pale, seems to be born up by some un-identified excitement. Her salvage work has included casting the silver entrée-dishes out of the dining-room window, which has immobilized a nesting pea-hen 'as Tarpeia was smitten by the Roman shields'. (Actually this was the deed of Hildegarde Coghill during a fire at Ross.)

At this point the Castle Knox brougham drives up the avenue, the coachman, unlike Flurry, having, apparently, been forgiven for his misdemeanours at the athletic sports. Smart work by the butler sends Lady Knox to look for Mrs Knox in the garden, while, to Yeates' terrified astonishment, Sally Knox creeps down the staircase and is bundled away in Mrs Knox's donkey-chair. Yeates is surreptitiously arranging his own get-away, when he is summoned to escort both Mrs Knox and Lady Knox, and with them to 'Haste to the Wedding'. Mrs Knox, 'she had on a wedding garment, a long white burnous, in which she could easily have been mistaken for a small, stout clergyman', has made such a satisfactory statement as to her testamentary intentions as enables Lady Knox to agree to a marriage she is unable to prevent. The hired carriage that takes Flurry and Sally to the station is driven by Slipper, bringing the first volume of R.M. stories to an appropriate close.

'He [Slipper] was shaved; he wore an old livery coat and a new pot hat; he was wondrous sober. On the following morning he was found asleep on a heap of stones ten miles away; somewhere in the neighbourhood one of the horses was grazing in a field with a certain amount of harness hanging about it. The carriage and the remaining horse were discovered in a roadside ditch, two miles further on; one of the carriage doors had been torn off, and in the interior the hens of the vicinity were conducting an exhaustive search after the rice that lurked in the cushions.'

11

The Irish best-sellers

THE reputation that Edith and Martin had earned as 'clever' writers was one that had derogatory undertones in the world to which they belonged. To be 'clever' was a quality regarded as likely to lead anyone, but particularly women, along disreputable paths. Reviewers, at that date, used the term with deprecation, particularly when disposing of a book such as *The Real Charlotte*, which provoked discomfort by its perception of the springs of human behaviour. It was only when praise came from readers and critics all over the world for *Some Experiences of an Irish R.M.* that the authors' position became unassailable. Its popularity reached the throne, for Queen Victoria accepted a copy on her last visit to Ireland, and even overcame the barriers of war, a copy being found in General de Wet's tent when the Boer commander had evaded one of many attempts to surprise him. The particular flavour of its success is perhaps best shown by the tribute of a male reader who, having read the book three times, flat-out, slowly savouring it, and finally picking out the parts he most enjoyed, added, 'and not till then, thank Heaven! was I told it was written by two women'. Edith accepted this compliment, so completely typical of its period, in the generous spirit in which it was offered, but it is easy to understand why she and Martin were active supporters of the Woman's Suffrage movement.

In 1899, when the Irish R.M. was published, horses were still the carriers of everything that did not travel by rail or bicycle. Consequently, when *Some Experiences of an Irish R.M.* was criticized in reviews, it was not because its necessary preoccupation with horses would be unfamiliar to some of its readers. The *Freeman's Journal*, strongly Nationalist, described the book as a prolonged prose version of the Ballyhooly Ballads, adding that 'the authors go to the Cockney state [*sic*] for their Irishmen and their Irish brogue'. Whether or not the

reviewer was aware that one of the authors was a sister of
Ballyhooly, he felt strongly that the 'What news from Erin,
boy?' school of drawing-room ballad was an offence to the
Children of the Captivity. The book was approached from a
different angle by an earnest Protestant Nationalist, who later
became an M.P. and the subject of a clerihew which ran:

> 'Mr Stephen Gwynn
> Keeps telling people what a mess Ireland is in,
> When they ask him to explain
> He does it all over again.'

These lines are not only an illustration of contemporary opinion
of Stephen Gwynn, but a symptom of the nervous boredom
induced by prolonged dissertation on a difficult problem. As
an American film producer remarked, commenting on a rival's
project to make a film about Parnell, 'There is no entertainment value in the Irish Question.'

Gwynn followed Oscar Wilde as a pupil of the great classicist
Mahaffy, also going up to Oxford and achieving a first in
Greats. Gwynn descended from Smith O'Brien, who had been
Wilde's earliest hero, and inherited a romantic attachment to
the rebellious days of 1848, when Wilde's mother, Speranza,
had written ardently in the cause of liberty. Devoted as he was
to his own conception of the problems of Ireland, Gwynn took
the opportunity of reviewing *Some Experiences of an Irish R.M.*
to expound his theories. Dealing with what he considered to
be an unbridgeable gap between rich and poor, he described
the latter as being massed behind their priests on one side of the
gulf, while on the other there stood a thin line of Protestant
gentry with their loyalty and culture rooted in England. He
ignored the prosperity of the Catholic middle-class, both in the
professions and in business, and he wrote firmly of the Catholic
gentry that, they being extinct in the West of Ireland, he knew
nothing of them. Even for Galway this was probably an over-
simplification, but in the neighbourhood of Dublin and in the
Irish midlands families of gentry, sometimes descended from
the same Norman ancestors, but following different faiths,
mingled in a social life whose operation required a religious
armistice. There is, however, literary evidence to support
Gwynn's statement that Catholics and Protestants did not

meet in Dublin drawing-rooms. The solitary Protestant in
Joyce's story *The Dead*, although his presence is considered to
lend style to a party, becomes uneasy with his hostesses whenever the technicalities of Catholic worship are discussed. In
Mount Music, a novel written after Martin's death, Edith
attempted to deal with religious divergences at a variety of
social levels, but, like Stephen Gwynn, she was handicapped
by the limitations of her own background.

Gwynn praised the R.M. stories for their humour and in-
sight, but ignored the discipline which had given them shape
and the imaginative power which had filled them with colour.
According to Oliver St John Gogarty, Gwynn was not in
sympathy with such manifestations of the Celtic literary revival
as the Abbey Theatre. When he came to exchange a series of
letters with Martin they were mainly reflections on political
problems. Martin was always the politician, Edith wrote, while
she herself could only claim to be an enthusiast for causes, but
it was also Martin who had the appetite for new literary
movements. From friendship with her Galway neighbour,
Lady Gregory, she felt a local as well as an intellectual interest
in the rise of the Abbey Theatre, and the development of
W. B. Yeats as a poet. In 1901 she visited Coole Park, where
Yeats was also staying. Her letter about this meeting was
printed by Edith in *Wheeltracks*, under the thinnest gauze veil
of disguise, 'Mr X' being in reality Mr Y(eats).

In the Philistia of the educated upper-classes, where the
Irish R.M. was welcomed and applauded, the poetry of Yeats
was regarded as freakish and incomprehensible. As late as 1911,
Saki, wishing to describe a lady notorious for unconventional
manners, wrote, 'The censorious said she slept in a hammock
and understood Yeats' poems. Her family denied both stories'.
As Martin walked with Yeats by

> '. . . . . the edge
> Of this desolate lake
> Where the wind cries in the sedge,'

there was an echo of the days when she had quoted, 'The
sacred keep of Ilion is rent,' to Andrew Lang among the
snows of St Andrews. There was even a slight recollection of
Scotland in her letter to Edith.

'August 1901. Mr X—looks just what I expected, a cross between a Dominie Sampson and a starved R.C. curate, in seedy black clothes, with a large black bow at the root of his long naked throat. He is egregiously the poet—mutters ends of verses to himself with a wild eye, bows over your hand in dark silence—but poet he is, and very interesting indeed and sympathetic to talk to. I like him and I got on well with him . . . He is not at all without a sense of humour which surprises me. He thinks *The Real Charlotte* very big . . . But he doesn't approve of humour for humour's sake. Here Miss Martin said beautiful things about humour being a high art . . . I smoked, and literary conversation raged, and my cigarette went out. It was windy by the lake; I couldn't make the matches light, and he held the dingy little lappets of his coat out, and I lighted the match in his bosom. No-one was there, and I trust no-one saw, as it must have looked very funny.'

Martin's description is strikingly like the rather malicious portrait of his son by John Butler Yeats which hangs in the Dublin National Gallery. The poet told Lady Gregory that, among other things, he considered Martin to be 'simple', an opinion she found surprising. From the experience of other guests led by Lady Gregory to Yeats' feet it seems that the rule of distant admiration was relaxed for a Galway neighbour.

Yeats might have withdrawn the adjective 'simple' had he seen a letter, written in the following October, in which Martin analysed a performance of *Diarmuid and Grania*. The play was a collaboration with George Moore, which Yeats called 'a strange sort of spider's web of George Moore's spinning'. Martin, on the other hand, called the play a mixture of saga and 'modern French situations', respectively bearing the strong mark of Yeats and Moore. Few plots can stand such a cold-blooded examination as Martin gave the play, in which she found the emotional vagaries of Grania particularly hard to bear. Also she took exception to Mr Frank Benson's technique in stage love-making, 'he moaned over Mrs Benson's face like a cat when a dog comes into the room'. Grania's changes of heart between Diarmuid and Finn end with the former dying in a fight with a fairy boar, more benevolent fairies having earlier sung the song, 'We who are old, old and gay', over Diarmuid and Grania's bridal sleep under a cromlech. Martin thought that the writing of the play might have been saved altogether had Grania realized that she was in love with Finn, whom she had jilted for Diarmuid. 'I believe', Martin wrote, 'the authors both believe that it is very grand to be a victim of a variety of fancies, like Mr S. who burst into a friend's studio to say that he had "never before been in love with a serpent-charmer".'

In a milder mood, a few years later, Martin praised *The King's Threshold*, a short play which Yeats himself had urged her to see, so that she might acknowledge 'that blank verse, perfectly spoken is the proper vehicle for poetry'. 'I had the pleasure of telling him that I thought it a sin to throw such beautiful weapons (as metres and rhymes) out of his armoury'.

Edith was never in the position to give such sound advice. She did not meet Yeats until thirty years after Martin, at Coole, had spoken of Humour as high art, or, as Yeats put it in another context, 'The jester walked in the garden'. This later meeting, at the inaugural dinner of the Irish Academy of Letters, came near to misfiring, Edith being so incensed at Yeats' invitation, addressed to 'Miss Summerville', that she threatened to address her reply to 'Major Yeates'.

The R.M.'s own story is resumed in *Further Experiences of an Irish R.M.*, and at once disrupted by the Boer War, to which Flurry Knox goes with the Irish Yeomanry. Patriotically volunteering to act as Deputy M.F.H. in Flurry's absence, Major Yeates immediately finds himself in trouble. The Pug-Nosed Fox, first story in this volume, opens with an attempt to photograph hounds, Master and Huntsman on a broiling August day, the discomforts being increased by disagreements as to a suitable background between the amateur photographer, Mrs Yeates, and a professional called McOstrich. Unnerved by the sight of a frightful monster, Mr McOstrich under the black hood of his camera, the hounds are only just beaten off from overwhelming him, and in the scrimmage the 'elderly and astute Venus' escapes into a nearby wood, where her voice is heard hunting a line. Discomfort is lost in disaster as the rest of the pack streak after her. Michael, the kennel-huntsman, identifying the fox as a pug-nosed old acquaintance who will be making a line for Temple Braney woods. Major Yeates, in the stiff new coat and cast-iron new cap of his mastership,

E

sweats across country, until the mare lent by Mr Knox lames
herself by falling over the tethering rope of a white mule. This
accident is made particularly bitter by the thanks bestowed on
Yeates for a donation to the mule's owner, who had wished
that the saints might be surprised at his success. With reason,
Yeates felt that the surprise would be mutual.

It is now that Yeates decides to seek help from the McRorys
of Temple Braney, prosperous newcomers, who belong to the
Dublin world of Francie Fitzpatrick, rather than to the 'half-
sir' circle of Mr Knox's Hounds or the Curranhilty Hunt.
Lacking Francie's tragic potentialities, the McRorys are untouched by the doom which has extinguished the Barons of
Temple Braney, leaving their house to be invaded by an alien
horde, begotten by a Dublin coal merchant. As he leads his
limping mare up the avenue, Yeates reflects with discourage-
ment on what he knows of the family. The sons, all said to be
medical students, are described in sequence as 'a bit of a lad,
but nothing at all to the next youngest'. The daughters have
been seen 'whirling in large companies on glittering bicycles,
and the legend respectfully ran that they had forty blouses
apiece'. More ominously, Mrs Cadogan has assured Philippa
that 'Wild Pigs in America wouldn't be treated worse than
Mrs McRory treated her servants'.

In later stories Somerville and Ross gave more details,
domestic and architectural, of Temple Braney, but on this first
visit Yeates, baffled by an arch unexpectedly inscribed 'Welcome', finds the house and yard deserted. 'A cavernous coach-
house stood open, empty save for the wheelless body of an
outside car that was seated on the floor, with wings outspread
like a hatching hen . . . A sickly smell greeted me, and I per-
ceived that in one of the boxes was a long low cage, alive with
the red-currant jelly eyes and pink noses of a colony of ferrets.'
The enchanted palace atmosphere is disrupted by bellows and
thumps from a loft above. Forced by conscience to ascend to
the loft, Yeates finds there, amid 'primeval lumber', Tomsy
Flood of Curranhilty, last seen on the wild night when Flurry's
hounds had been harboured in Tomsy's bed, and his breakfast
table garnished with dead mule.

Still a victim of brutal practical joking, Mr Flood has been
sewn, while passed out, into a feather bed, the medical student

McRorys having first sewn his evening clothes together with professional thoroughness. In the long process of cutting the stitches, Yeates learns that Tomsy is supposed to be best man at the wedding which has emptied the house. 'He also gave it as his private opinion that his cousin Harry Flood was making a hare of himself marrying that impudent little Pinkie McRory that was as vulgar as a bag of straddles, in spite of the money.' Indeed the whole family had too many airs about them for his fancy. ' "They take the English *Times*, if you please, and they all dress for dinner—every night I tell ye! I call that rot, y'know!" ' 'Feathered and fuddled', Tomsy suddenly hears a crash from the dining-room, and bursts through the door to revenge himself on the McRory brothers. The dining-room table is laid for the wedding breakfast, whose enjoyment has been pre-empted by Venus and her fellow hounds, President, patriarch of the pack, being seated on the wedding cake while demolishing a cold salmon. At this poignant moment the bridegroom and bride arrive in the doorway, followed by 'the towering mauve bonnet and equally towering wrath of Mrs McRory . . . I thought of the Wild Pigs in America, and wished I was with them.'

The Pug-Nosed Fox proceeds like an anapaest, swiftly, with a leap and a bound. It establishes the position of the McRorys by seeing them through the eyes of Tomsy Flood, a relic of older, roaring days, to whom they are pretentious commercial invaders. In later stories the relation of these newcomers to the aboriginals is achieved with a deeper understanding than, for example, the exchanges between Lady Knox and old Mrs Knox of Aussolas. With the possible exception of Lady Susan in *The Silver Fox*, Somerville and Ross's focus was slightly blurred when dealing with a character supposedly entirely English, on whom Ireland, like an ineffective vaccination, had not 'taken'.

By the beginning of the next story, *A Royal Command*, Philippa has produced two sons. The youngest does not train on, to use racing language, but the elder develops, later, into a troublemaking small boy who has to be rescued from a kind of supernatural booby trap. On their first appearance these children are nameless but embarrassing encumbrances to their father, on top of a stand at an Agricultural Show. Below them,

Philippa is helping to entertain an Eastern potentate, the guest of Bernard Shute, the Show's organizer. After sending the Yeates children into hysterics by turning his field-glasses on them—their father had been keeping them quiet with what would now be regarded as reprehensibly prejudiced descriptions of cannibal feasts—the Sultan's fancy is taken by the star jumper of the Show, a wild chestnut filly, with a white mane and blue-green eyes. The transaction, which will transform the filly into a state carriage horse, involves a royal command for a luncheon to be given at Shreelane. Yeates has just declared that spears he has brought from Africa are poisoned, and thereby disqualified for spearing the meat as the Sultan requires, when a piano-tuner makes an inopportune appearance. Driven from the house by 'the first fierce chords . . . followed by the usual chromatic passages, fluent and searching which merged in their turn into a concentrated attack upon a single note'.

Yeates sees his children setting forth on a picnic, one of them riding a donkey he had just refused as a bribe to induce him to recommend a stiff price for the chestnut filly. The filly adds to confusion by throwing her rider and bolting across the croquet lawn and the flower-garden. Breathless and filthy from her pursuit, the hosts rush into the house at the sound of wheels, Philippa falling on to her knees in front of the piano-tuner, who awaits payment, splintering her husband's eye-glass in the process. 'I turned at bay and dimly saw, silhouetted in the open doorway, a short figure in a frock coat with a species of black turban on its head. I advanced, bowed, and heroically began:

' "*Sire! J'ai l'honneur*——" '

Slipper, who has come on from a funeral with a crape weeper round his brown tweed cap, not unnaturally finds this address baffling. In his hand is a delayed telegram, apologizing for the sudden necessity which has taken the Sultan back to England. His 'normal attitude of perpetual frost' had constrained the piano-tuner, a witness of the Sultan's departure at the station, to keep this information to himself.

A Royal Command is an example of the economy with which Somerville and Ross handled their *dramatis personæ*. The Shutes are the agents who bring the Sultan on to the stage, while Slipper's appearance effects the dramatic climax which brings down the curtain. The chestnut filly plays the part of a beautiful villainess. She makes a perfect exit: 'finally the cross-cut saw men, the tuner's car-driver and a selection from the funeral, came so near to cornering her that she charged the sunk fence, floated across its gulf with offensive ease, and scurried away, with long and defiant squeals, to assault my horses at the far end of the paddock'.

Collecting years of suffering on Irish railways into a purgatorial whole, *Poisson d'Avril* traces the journey of Major Yeates from a blank fishing holiday to join his wife at a wedding party in England. Remembering, too late, that he is pledged to produce a salmon for his hostess, he takes advantage of the train's dilatory habits to dash into the town and buy a salmon, only to learn from the seven cloaked country women who share his carriage that he will be presenting his irreproachable sister-in-law with a fish bought from a poacher. Waking from a doze, he finds the train deserted and at a standstill, in a station far short of the junction where he is to join the mail. Through the dark and the rain he traces the train's crew to the station-master's lair, where they are having a game of cards. In an effort to make up for this abnegation of duty, all hands do their best to get him to the junction in time. ' "Mind the goods, Tim," shouted the Stationmaster, "she might be coming any-time now!" '

The answer travelled magnificently back from the engine. ' "Let her come! She'll meet her match!" A war-whoop on the steam whistle fittingly closed the speech, and the train sprang into action.' In spite of a teeth-chattering run, during which 'the salmon slowly churned its way forth from its newspaper, and moved along the netting with dreadful stealth', the Limited Mail is missed. Yeates spends an uneasy night on a paillasse under the billiard table of an hotel, which is jam-packed by those attending a Feis, or festival of Irish song and dance. In the dawn, the voice of the First Prize for Reels descends through a pocket of the billiard table on which the victorious dancer has spent the night. Through dazed eyes, Yeates watches while white shirt, grass-green breeches and pearl-grey stockings are changed for every-day clothes, culminating in the agony of squeezing dance-swollen feet into boots. Late that night, with the salmon now wrapped in straw-bottle-covers, Yeates arrives at the wedding house-party, where the ladies, radiant in satin and lace, rustle out to meet him. Assuming all parcels are presents for herself, the bride snatches the straw-covered bundle, to cast it from her on hearing that there is a salmon inside. There is an unexpected crash as the parcel hits the flagged floor, and an ominous pool of whisky begins to form. 'The footman here respectfully interposed . . . "I'm afraid the other things are rather spoiled, sir," ' he said seriously, and drew forth successively, a very large pair of high-low shoes, two long grey worsted stockings, and a pair of grass-green breeches.

They brought the house down, in a manner doubtless familiar to them when they shared the triumphs of Mr Jimmy Durkan [First Prize for Reels], but they left Alice Hervey distinctly cold.

' "You know, darling," she said to Philippa afterwards, "I don't think it was very clever of dear Sinclair to take the wrong parcel. I *had* counted on that salmon." '

In *The Man Who Came to Buy Apples*, Mrs Knox fights a duel with Flurry, who has taken the shooting of Aussolas and summoned guns to shoot the woodcock, driven in to the rhododendrons by a cold spell. The story sparkles with gripping frost, and glows with reflections from the bright blue sky. The woods may be dead and half-grey, but Maria is tremulous with excitement, and Yeates' pony dances on the frost nails in his shoes. Her head protected by a table-napkin as she feeds her assorted poultry, Mrs Knox conducts a row with Flurry about the unavailability of beaters. Simultaneously John Kane, her man of all work, is bargaining with Sullivan, a man who has come to buy apples, but who is unwilling to give the price demanded for 'sheep's noses that there isn't one in the country has but yourself'.

After an acid remark about the rabbit traps stacked suspiciously in the coach-house, Flurry moves the guns off, just as Sullivan presents a propitiatory bottle of potheen to Mrs Knox. Flurry's attempt to blackmail Sullivan with the choice of being prosecuted for making potheen or coming out with the beaters, is countered by a scream of abuse from his grandmother, who has other plans for Sullivan. 'Then in the same breath, and almost in the same key, "Major Yeates, which do you prefer, curry or Irish stew?" Feeling as Fair Rosamund might have felt . . . I selected curry . . . "Did you ever eat my grandmother's curry?" said Flurry to me, later, as we watched Bernard Shute trying to back his motor into the coach-house.

'I said I thought not.

' "Well, you'd take a splint off a horse with it," said Mrs Knox's grandson.'

Ever a menace with a gun, Bernard Shute precipitates the crisis of the day's sport, just as Yeates has registered the spectacle of Sullivan laying out the shooting luncheon on the road below the beat. Mrs Knox presides from her ancient phaeton, which she has conscripted Sullivan's pony to draw. Suddenly, John Kane bursts from the rhododendrons and shoves a sack into the carriage. At this moment Bernard Shute, missing a woodcock, peppers a mixed herd of cattle, horses and a donkey, their instant stampede being led by Trinket, the wicked old mare. Yeates races downhill to attempt the rescue of Mrs Knox, only succeeding in being himself swept away in the phaeton as Sullivan's pony joins the bolters, though Sullivan manages to snatch Mrs Knox to safety. Age-worn, the phaeton starts to disintegrate, and when a wheel comes off Yeates is bucked out on to the road. Slightly stunned, he is baffled by finding himself surrounded by dead rabbits, and by the sudden appearance of Minx, his wife's fox terrier, who is licking her master's face in a way both St Bernard-like and disgusting.

'Her attentions had the traditional reviving effect. I sat up and dashed her from me, and in so doing beheld my wife in the act of taking refuge in the frozen ditch, as the cavalcade swept past, the phaeton and pony bringing up the rear like artillery.'

Philippa, brought to the shoot by apprehension of widowhood from Bernard Shute's bad markmanship, finds that her husband, prostrate on a heap of rabbits, has exposed Mrs Knox's well-organized system of poaching from her shooting tenant, Flurry.

'I looked back in the direction from which I had come, and saw Mrs Knox advancing along the causeway arm-in-arm with the now inevitable Sullivan (who, it may not be out of place to remind the reader, had come to Aussolas early in the morning, with the pure and single intention of buying apples). In

Mrs Knox's disengaged arm was something which I discerned
to be the bottle of potheen, and I instantly resolved to mini-
mize the extent of my injuries.

'. . . something darted past Mrs Knox, something that looked
like a bundle of rags in a cyclone, but was, as a matter of fact,
my faithful water-spaniel Maria . . . Twice she flung herself by
the roadside and rolled, driving her snout into the ground like
the coulter of a plough. Her eyes were starting from her
head . . . She bit and tore frantically with her claws at the solid
ice of a puddle.

' "She's mad! She's gone mad!" exclaimed Philippa, snatching up as a weapon something that looked like a frying pan,
but was, I believe, the step of the phaeton.

'Maria was by this time near enough for me to discern a
canary coloured substance masking her muzzle.

' "Yes, she's quite mad," I replied, possessed by a spirit of
divination. "She's been eating the rabbit curry." '

Occasionally the artistic necessity of a story's development
allows Major Yeates to outwit the crafty enemies among whom
he moved. During his career as deputy M.F.H. he flouts
the disapproval of Michael, the kennel huntsman (never known
to have been in the wrong), and agrees to take Flurry's hounds
for a bye-day to Knockeenbee. In this remote farm old Mr
Flynn has reared two daughters of such paralysing refinement
that they are said never to put a foot out of the house except
to go to Paris. Mr Flynn has also reared a fine hound called
Playboy, of the old Irish white breed. Playboy, the principal
character in *A Conspiracy of Silence*, has passed from old Flynn
to Flurry as a make-weight in a disputed deal over some
heifers. Somerville and Ross describe old Flynn's farm as a
'flat-faced two storeyed house of the usual type of hideous-
ness'. This is, essentially, a judgement of the period. House-
hunters of a later age would think with longing of a two-
storeyed house, probably with Georgian proportions to its
windows, and of a demonstrably convenient size, for Major
Yeates, benighted after a disastrous day on the cliffs, has to be
accommodated in the drawing-room.

The bye-day has proceeded with a total broadmindedness
about the shibboleths of fox-hunting as practised in the English
shires. After Yeates and Doctor Hickey have escaped from the

fashionable conversation of the Misses Flynn, Yeates is beguiled into lending Philippa's pony to Master Eddy, the son of the house. Grinning from ear to ear, the boy is mostly kept in the saddle by the helping hands of a retinue of country boys. Gaiety is added by a lame fiddler on a donkey who has joined the field. Even Doctor Hickey admitted that it was 'as pleasant a day for smoking cigarettes as he had ever been out'. Yeates himself, aware that as a deputy M.F.H. he should be outraged, yields unashamedly to the charm of riding in winter sunshine along the cliffs that survey a blue sea, always an experience to suggest that Persephone has snatched a day's parole from her winter imprisonment. Finally, something 'that might have been a rusty can or a wisp of bracken' moves on the hillside and slides away over the top of a bank. This viewing away of the fox must have been a contribution of Edith's, for Martin's sight was even shorter than Yeates', and on one occasion she completed her circle of farewells to a large party by shaking hands with the butler.

After the fox has led the hounds off the cliff and on to an island, there is a tedious wait until Eugene, Flynn's man, has fetched the pack off in a boat, returning with the news that Playboy, pride of Flurry's hounds, has been seen drifting out into the Atlantic. On top of this blow, Yeates' mare has cast her foreshoes, and, the blacksmith being absent at a wake, Yeates is condemned to bed and supper with the Flynns. The two-hour meal begins with strong tea, cold mutton and porter, and culminates in roast goose and a rice pudding with currants in it. By this time Yeates is so paralysed with sleep that he can only beg to retire to the makeshift couch prepared for him in the drawing-room.

Discomfort from the temporary bed and the voice of a 'pragmatical cuckoo clock', prevent anything deeper than a dose of indigestion overtaking the visitor, until, at two in the morning, Eddy, the son of the house sneaks into the room. His gratitude for the loan of Philippa's pony has brought him downstairs to reveal that Playboy, far from being drowned, has been kidnapped by Eugene, and is even now imprisoned upstairs, while his kidnapper is attending the wake which has also drawn away the blacksmith. Though the reason for the bye-day is now clear, the delicacy of the situation forbids a

showdown with old Flynn. Yeates, guided by Eddy, creeps up
the staircase, past the door from which the master's enormous
snores reverberate. 'A dim skylight told that the roof was very
near to my head; I extended a groping hand for the wall, and
without any warning found my fingers closing, improbably,
awfully upon a warm human face.' This face belongs to
Maggie Kane, the cook. 'She placed in my hand a tepid and
bulky fragment, which, even in the dark I recognized as the
mighty drumstick of last night's goose; at the same time
Master Eddy opened the door and revealed Playboy, tied to
the leg of a low wooden bedstead.

He was standing up, his eyes gleamed green as emeralds, he
looked as big as a calf. He obviously regarded himself as the
guardian of Eugene's bower.' At Maggie Kane's suggestion,
Yeates unties the rope, while Eddy offers Playboy the bone,
a manœuvre almost over-effective. The rescue team cascade
down the stairs, old Flynn's snores ceasing as they thunder
past his door and down into the hall, where the cuckoo clock
utters 'three loud and poignant cuckoos'. 'I think that Playboy
must have sprung at it, in the belief that it was the voice of the
drumstick; I only know that my arm was nearly wrenched
from its socket, and the clock fell with a crash from the table
to the floor, where by some malevolence of its machinery, it
continued to cuckoo with jocund and implacable persistence . . .
The cuckoo's note became mysteriously muffled, and a door,
revealing a fire-lit kitchen, was shoved open. We struggled
through it, bound in a sheaf by Playboy's rope, and in our
midst the cuckoo clock, stifled but indomitable, continued its
protest under Maggie Kane's shawl.' Maggie Kane puts the
clock in a flour bin, and the plotters wake up Slipper. Miracu-
lously, he has refrained from the wake, and so he is sober
enough to trot off, under the stars, with Playboy's rope tied to
his arm. Slipper's reward for his sobriety is the opportunity to
recount the episode as a trial of wits between himself and
Eugene, in which version Yeates acquiesces. Between Yeates
and Mr Flynn when they happen to meet, though references to
the bye-day are not shirked, Playboy's name is covered by the
conspiracy of silence.

Examining this story in detail reveals a delicate variation of
slow and fast action. There is the agonizing boredom when

Yeates and Doctor Hickey are entertained by the sophisticated
Misses Flynn, 'their miracles of hair-dressing black as a raven's
wing, the necklaces, the bracelets and the lavish top-dressing
of powder', and the relief to amble along the cliffs in the sunshine, with jigs from the lame fiddler on his donkey to enliven
the frequent halts. The fast burst with the hounds is followed
by the bleak twilight hour when the huntsmen blow in-
creasingly forlorn blasts to the hounds marooned in the bay
below. Dejected by the loss of Playboy and overwhelmed by
sleep, Yeates finds himself expected to comment on the climax
of some story of old Flynn's, and can only stammer, 'That-that
must have been very nice.'

' "Nice!" echoed Mr. Flynn, and his astounded face shocked
me into consciousness; "sure she might have burnt the house
down." ' The action erupts again, with the rescue of Playboy
and the flight down the stairs, to come to a *rallentando* close,
when Yeates, breakfasting alone, learns that Mr Flynn, who
knows how to cut his losses, has left for a distant cattle fair.
A Conspiracy of Silence has not the sense of a tower being built,
each brick an additional comic disaster, which makes the con-
struction of *The House of Fahy* so remarkable, but its symmetry
makes it an equally satisfactory achievement.

The Boat's Share and *The Last Day of Shraft* cover two acts of
the same drama. Indeed, were the R.M. and his family removed, the plot would make a comedy about feuding fishermen. Yeates, who, on an earlier occasion, has remarked his own
resemblance to Parsifal, a kind of blameless fool, becomes entangled in the plot, but as an unwilling victim rather than an
actor. The families of Keohane and Brickley appear in court
with accusations against each other of assault on the strand,
concerning a fishing-boat whose ownership is explained in the
witness-box by Kate Keohane. ' "She's between Con Brickley
and me brother, an' the saine is between four, an' whatever
crew does be in it should get their share, and the boat has a
man's share." ' Already complicated, the issue is made more
tangled by Jer Keohane's courtship of Miss Brickley, recently
returned to her family after a sojourn as kitchen-maid at
Shreelane. Her employment ended abruptly consequent on
her annexing the sleeve of Philippa's best evening dress,
and through it straining the soup for the dinner party which

has celebrated Flurry Knox's return from the South African War.

Returned also to the Bench, Flurry has not lost his touch, and he intervenes when Kate Keohane exhibits a wound on her forehead, supposedly inflicted by the Brickleys. ' "Are you sure you haven't that since the time there was that business between yourself and the post-mistress at Munig? I'm told you had the name of the office on your forehead where she struck you with the office stamp! Try now, sergeant, can you read Munig on her forehead?" ' Kate Keohane ends her evidence with a flourish augmented by a stammer. Con Brickley, she says, had put his back to the cliff, and declared he would have 'Blood, Murdher, or F-Fish'. In this atmosphere, strongly reminiscent of *The Playboy of the Western World*, the parties are bound over 'in sheaves' to keep the peace, and the R.M. arranges with Flurry to shoot duck on Hare Island, whose strand has been the scene of the dispute. A lake, famous for duck, lies on the land of Con Brickley who, having lost a leg, has brilliantly used his handicapped state when giving evidence.

The story is taken up again in *The Last Day of Shraft* (Shrove Tuesday), though in the Collected Edition of the R.M.'s Experiences, published in 1928, the expedition to Hare Island is described as taking place on a 'grey and bitter December morning'. The incompatibility of December with Shrove Tuesday had, apparently, been overlooked throughout various reprintings. Such a slip might, on account of its rarity, be compared with the strawberry-picking party at Donwell Abbey in *Emma*, when Jane Austen wrote that the apple-trees of Abbey Farm were in full blossom.

Flurry has cried off from the shooting party, so Yeates' only companion is an elderly half-brother of his wife's, a fervent student of the Irish Language. Philippa, in a burst of enthusiasm for the Celtic Movement, has taken a few lessons in Irish, but a glance at the Irish grammar's display of triphthongs, eclipsed consonants and synthetic verbs has decided Yeates that his attitude, though sympathetic, should be distant. Edith and Martin had left far behind them the days when Edith's grandfather could speak some Irish and understand more. The language that had made the courthouse in *An Irish Problem* a vivid scene of bi-lingual drama had now to be cherished like a plant in danger of extinction.

Maxwell Bruce, Philippa's stepbrother, is left to commune with the local poet, who at least possesses a suitably flaming aureole of red hair, if no other qualification. The Brickleys and the Keohanes appear, for the moment, to be keeping the peace, but Peter Cadogan, overdressed for a shooting party in a refurbished flannel suit of his employer's, disappears when wanted as dog-boy and bagbearer. To replace Peter Cadogan in restraining the incorrigible spaniel, Maria, and the diabolical fox terrier, Minx, Yeates conscripts two small girls, who are minding goats, to act as dog-boys. This stratagem is successful until, after a nearly blank day, Yeates stalks and shoots a drake, only to learn, too late, that it is the husband of Mrs Brickley's ducks. Yeates is still aghast at this news when Maria bolts between his legs and tips him into a bog-hole. This last disaster forces him to borrow the peg-legged Brickley's Sunday suit, with trousers which, naturally, consist of but a leg and a half. Thawing out with a tumbler of whisky, Yeates becomes aware that the festival of Irish song, organized by the Brickleys, has got out of hand. Promised a particularly antique song, from a singer described as a perfect Modulator, the song, with painful appropriateness for Yeates, turns out to be the modern ballad which ends:

> 'But some wicked savage
> To grease his white cabbage
> Murdered Ned Flaherty's beautiful drake.'

A song sung in Nighttown by the Cardinal Simon Stephen Dedalus, with surprisingly few variations of phrase.

The bibulous gaiety is disrupted by Kate Keohane, who bursts in with the news that her brother Jer, the widower, has been seen sneaking off with Miss Brickley, and, even worse news, the Boat's Share, ancient bone of contention, has been stolen to pay their fares to America. While all concerned are reeling at this *dénouement*, a Police Sergeant appears in the doorway. Although the poet's presence of mind in blowing out the lamp enables some of the company to escape, Yeates and his brother-in-law have, undeniably, been caught red-handed in a shebeen. The Sergeant, tactfully averting his eyes from the empty tumbler and Yeates' leg, bare from the knee downwards, explains that Mr Knox had particularly recommended a raid on that day, mentioning, incidentally, that Peter Cadogan had been seen rowing away with the Widower and Miss Brickley. The R.M. assumes that his cast-off flannel suit was Peter Cadogan's idea of a best man's garment, but the plot has yet another twist. During dinner, Mrs Cadogan, in her turn, bursts in with the news that on this Shrove Tuesday, last day before Easter for the celebration of weddings, it is her nephew Peter who has married Miss Brickley and sailed for the New World. The Widower is picked up next day, 'drifting seaward in the boat whose "share" had formed the marriage portion of Mrs Peter Cadogan. Both oars were gone; there remained to him an empty bottle of "potheen", and a bucket. He was rowing the boat with the bucket.'

A Horse! A Horse! is a swift move out of the wild world of financial and amatory intrigues inhabited by the Keohanes and Brickleys. Although there is no hint of impropriety in their relationship, Philippa has a previously noticed weakness for Flurry, which frequently lands her husband in trying situations. On this occasion he has been lured by his wife and Flurry into taking a day's hunting with some neighbouring hounds, the bait being the opportunity to meet an old brother officer, now a General and K.C.B. The best part of the story describes dinner at the Butler-Knoxes, under whose rich, godly, Low Church roof the night before the meet is spent. Treating their valuable furniture with the uncaring contempt of ignorance, the Butler-Knoxes have the equally barbarous habit of dining at six-thirty p.m. Salmon follows soup; 'with the edge of dubious appetite already turned, we saw the succeeding items of the menu spread forth on the table like a dummy hand at bridge. The boiled turkey, with its satellite ham, the roast saddle of mutton with its stable companion the stack of cutlets; the succeeding course where a team of wild duck struggled for the lead with an open tart and a sago pudding.'

Next morning at breakfast (Sally Knox is on her knees under the table to confirm that the unappetizing glass of claret she had poured away had stained the carpet) the butler, who looks like Colonel Newcome in decadence, brings in a telegram. This announces a hitch in the arrival of the hirelings for the

Yeates, but after an agonizing interlude when they have to dispose of a drunken cook, who is terrorizing a neighbouring house as she had once terrorized Shreelane, the late arrived hirelings turn out to be superb jumpers. Yeates is surprised to see his old friend the General following hounds in a motor-car, but in his euphoria forgets this regrettable declension until a double disaster overtakes Philippa and himself. Immediately after the branch of a tree has neatly removed Yeates from his saddle, Philippa jumps over a bank into a pond. At this moment it becomes clear that the hirelings are, in reality, expensive new horses belonging to the General. Flurry, ever the instrument of disaster, had found the General's groom sleeping drunkenly in the horse box, and assumed the horses had come from the livery stable. As the General, face scarlet as his coat, approaches his old friend Yeates, who has kid-napped and maimed his horses, Mr Butler-Knox urges Philippa to take his place in the General's motor-car. ' "I will walk—I should really prefer it. The General will be quite happy now that he has found his horses and his old friend."

'The chauffeur, plying a long-necked oil-can, smiled sar-donically.'

The McRory family of Temple Braney have become in-creasingly acceptable to the neighbourhood, owing to their skill at games and charitable generosity. So acceptable indeed that in *Sharper Than A Ferret's Tooth* the eldest son spikes the plans of Miss Shute and Philippa to marry the latter's well-brought-up English niece, Sybil Hervey, to Bernard Shute. After spending an afternoon with Curly McRory, 'Sybil took to saying "I will", in what she believed to be a brogue, instead of "yes", and was detected in a fruitless search for the McRorys of Temple Braney in the pages of Burke's Irish Landed Gentry.' The charm of the middle-class young man for the English girl from a higher social level was usually, as seen by Somerville and Ross, enhanced by skill and daring on horseback. Curly McRory, however, does equally well, though he rides nothing wilder than a bicycle.

To further the match-making plan, Sally Knox invites the Yeates, with Sybil, to meet the Shutes at Aussolas, where the Flurry Knoxes are keeping house while old Mrs Knox takes a cure in England. The grouse, to shoot which had been the

excuse for the party, turn out to be mythical, and a domestic
crisis breaks, when the cook rushes into the dining-room at
breakfast, looking like the Tragic Muse and shaking her fists
with rage. 'The burying ground of her clan was—so she had
been informed by a swift runner—even now being broken into
by the butler and the pantry boy, and the graves of her ancestors were being thrown open to the Four Winds of the World
to make room for the Scuff of the County.' Her denunciation
comes to its climax with the statement that she is now on her
way to the graveyard, to drink the blood of these violators
of tombs.

' "I trust you will, Kate," cordially responded Mrs Flurry,
"don't wait a moment!"

'The Tragic Muse ... stared wildly at Mrs Flurry, seemed
to scent far off the possibility that she was not being taken
seriously, and whirled from the room, a vampire on the war-
path.'

A boating picnic, planned to fill the gap left by the cook, ends
abruptly when the boat rowed by Yeates and Philippa, with
Sally and Miss Shute as passengers, opens her seams and sinks
to rest in three feet of water beside the Temple Braney landing
stage. The ship's company have been unable to supply the
place of the lost bailer by using tea-cups from the picnic
hamper, because, in error, they have brought with them the
washing hamper of returned laundry. Bernard Shute and Sybil,
given the seaworthy punt in the interests of romance, join the
soaking conspirators, just as Curly McRory arrives to take
command of the situation. In addition to the agony of being
forced to sit through a McRory luncheon party, dressed in
gorgeous clothes lent from the wardrobes of their involuntary
hosts, the match-makers have to watch the growing success
of Curly's attentions to Sybil.

Rescue at last arrives in the form of Flurry, with the news
that Mrs Knox, advised by her English doctor to give up late
dinners, has returned to restore the usual disorder at Aussolas
with a flood of well-chosen abuse, her rage only tempered by
a meal from the forgotten picnic basket. 'Hide 'n-go-seek' has
dispersed the younger guests, and increased opportunities for
dalliance, as the youngest McRory daughter, 'dowered with
the accumulated experience of six elder sisters', points out to

Major Yeates. This sophisticate of twelve has observed her brother Curly and Sybil among the ferrets' cages.' ' "... she said one of the ferrets bit her finger and Curly kissed it!" ' As Flurry and Yeates seek shelter for the horses that have brought deliverance from the toils of the McRorys they open a door to what looks like a stable. The potent smell of ferrets greeted us.

'Seated on the ferrets' box were Mr De Lacy McRory, and Sybil, daughter of Alice Hervey. Apparently she had again been bitten by the ferret, but this time the bite was not on her finger.'

The story of *Oweneen the Sprat* begins with Denis, the Yeates' odd man, knocking down a very drunk 'mountainy man', when driving Philippa home through Christmas Eve crowds. The threat of vengeance from the family of Twohig, to which Oweneen the Sprat belongs, augmented by gloomy hints from Flurry and Slipper, causes hysteria among the domestics at Shreelane. After their household has sat up all night, reciting religious exercises, the Yeates set off on a visit of placation, taking with them soup, port, blankets and a pair of the R.M.'s boots to which he is sincerely attached. Approaching the Sprat's cottage, they are narrowly missed by an iron ball which comes hopping down the road, and, as the game of bowling is illegal from its danger to travellers, the bowler himself takes to the hills like a goat. This runaway is the sprat-sized Owen Twohig, the prospect of whose future on crutches has blackened Christmas at Shreelane. Flurry Knox, assisted by Slipper, has added deft touches, to a situation in which the R.M. and his wife find themselves with blackmail on one hand and superstition on the other.

After Flurry's machiavellian intervention in this story, and with the memory of other humiliations in *Holy Island* and *The Last Day of Shraft*, it is merciful of Somerville and Ross that in *The Whiteboys*, last story in *Further Experiences of An Irish R.M.*, Yeates should score over Mr Knox, in a way, as he says, to last the rest of his life and Flurry's. Yeates has gone with Flurry to collect three couple of hounds of the old white Irish breed, of which Playboy is a specimen. The Whiteboys have been hunted by O'Reilly, an old farmer, who, on his deathbed has no wish to let the hounds fall into the hands of his nephew Luke. This ne'er-do-well has often started for America, ' "but

he never got south of Mallow; he gets so drunk saying good-
bye to his friends." ' As Yeates listens to the carman passing
on this information to Flurry, Yeates 'for the hundredth time
longed for Flurry's incommunicable gift of being talked to',
a gift that Edith considered also to be possessed, in a super-
lative degree, by Martin. From an old tower, which is their
kennel, the hounds are loosed into the yard, to cause havoc
among the poultry, while old O'Reilly seated behind the half-
door, takes a bitter, dying farewell of a pack, 'chiefly differing
from the standard pattern by the human lawlessness of their
expression'. Even Flurry is made speechless, when, after three
couple have been chosen, the old farmer takes to his deathbed
and sends out his battered hunting horn to Mr Knox as a
luck-penny.

Three couple of criminals, the Whiteboys, complete their
catalogue of ill-doing during a morning's cubbing, when they
are reported to have marked a fox to ground among the
mysterious holes in an old Irish fort. This news is given to the
furious Mr Knox by two men who are driving a bread van,
though the raking, young, brown horse in the shafts makes
conversation difficult by his rampaging. Under heavy rain, all
blandishments fail to attract the Whiteboys from the depths of
the fort, and while Flurry, angry enough for suicide, according
to Doctor Hickey, rides home with the rest of the pack, Yeates
gets a meal in a farmhouse kitchen.

As he eats soda bread and boiled eggs, he becomes aware
that one of the children of the house is trying to purloin his
hunting crop.

' "What have ye the whip for?" asked the offspring, un-
daunted by discovery.

' "To bate the dogs with," I replied attuning my speech to
his as best I could.

' "Is it the big white dogs?" pursued the off-spring.'

Delicately, Yeates fishes for information, until, in one
beautiful sentence, the child reveals that the Whiteboys have
been taken away in the bread van by Luke O'Reilly, who
happens to be the little boy's uncle, and who has, obviously,
run a drag in order to claim his four-footed inheritance. Flurry
disappears for three days, supposedly to break every bone in
Luke O'Reilly's body, though that would not take away from

Doctor Hickey's pleasure whenever he recollects that Flurry had got O'Reilly's brother-in-law to screech down the holes of the fort in Irish, in case the white hounds had no English. Finally Yeates meets Flurry riding a young brown horse, 'with a wildish eye and a nasty rub from a misfitting collar.

' "I got him in a sort of a swap," said Flurry tranquilly.

' "I suppose he got that rub in the bread van?" I remarked, drawing a bow at a venture.

' "Well, that might be too," assented Flurry, regarding me with an eye that was like a stone wall with broken glass on it.'

12

The influence of the fox

MORE than once distance from home was a literary stimulant to Somerville and Ross. *Dan Russel the Fox*, the last complete novel they wrote together, was begun at Amélie-les-Bains in the Pyrenees, where they had gone for Martin's health. Influenza had refused to relax its grip, and Edith, in her second season as Master of the West Carbery, had dropped the hounds back into her brother Aylmer's lap, in order to take Martin to the south. Amélie-les-Bains was chosen because Edith had begun studying the Continental Bradshaw from its beginning, and this was the first resort that attracted her. Between spells of work they were fussed over by an elderly Frenchman, unusual in 1904 in being an Anglophile. In early life he had been a devoted protégé of George Sand (Edith firmly wrote Georges) and he gave the same kind of devotion to Martin.

Two chapters of *Dan Russel the Fox* were written, then the book was shelved until the cousins were abroad again in 1909, at Portofino which provides the background for the novel's last chapter. The first chapter begins at Aix-les-Bains, where a pretty widow from the South-West of Ireland makes up to a pair of cousins, singularly unlike Edith and Martin. Jean Masterman has been obliged to bring her two children back from India where her husband is stationed, and Katherine Rowan, a well-dowered orphan, has come to enliven the tedium of Mrs Masterman's cure. Another cousin, Ulick Adare, a rather precious young man, given to the practice of literature, is in attendance on the ladies, but it is obvious that he is hardly up to Miss Rowan's weight. Mrs Delanty, the widow, exploits the situation with such skill that in a hop, skip and jump she has not only let her nice little Irish hunting box to Mrs Masterman, but has sold a four-year-old to Miss Rowan, whom she has inspired with the ambition to follow Mr Fitzsimmons' hounds. Dermot, the horse, is referred to later as Katherine's 'Dermot dear and brown', which is a quotation from Yeats' *Ballad of the Old Foxhunter*, though further polishing of the poem changed the horse's name to Lollard, more of a poet's name than a huntsman's.

Some years before, in *Hunting Mahatmas*, Edith had dealt with the mystical means by which those who choose the paths of safety can hold their own with the thrusters in the hunting field. Both Mrs Delanty and Mr Fitzsimmons are examples in the expansion of this theme. Mrs Delanty, a skilled maker of horses, has a 'masterly manner for wrestling the lanes to her purpose', and 'a hunting memory for gaps, comparable to a card memory for the lesser trumps, which is bestowed by a kind providence on those who fitly appreciate it'. Gus Fitzsimmons maintains a fiction that he hunts his own hounds, which it is in the interest of his household to support. It is John Michael, Gus's half-brother, who hunts the hounds, and, as a kind of male Undine, fascinates both Katherine Rowan and Mrs Delanty. Physical beauty, skill with horses and hounds, together with a transparent honesty of heart might have made him an irritatingly perfect *preux chevalier* of a sportsman, but Somerville and Ross skirt this pitfall by emphasizing the lack of imagination which leaves these qualities unilluminated. While Mrs Masterman becomes apprehensive of Katherine's obsession with John Michael, Ulick Adare, who has been courting Katherine at a snail's pace, relieves his jealous feelings by christening his paralysingly shy rival 'Dumb Crambo'.

Katherine shirks the implications of her passion for John Michael. Mrs Delanty, eighteenth child of a Limerick butter merchant, faces her own situation with a sterner realism. Knowing she has no future with a penniless huntsman, she hooks, plays and lands a rich young Englishman, though this only takes place after John Michael has turned down declarations from both his admirers, declarations of love disguised as offers to help finance the hounds. Exacerbated by a farmer who has put up wire and put down poison, besides assaulting the Master and giving him an humiliating fall, Gus orders John Michael to take hounds home. John Michael rebels, as hounds are on a line, and, in the subsequent row with Gus, decides to emigrate to the American hunting field. Mrs

Delanty has stated her own attitude to Gus Fitzsimmons. ' "Of course Gus is an old friend of mine, . . . but I must say I never liked him very much." '

During the painfully slow ride home, after a hunt when Dan Russel the Fox has saved his brush, Katherine and John Michael are alone in the wind and rain, as close to understanding as they are ever able to get. She has been weakened by a fall, when attempting to try out a rough horse in emulation of John Michael's mastery, and collapses at the door of the Fitzsimmons' house. Later that night, when John Michael and his mother are nursing a hound on the edge of death from the poison, Mrs Fitzsimmons urges her son to marry the obviously willing Katherine and turn the tables on Gus. John Michael's indignant rejection of this proposition, an insult, he thinks, to Miss Rowan and an outrage to his own distaste for marriage, is spoken so loudly that the words travel along the passage and reach the bedroom, where Katherine hears them and accepts her defeat. Next morning, arriving at the Fitzsimmons' unabashedly hideous house, Mrs Masterman has a sinking feeling that Dumb Crambo has captured Katherine. She finds instead that Miss Rowan can be at once removed to Portofino, as a cure for nervous prostration. Watching a yacht sailing into the blue Bay of Liguria (Ulick Adare is on board, making a carefully casual reappearance) Katherine has time to reflect on the bitter lesson, 'that we may regret our sins, but we agonize over our follies'.

Mrs Delanty's attack on John Michael is more persistent, and he cannot escape as he is stirring the porridge for the hounds he plans to leave. 'His coat was off and his shirt sleeves were rolled up; the action of his arms and shoulders was rhythmic and powerful and strangely graceful.' The porridge has to be stirred throughout the interview, when Mrs Delanty offers John Michael the chance to hunt the hounds on behalf of her rich English admirer, making it clear that for John Michael's sake she is prepared to set up this puppet M.F.H. Her rebuff is as much harsher than Katherine's as her approach has been cruder. Left alone, John Michael remarks, ' "Oh my goodness . . . that was awful!" ' rakes out the fire, and continues to stir the porridge.

As a novel *Dan Russel the Fox* is well-constructed, with a

finely balanced cast of characters. Naturally the background
is to some extent the same as that of the R.M. stories, but there
is stronger feeling in the description of, for example, 'the little
vagrant lake that burned blue among the pale reeds—the
tremendous blue of bog-water under a clear sky', or the wind
'that rushed at them broadside on across the shuddering breast
of the country'. The principal characters are also loving and
suffering at a deeper emotional level. At the same time the
writers never lose sight of the blank in John Michael's nature.
When Katherine, in her over-enthusiasm, refers to a run as
'one crowded hour of glorious life', Ulick Adare listens with
pleasure to John Michael's scrupulous correction, ' "It was
more than an hour ... I made it an hour and seventeen
minutes." '

The circle of onlookers see the situation from opposite
points of view. Mrs Masterman makes the uncompromising
statement that, 'A Heart of Gold is all very well, but the day
comes when you feel ashamed of its owner socially.' From
the other side of the circle Jimmy Doyle, a follower of the
hounds, regards Katherine and her reputed £800 a year with
the respect of one who has, himself, £80 and keeps a horse on
it. There is even a moment when Jimmy Doyle hears John
Michael compliment Katherine on riding out a long hunt, and
wonders whether, after all, John Michael may be less of a fool
than his neighbours think. Mrs Delanty's tenderness for John
Michael is a subject on which the blacksmith, and those who
bring horses to his forge, can comment, without mercy, but
with acceptance of the whims of the heart, a heart that had been
helpless before the glamour of John Michael as he came
thundering down off a bank with a dazzling halo of light
behind his head. Dan Russel the Fox is the catalyst, pre-
cipitating crises and, as he departs, leaving his mark on
people's lives much as he leaves trails of hen's feathers on the
grass.

If John Michael, so incapable of exploiting his sexual
attraction, had an original it is unlikely that either of his
creators were among his victims. Martin's accident, and its
after-effects, may have given them material for Katherine's
disordered state after her fall, but not for her emotional disturbance. Seven years later, in *Irish Memories*, Edith wrote of

the summer when Martin first came to Castletownshend: 'For most boys and girls the varying, yet invariable flirtations and emotional episodes of youth are resolved and composed by marriage. To Martin and me was opened another way, and the flowering of both our lives was when we met each other.' There is no reason to suppose that Edith did not mean exactly what she said, but there is equally no reason to insist that this statement of devotion should be taken as a declaration of a physical relationship. Some time after Martin's death Edith was brought in contact with a circle notorious for the practice of lesbianism, but if the innocence of her remarks on the Ladies of Llangollen is remembered, it would be hard not to agree with those among her family and friends who maintain that during her years with Martin she was unenlightened on the subject of sexual inversion. Among the large families of the past, such as the Somervilles and Martins, the habit of visiting was conducive to forming friendships, which would, now-adays, be more likely to be made by girls at school, university or in a profession. Mr Maurice Collis, writing of Edith's youth in *Somerville and Ross*, has remarked on her prostration when her 'twin' cousin Ethel Coghill married Jim Penrose, and when her sister Hildegarde married Ethel's brother Egerton. Violent physical reaction to the marriage of a girl friend or a sister are, in fact, extremely common among young women, and should, in most cases, be taken as a bodily expression of the mind's admission that a particular and confidential relationship has come to an end. It is the premonition of this breaking-up that comes, inevitably, with marriage which often causes girls, as in Ethel Penrose's case, to conceal their serious intentions from their dearest confidants.

Although Edith had an impatience with what she regarded as irresponsible male neglect of opportunities denied to women on the most frivolous grounds, she was not ill at ease with men, at any stage of her long life. For many years one of her cousins, an Oxford don of much originality and charm, wished to marry her, but his devotion had only the posthumous reward of an appreciative obituary written by Edith for *The Times*. From Martin's letters the impression might be gathered that she had a distinct interest in men from a feminine point of view. However, to someone who knew her well it appeared that there was only one particular cousin who had aroused her interest, but his married state precluded any development of her feelings. After her father's death Edith administered Drishane, in addition to hunting, painting and writing, and her full life may have prevented possessiveness towards Martin from developing, to pour jealous poison into their relationship. 'There was a man hanging about,' said one of Martin's nephews, 'but Edith saw him off.' If this was so, it cast no shadow on their lives when, after her mother's death, Martin made her home at Drishane.

Soon after the appearance of *Dan Russel the Fox*, Nature followed art, and Stephen Gwynn directed to Drishane a travelling English journalist called Harold Begbie, who bore a close resemblance to the egregious Leigh Kelway in *Lisheen Races*. He did not end up in a ditch buried under a roulette wheel and an assortment of drunks, but Edith describes how Martin walked him round the garden, 'in the thin persistent rain', while administering a lecture on the subject of Home Rule. Meanwhile the Roman Catholic Bishop of Ross Carbery, cicerone of this Liberal Protestant political researcher, conversed amiably with Edith on nothing more pregnant than Votes for Women. Afterwards Martin wrote to Stephen Gwynn at the House of Commons. Gwynn was inclined to challenge her knowledge of certain levels of Irish life, but she pointed out that, unlike those Irishmen forced to make their careers in London, she and her cousin were fortunate in being able to reverse the accepted habits of the landlord class, spending in Ireland the money they made in England.

A photograph of the two cousins which dates from a slightly earlier period has been said by those who knew them to be the most delightful and the most characteristic. The photographer was Egerton Coghill, who had been Edith's fellow art-student and was now her brother-in-law. He balanced the composition, which has its centre low down on the proud head of the dog Sheila, by leaving a central empty space, on either side of which the sitters make an almost cubist pattern. Edith has the book, the pen in the hand, and the top dog, Candy, on her knee. Edith's collar and tie are uncompromisingly plain. Her expression is composed and powerful, but there are signs of femininity in the slight disarray of her hair under the massively draped hat. Martin wears a more frivolous tie and a more reposeful expression. Dogs are invariably conscious of the camera, but even among canine sitters Sheila and Candy surpass themselves by the complacency of their demeanour.

13

The last days of Major Yeates

HAVING first wandered, as Edith said, through various periodicals, the final volume of R.M. stories appeared in 1915 under the tile *In Mr Knox's Country*. Some reviewers complained that the mixture was not exactly as before, others that the mixture was only too much as before. In fact the stories are, if anything, drawn from more varied backgrounds than those written earlier, and even if they do not rise to the heights of virtuosity displayed in *Lisheen Races* or *The House of Fahy*, the first story, *How I First Met Doctor Hickey* and the last, *The Shooting of Shinroe*, are as remarkable as any written by Somerville and Ross. *How I First Met Doctor Hickey* belonged chronologically immediately after *Great-Uncle McCarthy*, and it was there that Edith placed it when she came to edit the R.M. stories in a collected edition. To regularize the rearrangement, she inserted into the description of Hickey—'a saturnine young man with a black torpedo beard'—the words 'whose acquaintance I had some months before been privileged to make'. As it appeared originally, a flash-back for readers already familiar with Hickey as Flurry's lieutenant and critic, and a glance at Yeates' early days, useful for new readers, the story had a special value, somewhat diluted by being moved to its historically correct position.

Yeates meets Doctor Hickey at a hotel in the West of Ireland in the course of a tortuous journey to meet Philippa, to whom he is newly engaged. Doctor Hickey is occupied in cultivating the two other guests, Mrs M'Evoy and her daughter. The acquaintance begins over dinner, when Yeates remarks to Hickey that the chandelier, a splendid medley of Tritons, dolphins and mermaids, looks to him as if it were Renaissance. Doctor Hickey replies that to him it looks more like bronze. The talk moves on from Mrs M'Evoy's canary, for whom a train was halted while, with the guard, she chased the bird to

the only bush in a treeless bog, to a fight between eagles
organized, in the past, by James the ancient hotel waiter. Outside the river laps against the wall of the hotel garden, on which
boys, who have been up since three that morning to come into
the local fair, sit in unflagging conversation, under a rose-pink
moon.

The next day Doctor Hickey takes the ladies to a regatta, to
be held not far from Carrow Junction, where Yeates is to meet
Philippa. He is made thankful for his prescience in evading
Doctor Hickey's expedition, when he overhears that the picnic
luncheon has, inevitably, been left behind. Consequently, when
Yeates re-encounters the party during his wait at Carrow
Junction, everyone is faint with hunger. Although they break
their way into the hotel, Yeates and Hickey drawing Mrs
M'Evoy through a window, 'two foot by three, steadily as the
great god Pan drew the pith from the reed', no food can be
found. Yeates, searching for a butcher, finds the shop, when a
terrified woman rushes into it, shrieking a warning about
'madmen from th' Asylum, . . . a small decorous party of men,
flanked by a couple of stalwart keepers in uniform. One of the
men, a white-faced being in seedy black, headed them, playing
an imaginary fiddle on his left arm, and smiling secretly to
himself'. It appears that Doctor Hickey has given some of the
patients leave to go to the sports, displaying, it should be
mentioned, ideas in the treatment of mental disability con-
siderably in advance of his generation.

While the bacon bought by Yeates is being fried by Mrs
M'Evoy, Doctor Hickey knocks the heads off bottles of
contraband porter. The hotel has lost its licence when, during
a police search for potheen, a jar had been thrown from a
window, unhappily falling on a goose, which had killed the
bird, but broken the jar's fall, so that the police had captured
the potheen. In the course of the meal, Mrs M'Evoy and her
daughter tell a story in duet of an earlier regatta, where, in the
darkness, with only fire-works for illumination, Miss M'Evoy
had been accosted by a gentleman with ' "a nasty kind of
foreign look, and a little pointed beard on him too. If you saw
the roll of his eyes when the green fire fell out of the rockets
you'd think of Mephistopheles——" "There's no doubt that
Mephistopheles was one of Shakespeare's grandest creations,"

said Doctor Hickey hurriedly.' Skilfully Mrs M'Evoy leads the story to the point where Doctor Hickey is exposed as the sinister gentleman with questionable intentions, at which moment her daughter grasps Yeates' arm with a loud yell. Philippa, fresh and exquisite as a visitor from a purer world, has appeared outside the window, and is staring in outrage at the squalid orgy in which her fiancé is only too clearly enjoying himself. She has come upon the hotel, she later explains, icily, while avoiding some drunken men, who had threatened the comfort of the walk she had taken, on finding herself alone at the station. ' "There are those men again!" exclaimed Philippa, coming a little nearer to me.

'In front of us, deviously ascending the long slope, was the Asylum party; the keepers, exceedingly drunk, being assisted to the station by the lunatics.' As a reviewer in *The Times Literary Supplement* pointed out the story ends with a passage that contains three separate *dénouements*, each, it may be added, springing from the previous one, as the rockets sprang forth with the rain of green fire that lit up Doctor Hickey's eyes.

The opening paragraph of *The Aussolas Martin Cat*—a title which possibly conceals a family joke—contains a sentence which has, deservedly, been much quoted as an example of Somerville and Ross's power of evoking mood and landscape. 'It was a gleaming morning in mid-May, when everything was young and tense and thin and fit to run for its life like a Derby horse.' Yeates has gone on an expedition with Flurry to pur-chase, for a dark purpose unrevealed, a pair of cubs, fallen from a vixen's cliff lair. Asking the way in a cottage, Yeates has found himself addressing a young woman who sits tremblingly staring at the wall. When things go amiss with the cubs, Flurry says he knew he would have no luck with them after Yeates had asked the way of Kitty the Shakes for it is rare for her to speak. This trembling and withdrawn oracle, with her heavy mop of hair and her eyes fixed on the wall, is so vivid a portrait that to meet her when inquiring in any strange cottage in any country would be no surprise.

At Aussolas the young Knoxes are on a visit, supposedly to support Mrs Knox's declining years, but handicapped by her refusal to decline, or to accept support when inconvenient to

herself. Ordered to Buxton for her rheumatism, she has found
a prospective tenant for the house, and, while the rest of the
party watch from a seat concealed among the laurels, she drags
this captive round the garden at the wheels of her bath-chair.
The seat in the laurels was known to be Mrs Knox's refuge
when the cook wished to know what was to be for the servants'
dinner. At Ross Mrs Martin had had a refuge for this purpose,
which she had shown to her daughter. Another filial tribute to
Mrs Martin was put into the mouth of Mr Tebbutts, the
grotesque 'stage Englishman', who contemplates renting
Aussolas. Awestruck, he says that Mrs Knox had been 'very
giddy' with him in the garden that afternoon, a remark
originally made of Mrs Martin by a clergyman, famous for
combining the more surrealist effects of Spooner, Malaprop
and Pecksniff.

Not unreasonably, Mr Tebbutts is alarmed by unexplained
noises, emerging from the powdering closet in the romantic
James II bedroom where he has been lodged. Already repelled
by what he calls 'the charnel 'ouse smell'—perhaps he was
more of a stage cockney than a stage Englishman—his nerve
goes at the sight of some animal, neither cat nor squirrel
gliding through his room. This is, Flurry says, the Aussolas
Martin Cat, presaging a death in the family. Yeates, his blood
chilled by the thought of this spectral feline of ill-omen,
actually an instant inspiration of Flurry's, only realizes the
provenance of the beast when Mrs Knox has appeared at her
bedroom door, 'swathed in hundreds of shawls', as she hurls
the tongs at one of the cubs. Mr Tebbutts, no longer a prospective tenant, 'passed out of the incident into the night, and
the Aussolas Martin Cat was swallowed up by a large hole in
the surbase of the corner of the first landing'. Flurry refuses to
admit that the seeing-off of Mr Tebbutts makes up for the loss
of the cubs. He can only reiterate, 'I knew I'd never have luck
with them after you asking the way of Kitty the Shakes.'

On the hundredth anniversary of Edith Somerville's birth,
Lennox Robinson broadcast a portrait of her that was both
affectionate and more laudatory than was, at that date, fashionable in the Irish literary circles to which he belonged. He was,
however, not entirely accurate in some of his details, being,
apparently, under the impression that a gap of ten years had

followed Edith's birth, and that her brothers were all younger
than Hildegarde. He also made the surprising statement that
a motor-car is only once mentioned, and then with nervous
suspicion, in *The Adventures of an Irish R.M.* [*sic*]. Sir Horace
Plunkett was said to have been the first man to drive a car on
the Irish roads, but he must have been soon joined by Bernard
Shute, already terrorizing the countryside in *A Royal Command* (*Further Experiences of An Irish R.M.*, 1908).

Major Yeates' own motor-car makes its first appearance outside the front door at Aussolas, and immediately Mrs Knox,
recovered from her rheumatic attack, commandeers this means
of transport to go to the rescue of Stephen Casey, son of a
former tenant, and now in the clutches of Goggin the Gombeen. Professor Fehlmann's note on Gombeen, '*Usurier haï des
paysans irlandais qui avaient recours à ses services*', though applied
to the usurer in *Naboth's Vineyard*, is also appropriate for this
less melancholy story, *The Finger of Mrs Knox*. From internal
evidence Mrs Knox must, by now, be at least ninety-six, and
Yeates, remembering this, asks her if fifteen miles an hour is
too fast. Over the mountain of shawls, in which she has been
encased by Mullins, her cross maid, Mrs Knox challenges him
to double her girlhood's feat of riding a fourteen-hand pony to
the fourteenth milestone on the Cork road in a minute under
the hour. As they whistle along at twenty miles an hour a shawl
blows away, but Mrs Knox tells Yeates she will get it back by
asking the priest to speak about it after next Sunday's Mass.

Rocking the Gombeen man on his heels, Mrs Knox points
out that the wood behind his public house, which he has laid
flat, was planted by Goggin's grandfather for the Colonel
('Badger' Knox, her late husband). Goggin agrees, adding
unctuously, ' "The Lord have mercy on his soul." "You'll be
wanting mercy on your own soul in the next world, if you
meet the Colonel there!" said Mrs Knox, unhesitatingly.'
Fighting at this speed, she arranges, without loss of time, that
Casey's debt shall be settled for five pounds, for which Yeates
finds himself obliged to stand surety, Mrs Knox being of a
saving habit of mind. Reprieved from the sheriff's officer,
Casey's donkey, calves and goats, are at once overwhelmed
by Mr Knox's hounds in full cry. Hoping to placate Flurry for
having to flog his hounds off the donkey, Yeates is delighted to

be able to cheer the pack on to the line of a reddish-brown something that he has seen slipping through the furze above. Mrs Knox, with a sudden, almost frightening change of manner, develops an hysterical wish to start for home, but Yeates is delayed by the sheriff's officer's request for the five pounds promised to rescue Casey's beasts. At Mrs Knox's final, masterly dictation, Yeates borrows the money from Goggin with which to stop the Gombeen man's own mouth. At this moment the quarry, on to whose trail Yeates has cheered the hounds, a small reddish brown collie, runs panting into the house. Mrs Knox's hysteria is explained, as her eyesight had not deceived her.

'As we ran out of Killoge at something near thirty miles an hour I heard scald crow laughter behind me in the shawls.'

In the pride of his motorship Yeates drives Philippa into a wilderness, where the Derryclares live in a luxury mitigated by the hazards of taking honey from angry bees or being press-ganged on board for queasy fishing trips. Yeates evades the yacht, but Lord Derryclare, and his boisterous son Bill, do not allow another guest, Mr Chichester, to escape. To Philippa Mr Chichester is *The Friend of her Youth* after whom the story is named. With a complete grasp of the subject, unhampered by a female point of view, Somerville and Ross see Chichester with Yeates eyes, '. . . I am not attracted by the friends of my wife's youth. If Chichester had been the type she fancied, was I merely a super Chichester?'

'Chichester was an elderly young man, worn smooth by much visiting in country houses, and thoroughly competent in the avocations proper to his career . . . to see his eye, critical yet alight with healthful voracity, travelling down the array of dishes on the side-table at breakfast, and arranging unhesitatingly the order in which they were to be attacked, was a lesson to the heedless who blunt the fine edge of appetite with porridge.' The Chichester type, super or otherwise, has sunk beneath the flood tide of change, gone with array of breakfast dishes on the side-board, and the pattern of country-house life which required a floating reserve of bachelor guns. But such lives included hardships, and after three days' pollack fishing, Chichester, pale from a coarse and inadequate diet, awaits with impatience the sail across the bay of Eyries. On the other side stands a hotel, where Chichester has ordered a splendid luncheon, to entertain the Derryclares, their younger son, a midshipman, whose torpedo boat happens to be moored alongside, and a party of local beauties, attracted by the flotilla's arrival. Perfectly dressed in grey flannel, Chichester waits, in even greater agony than the rest of the yacht's company, as the anchor refuses to be drawn from the ocean floor. Others are sweating and hungry, but it is at his expense that the torpedo-boat's officers and their young ladies are gorging out of reach. Even Yeates can find pity for Chichester when the torpedo boat dashes past in an exultant curve, bawling messages of thanks through a megaphone.

At length, a diver comes on board, and with a few turns of the windlass brings the anchor up like a hot knife out of butter. With the diver comes a telegram that enables Chichester to make transparent excuses for escaping from a situation where his mid-day meal has been the offer of sardines and tea made by Philippa at two p.m. When Chichester's sufferings have caused him to refuse the tea offered by the friend of his youth, she thoughtfully improvises a cosy for the teapot.

'The farewells were made, the parting regrets very creditably accomplished, and we stood on the deck and saw him go, with his suitcase, his rods, his gun-case heaped imposingly in the bow, his rug and his coats, the greater and the less, piled behind him in the stern.' In the freshening wind, Chichester rises to put on his greater coat, sitting down abruptly as the boat lurches, only to rise suddenly again, as if stung by a wasp. It is in the coat pocket of the friend of her youth that Philippa has improvised a tea-cosy.

At this point it may be helpful to give a skeleton-tree of Philippa's family, as she plays more of a leading part in the later R.M. stories than in earlier days when Mr Knox was predominant. Philippa is known to have had a powerful godfather, an uncle in Donegal, a Gaelophile step-brother called Maxwell Bruce, and a rich sister, Alice Hervey, possibly a stepsister, mother of two daughters, one of these being Sybil, enamoured of Curly McRory. Philippa's most inconvenient kinsman is, however, Captain Andrew Larpent, R.E., an inveterate piano player, given to criticism of the structure of Shreelane. There have been complaints that *Harrington's*, in

F

which Captain Larpent first appears, is an awkward mixture of the knockabout and the supernatural. These objections ignore the fact that to Edith, if not to Martin, the supernatural was an element of everyday life, and not an area separate from the prosaic or the farcical.

Driven from home by the domestic purifications following on a visit from Cantillon the beautifully named sweep, the Yeates take Larpent on a picnic. It is not mentioned if this is the same sweep who played such an important part in *Great Uncle McCarthy*, but as his visit has deprived Anthony Yeates of his ninth birthday cake, the boy is brought on the picnic as a compensation. Cantillon is the casual agent in the subsequent drama. The picnic is to be combined with calling on new, chicken-farming neighbours. ' "Now remember, both of you, (said Philippa) one of them is a doctor, Scotch, and a theosophist, or something mysterious of that sort; and the pretty one was engaged to a gunner and it was broken off—why, I don't know—drink, I fancy, or mad——" ' After Andrew Larpent has pulled the bell out by the roots, it is discovered that Doctor Fraser and Meg Longmuir, the chicken farmers, have gone to an auction at Harrington's, a bankrupt copper mine. A glutton for auctions, Philippa leads the party to Harrington's. 'One of the sheds had but half a roof; a truck lay on its side in a pool of water; defeat was written starkly over all.' Recognized by the auctioneer as a valued customer, Philippa quickly buys the aneroid barometer, the last thing Mr Harrington laid his hand on, before leaving the house to cast himself down the mine shaft. A large matron in the crowd tells Yeates and Andrew that the coroner's jury brought it in as an accident, out of consideration for the widow's benefit under an insurance policy. Andrew asks if, 'apart from the climate and the architecture' there had been any reason for suicide. ' "I'm told he was a little annoyed," said an enormous farmer, delicately.

' "It was the weather preyed on him," said the matron. "There was a vessel coming round to him with coal and all sorts, . . . and in the latther end she met a rock and she went down in a lump, and his own brother that was in her was drownded." '

It happens that Yeates' own last act before leaving home has been to refuse the loan to Mr Knox of his long ladder, a recent acquisition, of such benefit to the neighbourhood that it 'enjoyed a butterfly existence of country house visiting'. Persuaded by Andrew that a second long ladder would be a measure of economy, Yeates secures one that has come up for sale, while Andrew, at the sound of a piano, darts into the house to join the pretty chicken farmer in the overture of 'Semiramide' arranged for four hands. It seems to Yeates that a tall man in a yachting cap is standing between the players and the light, but they thunder on, apparently unconscious of any shadow. And now the horror, hinted at in the tale of Mr Harrington's suicide, comes sidling into the story. Doctor Fraser, the second chicken farmer, has seen Anthony and Minx, the fox terrier, beside the old shaft, a tall man in a yachting cap had been with them, but Minx has returned alone, distressed and filthy. Doctor Fraser's hand is lying on the aneroid barometer, bought just now by Philippa, having been handed on from unlucky manager to unlucky manager, until Mr Harrington tapped it for the last time and went out to fall to his death down the mine shaft. Doctor Fraser sits down suddenly. ' "I see tram-lines," she said gropingly, "and water—I wonder if he's asleep——" ' Fighting panic with the idea that Anthony had been seen with a man in a yachting cap, 'in itself a guarantee of competence', Yeates finds himself following Philippa and a local boy down some cliff steps. They disappear into a tunnel from which the tram-lines of the old mine protrude over a cove, 'where yellow foam far below, churned and blew upward in heavy flakes'.

Yeates is at a loss in a cross-gallery when he meets with Minx. '[She] paused just short of the cross-ways, staring as though I was a stranger . . . A fresh light showed her, still motionless; her back was up, not in the ordinary ridge, but in patches here and there; she was looking at something behind me; she made her mouth round as a shilling, held up her white throat, and howled thinly and horribly as if she were keening. I cannot deny that I stiffened as I stood, and that second being that is awake when we are asleep (and is always afraid) took charge for a moment.' Following the tram-lines brings Yeates to a patch of light from Anthony's electric torch. 'Philippa . . . was kneeling between the tram-lines in the muddy water,

holding Anthony in her arms. He was motionless and limp,
and I felt that sickening drop of the heart that comes when
the thing that seems too bad to think of becomes in an instant
the thing that is.

' "Tram-lines and water——" said a level voice in my brain.
"I wonder if he is asleep——"

'I wondered too.'

Bandaged by Doctor Fraser, Anthony is brought up from
the shaft by means of the long ladder, whose fortunate presence
is explained by Cantillon, pale-faced without his usual top-
dressing of soot. ' ". . . wasn't it the mercy of God them chaps
Mr Knox has at the kennels had lent it to the Mahonys, and
them that's here took it from the Mahonys in a hurry the time
Mr Harrington died! And through it all it was the Major's
ladder . . . Faith I mightn't know it myself only for the old
poker I stuck in it one time at Mr Knox's when a rung broke
under me——" As Yeates jumps into the car he treads crack-
lingly the aneroid concealed under a rug. When we reached a
point in the road where it skirts the cliff I stopped the car, and
flung the aneroid, like a quoit, over the edge, through the
wind and the rain into oblivion.'

The two following stories concern the chicken-farmers, and
have also some element of the supernatural. As a result of a
feud between rival local jockeys, *The Maroan Pony*, property of
the chicken-farmers, is found in a loft only reached by a flight
of steps. 'In telling the story I have formed the habit of saying
there were ten of them', at a moment when she was due to be
saddled for a race. Force and cajolery are unavailing. The
maroan pony knocks Larpent into a pannier of cabbages, and
spurns the bait when Philippa lays the cabbages in rows on the
steps, 'as if it were a harvest festival'. Doctor Fraser asks if she
might try something she had once been told. ' "By all means,"
said Andrew, as chillingly as was possible for a man who was
very red in the face and covered with cobwebs.' With apparently nothing beyond the most ordinary words and pats of
encouragement, Doctor Fraser induces the pony to drop from
step to step with trembling but cunning feet. The pony is
rushed off to run a victorious race, but Doctor Fraser (like the
wise woman in Kipling's story *Simple Simon*, it appears always
to have hurted her to show her gifts) remains with Yeates.

While bringing her a glass of water, it is revealed to him that
there had been, all the time, a door into the loft from the field
above, concealed by bracken by the enemies of the maroan
pony's jockey. This made the working of the Charm, for which
Doctor Fraser says her grandfather gave Rarey thirty pounds,
even more remarkable.

Rarey's secret of charming horses, however wild, had
amazed Great Britain in 1859. It was, in reality, the father of
Fanny Currey who had paid thirty pounds for the secret, and
passed it on to his daughter. Mr Currey spent most of a long life
as agent, at Lismore, to the Duke of Devonshire. There were
family connections, and Edith shared suffragist opinions and a
passion for landscape painting with Fanny. Mr Currey was
succeeded in the agency by Jim Penrose, the husband of Ethel
Coghill, but his daughter continued to dominate her world at
Lismore, by methods that included bad language, and, when a
council drainage scheme threatened her bulb farm, a show of
armed resistance. Edith had seen the charm working when
Fanny Currey rushed to intervene between a carter and the
jibbing horse he was beating. 'I followed her. To save blood-
shed. The carter's blood, not Fanny's. The Charm was effective,
and it was then that Fanny Currey told how she had started a
jibbing cabhorse in Oxford Street, an adventure given to
Doctor Fraser. Rarey, if the *Illustrated London News* of 1885 can
be believed, could subdue the wildest of stallions, turning
them from man-killing fiends to gracious creatures prepared
to offer Mr Rarey his top-hat by the brim held between
their teeth.

Major Apollo Riggs takes place against a background of
domestic discomfort phenomenal even by the standards that
prevail at Shreelane. Andrew Larpent, speaking with the
authority of a Sapper, insists that the chimneys of Shreelane
are dangerously far from the perpendicular. Yeates employs
Walkin' Aisy, the local builder, to rebuild the chimney stacks,
in spite of his monumental incompetence and elusiveness. So
compelling is his portrait, that, to those reared on the R.M.
stories, the sight of any builder carrying a ladder calls up the
vision of this mason 'never known . . . to accept a job without
suggesting that some one else could do it better than he (in
which he was probably quite right).'

Discussing the rebuilding, Flurry maintains that only the ivy and the weather-slating hold the walls together. Contrariwise, Mrs Knox insists that in the storm of thirty-nine (the Big Wind) her father had said that ' "if Shreelane fell, not a house in Ireland would stand. Everyone in the house spent that night in the kitchen." "Maybe that was nothing new to them," suggested Flurry.' Mrs Knox ignores this comment on an incident that had been one of the legends of Ross. Shreelane, she explains, was built by an ancestor, in honour of his wedding to ' "... a Riggs of Castle Riggs, a cousin of the celebrated Major Apollo—and thereby hangs a tale!" She blinked her eyes like an old rat, and looked at each of us in turn ... "They knew how to build in those days," she began again. "The basement of Shreelane is all vaulted." "I dare say the kitchen would make a nice vault," said Flurry.' To Yeates' surprise, Mrs Knox looks hard at Flurry and becomes silent.

The folly of tampering with the fabric of Shreelane becomes ever more apparent, culminating in a grisly dinner party where Meg Longmuir spurns Andrew. She adds social unease to the physical discomforts of smoking new chimneys by flirting with Bernard Shute. Andrew, disgruntled and bombastic, proposes a paper-chase to exercise hunters immobilized by a long drought. ' "I think we'd better make a hare of you," said Flurry, fixing expressionless eyes on Captain Larpent. "It mightn't be hard." ' Larpent, unaware that this means to make a fool of someone, misses the nuance of the insult, and Flurry, as ever alive to an opportunity of passing-on a horse, moves smoothly on, to offer Andrew a ride on 'a little horse that I was thinking of parting ...' At this point the party is disrupted by a crash, as a rat bolts under the feet of the parlour-maid, upsetting both her and the coffee-tray. Minx, her son and daughter, the red setter and the dinner party descend in full cry to the cellar, where the rat is slaughtered in a nest of old letters, broken out of a box of the kind once indigenous to the rumble of a coach. Under the turf mould of generations, Andrew finds a flagstone, with its ring fastened by a sealed padlock, which he insists on opening, in spite of protests from Flurry and Meg Longmuir. The result of this assertion against Miss Longmuir nearly causes Andrew to disappear into the inky waters of the well that is revealed in the turf-room floor.

Next morning the well is dredged, adding evil-smelling sludge ' "ideal for the roses," said Philippa'—to the mess left in the yard by Walkin' Aisy. Mutterings of trouble come from the servants, and Flurry, who gives the children the letters from the old coach box to tear up for the paper-chase, reports that the last time the well was opened the servants fled from the house. In the interests of selling the young horse to Andrew, Flurry chooses a safe line for the paper-chase, which finishes in the yard at Shreelane. Here the crowd, including Mrs Knox in her phaeton, are assembled round the debris of the gable chimney, which, left half-built by Walkin' Aisy, has grown tired of awaiting his return, and collapsed.

At this moment Larpent clatters through the gate, out of control on Flurry's chestnut horse, which trips over the rubble from the chimney and pitches Andrew off on to his head. His recovered lady-love binds up his wounds, and meanwhile Mrs Knox gives Major Yeates some good advice. She takes from her chain, to which something like a bootlace attaches it, the seal with which her father had sealed up the turf-house well at the time of the Famine. Major Apollo Riggs, she says, drove up to Shreelane one day in a fine coach and four, which next day drove away without him. ' "He found himself a success at Shreelane," I suggested. "Not so much with his host as his hostess," returned Mrs Knox,' (suitably sibylline in what is, alas, almost her final utterance). Major Apollo Riggs had never been seen again, the implication being that his disappearance accounted for the richness of the sludge in the turf-house well. The letters from the coach have been scattered by the paper-chase, only the one scrap with the word 'Apollo' and nothing more, has, tantalizingly, been stuck on to Andrew in his fall.

Miss Larkie McRory has ridden in the paper-chase, mounted on what Flurry called 'the latter end of a car-horse'. She first shows her initiative in the opening scene of *The Bosom of The McRorys* when, at a Harvest Festival, the golden butterfly that quivers above Mrs McRory's bonnet has fixed its grappling irons into an adjunct of Philippa's hat, causing them to remain 'brow to brow in what seemed to be a prolonged embrace' . . . 'the butterfly's vitals slowly uncoiled, and were drawn out into a single but indomitable strand of gold wire; the Bishop was imminent, when a female McRory in the pew behind (known to the Fancy as Larkie) intervened with what were, I believe, a pair of manicure scissors'. Larkie develops into a reflection of Francie Fitzpatrick, without her tragic tendencies, and seen in a hunting looking-glass.

A dinner-party at Temple Braney becomes an inescapable social burden, alleviated for Yeates by finding his neighbour is Bobbie Bennett. 'I asked for that Mr Tomsy Flood whose career had twice, at vital points been intersected by me. "Ah, poor Tomsy! He took to this, y'know," Miss Bennett slightly jerked her little finger, "and he wouldn't ride a donkey over a sod of turf. They sent him out to South Africa to a ostrich farm, and when the people found he couldn't ride they put him to bed with a setting of ostrich eggs to keep them warm, and he did this grand, till someone gave him a bottle of whisky, and he got rather lively and broke all the eggs. They say it's a lay preacher he's going to be now!" ' This anecdote, superficially farcical, is illuminated by a twist of happy genius in the last sentence.

Seeking his motor car after dinner, Yeates is guided by Miss Bennett through the back parts of Temple Braney. In one room two children with mumps are being treated with punch, while in the kitchen, the cook with her frying pan for instrument is giving an imitation of Miss Cooney O'Rattigan, a guest who sings Italian to a mandoline. Yeates feels as if he was being lead through Chinatown, San Francisco, by a detective as they traverse a gothic corridor, 'a flagged passage stretched like a tunnel before us, lighted by a solitary candle stuck in its own grease in a window. A long battle-line of bicycles occupied one side of the passage; there were doors padlocked and cobwebbed on the other. A ragged baize door at the end of the tunnel opened into a darkness that smelt of rat-holes, and was patched by a square or two of moonlight.' Except for the bicycles, ever a feature of the back offices of Irish country houses, the scene might have come from Henry Tilney's take-off of Mrs Radcliffe's horror stories. A reference to the Georgian vastness of the coach-house, from which the motor is missing, appears to be the first time Edith and Martin wrote of the architecture of their country as being in any way remarkable. The motor has been abandoned by some young McRorys to batter its way through a holly bush.

Twisted round the brakes are the streamers from Miss Cooney O'Rattigan's mandoline. ' "Dublin for ever! (Miss Bennett exclaimed) . . . There's the spoils of war for you! And it's all the spoils you'll get—the whole pack of them's hid in the house by now."

'From an unlighted window over the hall door a voice added itself to the conversation.

' "God help the house that holds them!" it said, addressing the universe.

'The window was closed.

' "That's old McRory," said Miss Bennett . . .

'Again I thought of Chinatown, sleepless, incalculable, with its infinite capacity for sheltering the criminal.'

Put Down One and Carry Two describes the next day's hunting, up and down Lonen Hill, which stands above Lonen Lake, scene of the Regatta in *The Waters of Strife*. As well as facetious remarks on the subject of the after-effects of McRory's champagne, Yeates has to endure the involuntary pursuit of Larkie McRory, whose shaggy, grey horse attaches itself to Yeates' sedate hunter Daniel. At last, faced with a pole jammed across a bohireen, Yeates bets Larkie, whose face is glowing with the excitement of the chase, that, should she jump it she will come off her horse. ' "Done with you!" said Miss McRory suddenly smiting the grey cob with a venomous little cutting whip (one that probably dated from the sixties, and had for a handle an ivory greyhound's head with a plaited collar round its neck).'

Larkie McRory must have been near to Edith's heart, for the whip bestowed on her was the first that Edith herself took out hunting, and which still hangs in the hall at Drishane, together with the last, utilitarian, crop carried by the Master of the West Carbery.

Larkie McRory sails from the saddle and her cob disappears into the mist and rain. With Yeates leading Daniel and Larkie sitting sideways, they struggle on till they reach the wishing well on Lonen Hill, where they eat Yeates' sandwiches, and Daniel eats the votive rags off the holy thorn bush. Their relationship becomes even closer when, Yeates being lamed by walking in his boots, they have to proceed with Larkie sitting behind him on the wide plateau of Daniel's hindquarters. By this time he has learnt that her peculiar nickname comes from

a Mr Mulcahy, who said, affecting an English accent, that the
McRory sisters were 'Lorky little gurls with lorge dark eyes'.
The idyll, a rare treat for the R.M., ends with the double-
banked pair finding themselves in the glaring headlights of a
stationary car. '[Daniel] swung to one side, he drifted like a
blown leaf and Miss McRory clung to me like a knapsack.' The
car belongs to Lady Knox, a momentous figure in pot hat and
fur coat, but Yeates, in an extremity of wetness and numb
exhaustion has passed beyond embarrassment. 'Flurry came on
into the light; there was just room in me for subconscious
recognition of the fact that he was riding the missing grey cob,
and that this was a typical thing, and one that might have
been expected.'

In the last story that concerns Mr Knox's hounds, called
The Comte de Pralines, Larkie McRory is allowed to get her
teeth into richer game than hitherto. The idea of passing someone off as a foreigner without English is a joke with a peculiarly
period flavour, its humour reduced in this case by the victims
being unclear in their minds as to the distinctions between
European countries; war, with its harsh lessons in geography,
was still a threat in the future. Philippa has conspired with the
Derryclares' son, Bill, to import a French-speaking friend, to
be introduced as the Comte de Pralines, into Mr Knox's field.
Exquisite in turn-out and Gallic politeness, the stranger causes
all to flee before him. Bobbie Bennett, asked if she spoke
French, 'looked as if she was drowning and answered, *"Seulement très petit."* ' Miss McRory, on the other hand, finds
language difference to be no barrier, and so catches the moment
when the Comte de Pralines relapses into English. Lady Knox
and Flurry, however, remain deceived until the end of the
Great Castle Knox run, which is lifted above ordinariness by
the involvement of a wedding party in an inside car, 'with a
scarlet faced bride embedded in female relatives'. Shortly before
meeting this scene, Yeates has shaken off the devoted attendance of a donkey and her foal, the mother's broken chain
clanking 'as if she was a family ghost'. The male guests from
the wedding party have all joined the hunt, the bridegroom
running with Larkie McRory's hat in his hand. All followers
of the hunt converge on the spot where the Comte de Pralines
is breaking up the fox in fluent English.

'Flurry turned an iron face upon me. His eye was no bigger than a pin's head.

' "I suppose it was from Larkie McRory he got the English?" he said, "he learnt it quick."

' "The McRorys don't speak English!" said Lady Knox, in a voice like a north-east wind.

' "*Seulement très petit!*" Philippa murmured brazenly.'

Yeates and his wife have nearly effected an unobtrusive withdrawal when 'a yearning choking wail came to us from the lane.

' "The Bride?" queried my wife hysterically.

'It was repeated; in the same instant my admirers, the jackasses, *mère et fils*, advanced upon the scene at a delirious gallop, and, sobbing with the ecstasy of reunion, resumed their attendance on Daniel.' Watched by the flower of Mr Knox's field, the R.M.'s exit is as dramatic as it is final.

There remained only *The Shooting of Shinroe* to be written, which, like *How I First Met Doctor Hickey*, begins in a West of Ireland Hotel. Before the Owenford Sessions, Yeates has been promised a day's shooting on the hill of Shinroe, where an ancient solicitor, Francis Joseph M'Cabe, claims to have sporting rights. M'Cabe's name suggests a Catholic background, and his portrait shows that Somerville and Ross could, when they wished, handle the professional middle-classes. After complaints about the basket chairs and the German clerk by which the hotel attempts to keep up with the times, M'Cabe discusses the Owenford dentist, Jeffers, a keen sportsman, who has that morning fitted M'Cabe with false teeth. On the river's bank, one night, Jeffers had trodden on the face of a poacher who was sleeping drunkenly on the bundles of spurge he had brought to poison the waters.

'What did [Jeffers] do, is it? Ran off for his life, roaring out ' "There's a first-rate dentist in Owenford!" '

'He yawned—a large yawn that ended in a metallic click. His eyes met mine full of unspoken things; we parted in a silence that seemed to have been artificially imposed on Mr M'Cabe.'

The day on Shinroe is of the blankest and the dog, lent by Jeffers, the dentist, must, M'Cabe believes, have been taken as

a bad debt, answering to no gun-dog name 'from Don to
Grouse, from Carlo to Shot'. Incautious from annoyance,
M'Cabe reveals that not only has he paid Jeffers a high price
for his painful new teeth, but he has initiated the dentist into
the technique of shooting Shinroe, which accounts for its
birdlessness. Yeates is even more shaken to learn that, on top
of Jeffers' depredations, the shooting has been let for ten times
its value to an English syndicate, which makes the R.M.,
though empty handed, a poacher. Slightly redeeming his use-
lessness, the dentist's dog smells out a bottle of potheen, hidden
under a bush, but even sustained by this liquid fire it is a long
wet trudge towards Coppeen Road Station. Here it may be
possible to set what the local car-driver calls an 'amber-bush'
for the evening train, which only stops when flagged.

This information has been passed to Yeates when he and
M'Cabe have been given a lift on the outside car on which they
had begun their Barmecidal day's sport. Permission for the lift
has to be given by the police sergeant and a constable in charge
of a prisoner, who is due to appear before Yeates at the Sessions
next day. The driver tells the rest of the news, picked up
at Coppeen Road Station. The English syndicate, tenants
of Shinroe, have heard of ' "two fellas walking it with
guns and a dog" ' and have gone to report the matter to the
police.

' "Did they see the fellows?" I asked lightly, after a panic-
stricken pause.

' "They did not. Sure they said if they seen them, they'd
shoot them like rooks." '

Jerry, the car driver, is personally incensed at a further piece
of news from Coppeen Road. It seems that a man on a motor-
bike had Shinroe shot out by ten o'clock that morning, which
Jerry regards as a threat by a machine to a horse-driver's livelihood. Yeates is reflecting that he, at least, has not gone poaching on a motor-bicycle, when M'Cabe whispers to him that the
prisoner on the car will be appearing in court next morning
charged with hunting Shinroe with greyhounds. Furious as he
is with M'Cabe for putting him in a legally compromised
position, Yeates begins to waver when he hears his fellow
poacher's attempts to open the bottle of potheen marked down
by the dentist's dog.

' "Hold on!" roared M'Cabe, with a new and strange utterance. "Thtop the horth! I've dropped me teeth!" '

The agonizing search begins, first Yeates, and then the Sergeant joining in. Jerry the car-man produces the end of a candle, climbing down from the car, but almost at once the candle slips into a puddle. M'Cabe's lisping rage is intensified by the knowledge that his present discomfort will be as nothing to his professional incapacity in court next day. Having no matches, Yeates hails the constable, who has remained on the car with the prisoner. 'The constable politely jumped off and came to meet me.'

'As he was in the act of handing me his match-box, the car drove away down the hill.' Pursuit of the prisoner by Jerry and the police is futile, the mare's implacable stride being quickened by the attentions of the dentist's dog.

'Far, far away from the direction of Coppeen Road, that sinister outpost where evil rumours were launched, and the night trains were waylaid by the amber-bushes, a steady tapping sound advanced towards us.' As the lamp of a motor-bicycle appears, M'Cabe begs Yeates to stop the rider and entreat him to keep to the teeth-free side of the road, himself unable to explain the position owing to their loss. Yeates sees a gun slung across the rider's back and a full game bag on the carrier, but the rider only slows down for long enough to call out, "There's a first rate dentist in Owenford."

'[M'Cabe] clutched my arm and shook it.
' "That wath Jefferth! Jefferth, I tell ye! The dirty poacher! And his bag full of our birdths!" '

The climax of Major Yeates' last adventure having been inexorably built up, he draws M'Cabe from the scene of his loss, gently, as one deals with the bereaved, and with him faces the six-mile walk to Owenford.

In this last book that Somerville and Ross wrote together, Edith's illustrations are in chalk on greenish paper. She tended to vary the portraits of the characters more than they varied in their written appearances. In early illustrations of Major Yeates she drew him as a lanky figure of despair, and held to this convention until after he is shown in horror at shooting a tame drake. On the other hand, when he is driving with Philippa in the Butler-Knox's pony carriage, they have become figures of worldly consequence in top hats and coats with fur collars. The gallery of portraits which illustrates *In Mr Knox's Country* were the last pictures of the world which Edith and Martin had created together. A few months later death had taken Martin and left Edith alone.

14
A widowhood of the spirit

'The unmarried woman seldom escapes a widowhood of the spirit.
There is sure to be someone, parent, brother, sister, friend, more
comfortable to her than the day, with whom her life is so entwined
that the wrench of parting leaves a torn void never entirely healed
or filled, and this is above all the case when the separation is untimely, and the desolation is where life-long hopes and dependence
have been gathered up.'

Charlotte M. Yonge. (*The Pillars of the House*)

WHEN Flurry Knox says good-bye to Major Yeates, his
deputy M.F.H., who is seeing the Irish Yeomanry off to
the South African War, his last words are ' "... whatever
you do, don't give more than half-a-crown for a donkey.
There's no meat on them." ' Flurry, as has been seen, returns,
seemingly unmarked by his experiences. On his last appearance
he inquires if the supposed Comte de Pralines had come to buy
horses for the German Army, considering this to be a perfectly
reasonable activity for a Frenchman. It is problematical if
Flurry and his circle could have survived the 1914 War, and
the subsequent Irish upheavals, without disintegration, but,
as it happened, the moment at which Martin left Edith was
one when a final curtain of history was due to fall. When the
curtain rose on the next act Edith was alone, to play her part in
a world, she wrote, where the Steam Roller of Time was
obliterating all the old wheel-tracks.

In May, 1915, the war came painfully close to Castletowns-
hend, when the *Lusitania* was torpedoed off Galley Head, Co.
Cork. Among those lost was Sir Hugh Lane, nephew of Lady
Gregory, and Martin sent *In Mr Knox's Country* to her cousin
Augusta, with the hope that it might provide some distraction
in this grief. The grateful response was at variance with
Lennox Robinson's statement (made in a broadcast on the
centenary of Edith's birth) that Lady Gregory had particularly

disliked the R.M. stories. She was reading the book slowly, she wrote to Martin, because she was reading it aloud to W. B. Yeats. 'He at first mention of Major Yeates asked anxiously if it was spelt with a second "e", and hearing it was, gave himself up to uninterrupted enjoyment.' She particularly enjoyed the character of old Mrs Knox, because there was so much of Martin's mother in its composition and she agreed with Martin that one should be grateful for 'the laughter-calling gift'. She had considered *The Real Charlotte* to be 'far beyond any writer now going with the one exception of Hardy'. It was probably Mrs Knox's erudition and turn of phrase that recalled Mrs Martin to Lady Gregory, rather than the fact that she blinked her eyes like an old rat, but it is pleasant to think of Yeats listening, as Lady Gregory read aloud to him the methods by which Mrs Knox dealt with Goggin the Gombeen.

Turning their back on the War, and the success of *In Mr Knox's Country*, Edith and Martin sank into the timeless repose of a holiday in Kerry. Except for the 'white Daageens', Sheila and Dooley, imported by themselves, every living creature seemed to be in colour a rich and glowing black. A new-born Kerry calf was like 'a black spaniel puppy', and as black in their own feathers and furs were the turkeys, the hens and the Kerry beagles. These hounds were summoned, one Sunday after second Mass, to show the visitors their gifts. They were collected into a working pack by the notes of a copper-coloured bugle hung with red tassels, blown by Johnny the Post, son of the postmaster known even more euphoniously as Connie the Wings. Raising their noses, the Black Beagles keened on the bugle's note with a sound that seemed to belong to 'the earlier ages of the world'. Looking back on these last halcyon days with Martin, Edith found it hard to choose between the days on the strand, entranced by the smooth sea with, on the horizon, 'those pale pyramids of azure', the Skelligs, and days on the Slough, 'lying full length on a massed embroidery of flowers, close and gorgeous as a pattern on a Chinese cloak'.

Martin had always had a tendency to lie on sofas, incapacitated by complaints which her immediate family regarded as nervous, verging on the imaginary. In spite of this history, it would be wrong to conclude that it was Edith who galvanized her into physical as well as literary activity. Her practical energy in an emergency was clear in a letter to Edith, quoted in *Irish Memories*, and written from Ross, to describe the difficulty of getting to church on a Sunday morning when a rat, well-known to be poison, had been found in the oats. In a sequence like the House that Jack Built, this discovery resulted in the pony being left unfed, and when Martin commanded that hay should be substituted for the oats, the pony cast a shoe on being put into the shafts. There was another pony, but she was lame. 'Nothing for it', wrote Martin, 'but the monster Daisy browsing on the lawn with her foal.' Martin described herself. 'I had on a voile skirt of stupendous length with a floating train, my best gloves, and other Sunday trappings.' In this finery, she helped Rickeen, the factotum, to separate the shrieking mare from her foal, and stuffed the latter into the barn, causing the donkey to burst out in an endeavour to join a neighbour's ass. The foal's shrieks from the barn mingled with Rickeen's curses in Irish and English, and with Martin's own laughter. Rickeen drove the donkey by blows into the pigsty. 'Then we pitched Mama on to the car and got off. Daisy, almost invisible under her buffalo mane, as usual went the pace, and we got in at the First Lesson.'

Pitching Mrs Martin on to the car can have been no mean feat if her size is recollected, but the episode gives an excellent portrait of Martin, painted by herself. Her adherence to the convention which required voile skirts and gloves for church-going contrasts with her resource in dealing with a situation in which her laughter was almost more of a handicap than her elegance. (Gloves she regarded as an essential for polite wear, even reproving a young niece for discarding them in the informality of Castletownshend.) The final contrast lies between the helter-skelter drive behind the shaggy mare and the decorum of the First Lesson.

After Martin's hunting accident, Edith had marvelled at the determined courage which had kept her from abandoning her part in their writing, and had got her back into the saddle with her nerve unshaken. But soon after the holiday in Kerry Martin began to suffer from symptoms for which there appeared to be no satisfactory explanation, or even diagnosis. There was some improvement, then a sudden deterioration in her state, and she passed into unconsciousness, suffering from

an inoperable tumour on the brain. Edith could do no more
than watch beside Martin, her courage bracing her to keep the
helpless agony in her spirit at bay. In the course of this watching she made one last drawing of Martin's unconscious head.
The drawing was unidealized, done on the greenish paper in
black and white chalk, the medium she had used for the gay
illustrations to *In Mr Knox's Country*. It is the picture of someone already beyond the sound of human voices, with an
expression as remote as that of death itself, but details of
shawls and clothing are scrawled in with a hand that did not
falter. Edith was spared the hearing of the banshee voice that
others heard crying under Martin's window, but she knew that
Martin was leaving her and by the middle of December her
long widowhood of the spirit had begun.

Martin was buried in the graveyard of St Barrahane, at
the east end of the church where the view over Castlehaven
Harbour is wide and shining. On her memorial cross are engraved the words from the book of Wisdom which testify that
the Souls of the Righteous are in the hands of God, and though
in the sight of the Unwise they seem to die they are in peace.
It was a harrowing season, full of grief, for many beside Edith.
In *Irish Memories*, writing of Martin's love of hunting, she
commemorated also three sons of her neighbours in West
Carbery who had been proud to wear the velvet cap of the
Hunt Servant and turn hounds for the West Carbery, before
they were lost in battle. Martin was still alive to share Edith's
pleasure and pride when *The Times* included extracts from the
R.M. stories among broadsheets to be distributed to troops at
the front. Edith learnt later that the 'laughter calling gift' that
belonged to Major Yeates had been found valuable by Gilbert
Talbot, killed at Ypres in 1915, to whom Toc H was the
memorial. The last entry in his diary told that he had read aloud
an R.M. story in the men's rest-time, 'a roaring success'. Other
friends wrote to Edith in gratitude for the respite from grief
gained from the same source, and Edith believed that Martin
knew and was glad.

Death and burial had always had a strong fascination for
Martin, as can be seen from her letters and the essays written
by herself alone. In the next parish to Castlehaven, there was a
graveyard of such decayed loneliness that, Edith wrote, 'the

dreadful wreck of tombs too old even for tradition to whisper whose once they were'. She went on to tell of a beggar-woman who came there from a distance to attend the funeral of an old friend and benefactress, expressing her farewell in a way Edith knew Martin would have understood. 'And when she seen the corpse pass her, she threw up the hands, and says she, "That your journey may thrive wid ye!"' The journey on which Martin had gone, though it removed her from Edith's sight, became in the survivor's belief a less than total separation.

From the days of her childhood, Edith could recall spiritualist experiments among her family, particularly at the Rectory at Castlehaven during the long incumbency of the Reverend Charles Bushe. This son of the Lord Chief Justice had contributed the most terrifying twist to the family tree by marrying his niece's elder half-sister. Their children included the brilliant Seymour Bushe, Q.C., who not only gave himself the Joycean punning nickname of 'Saymore Bosh', but is mentioned in *Ulysses* as an inspired advocate.

'J. J. O'Molloy turned to Stephen and said quietly and slowly: "One of the most polished periods I think I ever listened to in my life fell from the lips of Seymour Bushe. It was in that case of fratricide, the Childs murder case. Bushe defended him." The speech contrasted Roman justice with the earlier Mosaic code, and cited the Moses of Michelangelo in the Vatican. If J. J. O'Molloy's memory is to be relied upon the passage ran: "—that stony effigy in frozen music, horned and terrible, of the human form divine, that eternal symbol of wisdom and prophecy which, if aught that the imagination or the hand of sculptor has wrought in marble of soultransfigured and of soultransfiguring deserves to live, deserves to live."'

It was, however, to Constance Bushe, sister of the orator, that Edith turned for 'wisdom and prophecy'. Constance was sensitively gifted both in the arts of this world, and in her ability to establish communication with worlds unseen. Weak health and her family obligations prevented her from giving the devotion to painting that Edith was able to give, but, among a clan of artists her water-colours have a peculiar strength and delicacy, and her illustrations of family contretemps are full of wit. The table used for questioning at the

Rectory not only declared that Constance was the darling of the spirits, but followed her about, it was said, so assiduously that Miss Bushe took fright and refused to lay her hands, any more, on its polished top. The table converted Sir Joscelyn Coghill to the Society for Psychical Research, by rapping out 'Stafford', when challenged to say where Sir Joscelyn had bought his boots, which had been purchased during a breakdown of the Irish Mail. Colonel Kendal Coghill followed his brother, after a probationary period when Edith and Cameron Somerville were conscripted as mediums in automatic writing. They sat in boredom, while their Uncle Kendal sat entranced at a flood of hints poured out by a supposed ancestress, concerning a hoard of diamonds she had hidden in Dublin before her murder by an Irish Rapparee.

Much as Edith relied on Constance's sympathy in all she had lost in losing Martin, it was not through this agency that messages began to come to her, messages which held a promise that some of the loss might be made up. The beginning of this spiritual correspondence seems to have been almost accidental, Edith and a neighbour, Jem Barlow, attempting by means of automatic writing to get in touch with someone recently killed in the war. Miss Barlow was an addition to the fluid, gregarious life of Castletownshend. She had moved into the village about four years before, to become respected for her mediumistic powers by those Coghills and Somervilles who experimented in the occult. To the younger generation her appearance in their midst was a grown-up whim, never entirely explained. They would have hardly been surprised to learn that she had arrived on a broomstick, and, on at least one occasion, this would have been the easiest explanation for her appearance in a spot remote from anywhere she had reason to be. It was difficult to analyse how much of the hurricane of drama in which she lived was deliberately generated by herself, or the unconscious product of boiling inward forces. For instance, the horde of wild men who surged past her out of an ancient fort above Drishane dressed in skins—she could even smell them—and waving clubs as they went over the cliffs, could have been a straight invention, or such a suitable manifestation from the past that her senses responded to her imagination.

The first message from Martin left Edith perplexed and

doubtful, but conviction came with greater ease in the practice of automatic writing, in which she ceased, in time, to be solely dependent on Jem Barlow. As will be seen later, Martin's role expanded from help to Edith to continue her writing, to advice and support in the troubled times which were to follow in the early nineteen-twenties. Edith's belief that she was in direct communication with Martin remained unshaken to her life's end. She wrote that she did not grudge their easy chairs to those who sat in the Seats of the Scornful. They should not certainly grudge her what Constance Bushe, who, as Edith said, 'knew and understood everything' wrote at the end of a letter on the subject of Martin's continuing, if unseen, partnership. '. . . *Of course*, I can understand what this means to you, and it seems a very special "way of escape that you may be able to bear it".'

The first result of Martin's encouragement was the patchwork volume of biography and autobiography, *Irish Memories*. Edith wrote to Lord Dunsany, who, as a young man had made a sensation by swimming across Castlehaven Harbour, for permission to quote, as an epigraph, lines from his play *The Tents of the Arabs*. The passage, which she wished to be the key-note of the book, began, 'What is this child of man that can conquer Time and is braver than Love?

'Even Memory.'

Irish Memories includes a quantity of stories which have already been referred to as they occurred chronologically. Edith did not, it seems, realize that a pattern is as necessary in reminiscence as it is in fiction. She doubles back from Martin's history of her brother Robert and the Martins of Ross, to letters from Charles Kendal Bushe about Maria Edgeworth, then to letters from Miss Edgeworth herself. Again, advancing in time, come chapters that give a sketch of early days in West Carbery, and the arrival of the Reverend Charles Bushe, letting new light into the private world where Townshends and Somervilles fought and married each other. It is not an easy book for research students. Stories about Mrs Somerville's reactions to her daughter Edith's hair—'a collection of filthy little furze bushes'—are mixed with political comments, which in their turn give way to more strictures of Mrs Somerville's. She was particularly incensed with her daughter Hildegarde,

who suggested that one of the four Grand Passions seen in her hand by a palmist would, naturally, have been Colonel Somerville. 'The preposterous dowdiness of this suggestion almost deprived my mother of the power of speech.
 ' "Papa . . . Paugh!" '
 The bibliography at the end of *Irish Memories* gives the titles of the sixteen books which the two pairs of hands of Somerville and Ross had written in twenty-six years, from *An Irish Cousin*, written in whatever hiding places Drishane had to offer, to *In Mr Knox's Country*, for which readers all over the world had been expectant. It is inconceivable that Edith would not have continued to write, even without the ghostly reassurance of Martin; the habit had become part of herself, even more than painting. But in whatever way she had developed, her writing would always have kept a strong element of devotion to Martin, an act of Love and Memory, perhaps most happily expressed in the sonnet of Louise Labé:

> '*Je ne souhaitte encore point mourir.*
> *Mais quand mes yeus je sentiray tarir,*
> *Ma voix cassee, et ma main impuissante,*
> *Et mon esprit en ce mortel sejour*
> *Ne pouvant plus montrer signe d'amante:*
> *Priray la Mort noircir mon plus cler iour.*'

15
The hill of fairy music

AMONG the Somerville and Ross papers there survives an unfinished novel, written jointly, with a note that parts of it had been used in *Mount Music*, which appeared in 1919 as by E. Œ. Somerville and Martin Ross. Edith, in a brief preface, wrote that the work had been planned and partly written in Martin's lifetime, so that the attribution to both writers was justified. *Mount Music* is an ambitious book, the most ambitiously planned that the cousins ever attempted. They had never before dealt with the influence of the Roman Catholic Church on the ordinary lives of its people, even the troubles in *Naboth's Vineyard* being uncomplicated by clerical intervention. At Ross the foster mothers of the Martin children had always taken their nurselings to the priest for a second baptism, a practice accepted by the parents in the spirit which allowed Mrs Martin to declare that her son Robert might be bathed in holy water, provided it was heated first. Martin has described attending confirmations, weddings and funerals, but at these the priest had been a functionary, not even essential in the conduct of a burying. The crusade of the Nationalist priest who did not quail before the interdiction of Rome, secure in the support of his parish, was an exception in its extreme militancy. Edith had a happier experience with a parish priest who gave his judgement, always accepted, on disputed claims on the Fowl Fund, comforting her in her perpetual doubt as to whether she was behaving to claimants with callous brutality or imbecile credulity.

The house and demesne of Mount Music take their name from Cnochan an Ceoil Sidhe, the Hill of Fairy Music, which looks out over the Vale of the River Broadwater. There is no mention of such a fortress as Lismore Castle, but Mount Music's situation, and the geographical relation of the towns of Cluhir and Riverstown, must have been drawn from Edith's knowledge of the River Blackwater, the Palladian houses on its banks and the towns of Lismore and Cappoquin.

The Talbot-Lowrys of Mount Music are going downhill, like Hemingway's bankrupt in *The Sun Also Rises*, both gradually and suddenly. Christian, the youngest of six, has bestowed on her something of the qualities that Edith said belonged to Martin. Beside fearlessness on horseback, she has a flower-like freshness of skin, and a gift of loving patience towards the old, the awkward and the sad. Edith added the compliment paid to herself as a girl by an ancient horse-breaker, ' "Twas the grandfather that gave you the sate, but 'twas the Lord Almighty that gave you the hands," ' to the list of Christian's gifts, together with an ability to hold silent conversations with beings invisible to the rest of the world.

Christian has need of her loving charity for Major Talbot-Lowry, her father, is unable to realize the political changes that have gradually eroded his position. The suddenness of his financial collapse comes when he allows his remaining assets to slide into the large, inexorable hands of Doctor Mangan from the town of Cluhir. There are echoes of Roddy Lambert's manipulation of Lady Dysart in Doctor Mangan's manœuvre, by which he allows the Major to get the better of him over buying a horse, and uses the resulting mood of good humour to get the Major's vote for the Doctor's own nominee for a surgery appointment. He is aware that any pecuniary set-back over the horse deal will be made good by the nominee's father.

Between the decaying Protestant world of the Talbot-Lowrys, and the cosy Catholic household of the Mangans, there stands Larry Coppinger, a cousin of the Lowrys. Somerville and Ross (assuming this to be part of the original scheme of the book) have sent Larry's father to India to marry a Catholic girl from a North of England family, leaving an orphan Catholic son to cope with this dichotomy. If this seems a long way to go to get results which could have been achieved nearer home, it should be remembered that apparently, like Stephen Gwynn, Edith and Martin had little experience of the Irish Catholic gentry on which to draw.

Having established a grip on the Mount Music property, the Doctor starts to play on Larry's romantic Nationalism, which is strengthened by his feeling that his religion binds him to the

country people. Larry and Christian fall in love, but the Doctor
manages to break off their engagement by alienating Larry
from Major Talbot-Lowry for political reasons, and convincing
Christian that rebellion on her part would dangerously agitate
her father. Tishy, the Doctor's voluptuous daughter, is slipped
into the void left by Christian, and, with Mount Music in his
possession, the Doctor expects that Christian will not finally
refuse his son Barty, an earnest creature, dumbly in love with
her. Most of these plans are on the point of fulfilment when
the Doctor, steadfast professionally if flexible financially, is
drowned in the flooded Broadwater on his way to a confine-
ment. Evans, the fanatically Protestant butler from Mount
Music, finds the body washed ashore, below the house which
had been captured with such patient skill. ' "Well, ye wanted
Mount Music!" [Evans] said at last. "How d'ye like it now ye've
got it?" '

In their young days Larry organizes his cousins into a band,
called the Companions of Finn and pledged to drive out the
Saxon invader from Dublin Castle. 'The Revolutionary, or
Reformer, who hesitates at becoming a bore is unworthy of his
high office.' Larry soon bores the Companions of Finn into
extinction, with the exception of Christian, and this is the
foundation of their romance. But even if disagreeing with
Professor Fehlmann's dictum that '*Le problème réligieux est
certes évoqué de façon trop superficielle,*' it is hard to dispute his
further comment that '*la peinture de l'amour est, là encore, d'une
qualité médiocre*'. Dame Ethel Smyth, a friend of great importance to Edith in the later years of her life, reviewed *Mount
Music,* and compared Christian and Larry to the lovers in
Middlemarch, Dorothea Casaubon and what Dame Ethel called
'the sadly inadequate Will Ladislaw'. It is, perhaps, Christian's
over-adequacy that throws *Mount Music* out of perspective, but
as Larry is almost more of a dolt than Christian's own father
he may be presumed to be capable of surviving marriage with
someone whose unfaltering sweetness covers the dead as well
as the living.

Mount Music has, on the other hand, many redeeming words.
For example, outside the salmon fishing hotel overlooking the
river, 'sad anglers, in ancient tweed suits, lolled broken-
heartedly in basket chairs'. Or the concert described as 'a sort

of lyrical geography—the map of Ireland set to music! Bantry bay, Killarney, the Mountains of Somewhere, the Waters of Somewhere else . . .' Whether the view of religion is superficial or not, the clergy of all denominations get an impartial roughing-up. On the Catholic side there is Father Greer, mahout to Doctor Mangan's elephant, and inventor of the useful word, 'insinuendo', who easily persuades his neighbour, Father Sweeny, to follow the political manœuvres which will keep Larry in the fold of his baptism. At that moment Father Sweeny is in hospital, with a leg broken in a spill on his way to visit a dying parishioner. Always plethoric, Father Sweeny is nearly apoplectic at the news that the parishioner, anointed by another, has recovered. In fairness it must be said that Larry, besides feeling his religion to be a bond of sympathy with the country people, experiences a deep emotion when he hears Barty Mangan recite beside the Doctor's corpse, 'By the multitude of Thy mercies, ever compassionate to human frailty, deliver him, O Lord.'

On the Protestant side, Larry's aunt Frederica represents the Low Church Dublin circles in which Edith's and Martin's aunts found so much religious excitement. Though herself gentle-hearted, she assents with enthusiasm to the Doctrine of Eternal Damnation, and would have gone to the stake for the Verbal Inspiration of the Bible. The two local vicars are a contrast. One is well-born, sporting and popular with the Catholic poor of his parish, '. . . being rich, liberal, easily bored, and not particularly sympathetic to affliction [he] was accustomed to stanch the flow of tears and talk alike, with a form of solace that rarely failed to meet the case'. The incumbent of Cluhir, on the other hand, is a melancholy cleric, who agrees to offer prayers for fine weather, adding 'as he looked, like an old horse, down his long deplorable nose, "but I fear they will not be of much use, as the glawss is remorkably low!" '

Finally there is a vignette of one of Christian's brothers, who has early decided that the Church would be a suitable field for gifts developed in childhood's religious exercises, when Christian, as the Witch of Endor, would be tortured in the manner of the Inquisition. 'John . . . now a very decorative curate in a London church . . . Undecided whether to regard Larry with suspicion as a brand still smouldering from the fires of secularist France, or affectionately, as a member of what, in one of his earlier sermons, he had described as "Our ancient Mother Church, dear Peopul! Beloved, but in some matters, that I will presently indicate to you, mistaken!" '

By the time *Mount Music*, which runs roughly from 1890 to 1907, had appeared the Easter Week Rising of 1916 had given a tilt to the rocking stone of the English government of Ireland. Balance was regained, precariously, for three more years, until an increase of violence toppled the stone. The inevitable contractions of history have often obliterated the fact that, at the time, the Rising was an isolated incident, its significance clouded by the crueller exigences of the Western Front. Even in reviews of *Mount Music* it is the operation of the Land Acts, rather than the fighting in the streets of Dublin, that is considered to have undermined the position of such families as the Talbot-Lowrys.

Martin's death was then sufficiently recent for her political opinions to be relevant, but Edith's confidence in the unbroken chain of their sympathy was so complete that, as more time passed, she was able to ignore those problems of historical perspective which inevitably increase as a death becomes more remote in time. The effect on Edith's writing was insidious, rather than immediately remarkable. On her own, Edith wrote with compulsive speed; to use a hunting metaphor, she was apt to overrun hounds. Martin, as Edith described her at Étaples, would lie meditating, recording her thoughts in small scribbles, hard to read. She once made a note for Edith that a paragraph was too subtle and involved, and it was the loss of this gift for artistic discrimination that was the greatest deprivation to Edith's writing. Martin might not have modified the plot or the characters of *Mount Music*, but it is hard to believe that she would not have pruned sentences which underline a point already made in dialogue. In *The Whiteboys* a cardriver remarks to Flurry, of influenza, ' "there's people dying now that never died before" ', and the conversation proceeds without comment from the authors. In *Mount Music*, when the same remark occurs, Edith, writing on her own, adds that this statement was readily comprehended by a midget dairy woman. Hemingway incidentally attributed it to a favourite barman, quoting it on hearing of Ford Madox Ford's death.

For *An Enthusiast*, the next novel that she brought forth, Edith made only the modified claim that Martin had been her passive, rather than active, collaborator. However, in the year between the publication of *Mount Music* and *An Enthusiast*, Edith found time to collect vagrant writings into a volume which she called *Strayaways*. It is here that the separate threads of her style and Martin's can best be studied, as if the fabric of blue and yellow shot silk had been many times magnified. More than a third of the book was occupied by *In the State of Denmark*, considered in an earlier chapter among other travellers' tales. Of the balance, Martin alone had been responsible for more than half the material, and had also joined with Edith in a significant book review. To assist the study of Martin's 'individual outlook', Edith wrote that she had rounded up her cousin's two earliest articles from 'the ultimate fold, the British Museum'. *Strayaways* might have been called 'Martin's Contribution'; so much is it permeated by her spirit that Edith's illustrations are, at times, almost an intrusion between the reader and Martin's words. This is not the case, however, with the frontispiece, illustrating *At the River's Edge*, considered by Martin's sister, Katherine Currey, to have been her finest piece of writing.

At the River's Edge is dated as written in 1914, when Martin, herself, was moving unknowingly towards the river which was to divide her from Edith. The incidents of the winter night's watching, beside a cottage fire, with Anastasia, an elderly spinster, who is tending a dying patient, belong to the days of Martin's return to Ross. 'Everything about her was clumsy, except her watchful grey eyes; I have never seen a cow seat itself in an arm-chair, but I imagine it would do so in the manner of Anastasia.' Occasionally, after stirring the gruel, Anastasia dozes, leaving Martin to reflect on the philosophy, familiar in its pattern, but alien in its point of view, which Anastasia's conversation reveals. The talk moves from fairies, thought to be fallen angels allowed to stay on earth, to the two evenings in quick succession when Anastasia had been seen by neighbours, when ' "not a bit of me was next or nigh the place" '. In an even voice she tells that ' "one man seen the woman, and he knew well it was meself, and she coming to him, and she in a valley, and it was the fall of the evening, in harvest time"'. This was, Martin thought, 'the scriptual method of narrative, that curves on its way like running water, and sinks to its one and inevitable channel'. She thought of the theory that some constituent of the Irish race had been Mediterranean, bringing with it this gift of the perfect word picture. '. . . and all the while the boots of Anastasia confronted me, planted at the edge of the turf ashes on the hearth, like boulders on a foamy beach.'

As in her earlier essay, *In Sickness and In Health*, Martin broods on the contrast between the practical arrangements by which marriage was achieved among the Irish country people, and the roundabout habits of her own world. 'Marriage, not flirtation, is the concern of Anastasia's social circle; the creature that we indulgently and sympathetically term Passion is by them flogged to kennel under another name.' Having dealt severely with the idea of Lust, Martin's gaiety reasserts itself as she remembers a mission service, where the priest, a great angry crow in his cassock and biretta, had denounced the evils awaiting young people who walked together in dusky woods and lanes. ' "I knew a most respectable young man," narrated the Missioner, "and his wife, a decent young girl; they had a nice young family." The congregation laughed delightedly and sympathetically, and the Missioner glowered upon them. This was not going to be a laughing matter. Soon there was drink in it, and a Protestant somewhere I think; worse things followed. "The two of them are burning together in the flames of Purgatory," concluded the Missioner with ferocity, and rumbled at them like an angry bull. . . . I saw the congregation go home in the dusk, the women walking in parties by themselves, the men silently passing the public-house as if it had *Dhroch hool*, which means the Evil Eye.'

Anastasia, perceptive of Martin's mood, begins to speak of priests translating that passage from the Irish mission sermon which Martin used in her unfinished history of her family, and which began, 'Oh, black seas of Eternity . . .' Talking of the Irish that was then being taught, Anastasia, yawning, says that '"the Irish were deep-spoken people long ago . . . it was all love songs they had . . . Sure, there's no talk of love now." She said it comfortably, and presently dozed, and I wondered what talk of love she had heard.'

Throughout the night the dying patient, shadowy, only referred to as the reason for this vigil, and given neither age nor sex, has been tended by Anastasia efficiently, but from philosophy 'rather than from that tenderness that has its heart within the need of its tended one'. With the grey coming of morning the robin's song and the ringing of the convent bell bring a relief from tension. 'The quiet hopelessness of the sickroom ceased to be the central thing in life.' A girl goes down to the river with her milk cans, humming 'Lannigan's Ball',

'I wish I were in Galway Town,
It's there I'd meet my darling.'

'A young man in a creamy flannel bauneen and a black soft hat came riding down the opposite bank on a bare-backed Connemara pony.' Offering the girl the preference in his decision to marry next Shraft, he accepts her placid refusal with a hint that the offer will remain open until the last moment. He rides off again out of the spawning bed over which the mare has been drinking. There is some laughter in the kitchen, 'with Anastasia as humorist'. '. . . a mist began to thicken the sky. It went and came, as though it must return to press the house to its bosom, and tell those within of its love and its despondency.'

Edith's frontispiece shows the young man watering his mare—obviously a Shan Bui—while the girl scours a bowl with river sand and straw to the tune of 'Lannigan's Ball'. Colour notes occurring in the story may be an example of Edith's influence, but otherwise Martin is on her own, considering two opposing views of marriage and love. As Martin contemplated Anastasia, so can Martin be contemplated, with the wonder as to what talk of love she had heard.

Like those pictures contrived on strips of glass which, when the observer moves, transform one subject into another within the same frame, so Martin could turn from the elegiac tone of *At the River's Edge* to study a coarser manifestation of love, as she did in *Two Sunday Afternoons*, a story placed by Edith near the end of *Strayaways*. Edith wrote that *Two Sunday Afternoons* had been laid aside, Martin regarding it as too sordid and tragic. It is based on tales she heard in her young days in

Dublin, when the Invincibles hoarded their vengeance, but, nevertheless, struck savagely and implacably.

On a Sunday in May, Kate Byrne, a servant girl in a Dublin lodging house, is picked up by a young house-painter. A week or so later, after long embraces under the laburnums on Stephen's Green, he takes her to a public-house, introducing her to a group of friends who include a well-dressed lady, with an Irish-American accent. Through a glow induced by several glasses of port, Kate is flattered to hear this smart lady inviting herself to tea on the following Sunday. On that day Kate is alone in the house, except for Mr Mackenzie, the landlord, an Ulsterman retired from the Dublin Custom House. Kate, fortified though she is by Mrs Mackenzie's best teapot and some finery of the Misses Mackenzie, finds that even these surreptitious borrowings do not make for ease with Mrs Nolan, her visitor. Mrs Nolan, who surprises Kate by wearing a pair of cheap tennis shoes, is alternately *distraite* and flattering, until, just as a whistle comes from the stables at the back, she asks to be shown the house. Kate opens the larder door and suddenly finds herself shoved inside and the key turned upon her. Surprised at what she considers to be no more than a peculiar practical joke, Kate forces open the door, only to hear terrible sounds of a struggle on the stairs. Mr Mackenzie is battling with two men, one of whom is Joe, Kate's lover. Clinging to him with screams of panic, she falls fainting as he strikes her with a knife. Later, dying in hospital, she is asked to identify a man whom she can just discern to be Joe. In a last effort of love she denies having seen him in the attack, only to give a final delirious scream which betrays him, '. . . her head swung aside on to the nurse's arm. It had dropped scarcely less helplessly on Devine's shoulder a week ago, when the laburnum leaned overhead, and the sunshine struck the living sparkle in her brown hair.' This tragedy has come about from a belated revenge of the Invincibles on Mr Mackenzie, for detecting a quantity of dynamite in his Custom House days, and causing Joe's brother (also Mrs Nolan's lover) to get a life sentence.

Ignoring the melodrama, *Two Sunday Afternoons* is a story of the Dublin of which Joyce wrote in *Two Gallants*. Kate might have been the 'slavey', courted by one of the gallants, not as a means of political revenge, but because she will be

willing to give her seducer a small gold coin, to finance his
evening's drinking. Even the descriptions of the girls are
almost interchangeable, if allowance is made for differences in
the writers' points of view.

'. . . the coarse colour that covered cheek and high cheek-
bone spoke of youth and strength; her mouth was good-
humoured, Irish and vague. The blue eyes were well and
darkly set, the slant of the eyebrows downwards to the snub
nose might have been sinister or might have been merely
vulgar.' (Martin Ross.)

'Frank rude health glowed in her face, on her fat red cheeks
and in her unabashed blue eyes. Her features were blunt. She
had broad nostrils, a straggling mouth which lay open in a
contented leer, and two projecting front teeth.' (James Joyce.)

Joyce, the greater literary artist, leaves the reader to draw
conclusions, while Martin makes her points more heavily, with
such adjectives as 'good-humoured', 'sinister' and 'vulgar', but
the girls might be identical twins. The picking up, in both
stories, takes place on the path beside the Grand Canal, and the
public house, in which the two Gallants have been wearying
the company on that August Sunday, could easily be the same
into which Kate Byrne is beguiled in the month of May.

'The swing doors with their muffed glass banged behind
them, and Kate found herself in a semi-dark bar with a crowd
of men . . . In deference to Sunday, the shutters were up, and a
ragged flare of gas combined with the swing door to light the
bar; there was a babel of laughter, talk and tipsy argument, the
sour smell of spilt drink contended with the weight of bad
tobacco smoke that hung in the air.' *Two Sunday Afternoons* was
written, though unpublished, when *Dubliners* appeared, so the
resemblances, of persons and of background, belong apparently
to the well-populated world of literary coincidence.

Between the passions of *Two Sunday Afternoons* and the
philosophy of *At the River's Edge*, there are slight notes which
Martin did not fill out, *The Old Station Master* and *A Sub-
terranean Cave at Cloonabina*, and a complete ghost story, *The
Dog from Doone*. These belong to Ross, as do her two earliest
articles, *A Delegate of the National League* and *Cheops in Connemara*. The death of the Delegate had given her encouragement
when contemplating Ireland's future, for she knew he had put

his loyal friendship to the Martin family above the League's orders to maim the cattle in the demesne, while the disconnected learning by rote of Horace Smith's *Address to a Mummy*, which gave its title to *Cheops in Connemara*, filled her with pity for the scholars of the local National School and terror for their future.

The Dog from Doone has for its background Christmas holidays at Ross. In a dormitory, reached by a corridor of sweating stone flags, four schoolboys are housed, giving the room the appearance of being inhabited by four large families. They are also harbouring the Dog from Doone, a stray thief, just escaped from a brutal attempt to drown him. The narrator, supposedly a Sandhurst cadet, cannot himself resist the dog's pathetic hunted state, and is rewarded by being rescued from a nasty fall down a swallet-hole, while in pursuit of a ghostly pack of white hounds, drifting through the wood like 'a stack of wool'. Martin never gave a clearer picture of the atmosphere of Ross, an outpost of domestic civilization, threatened on one hand by stray dogs snatching the whipped cream off the kitchen table, and on the other by the wild outside, where phantom hounds could lead their followers into real pitfalls.

Returning from the Dublin Horse Show in 1913, Martin wrote *An Incorrigible Unionist*, an essay expressing the belief that the Horse, by his economic importance and the nation's devotion to his breeding, might yet knit Ireland together. She wrote this as a gesture of faith, being well aware of the strikers in the streets of Dublin and the ominous squaring-up of Ulster to the South. Her opinion of the Horse's power as an influence for peace was, to a certain extent, vindicated in 1920, when much of the country was in a state of open warfare, but the Dublin Horse Show took place in an undeclared truce. It was rare for Martin, or Edith, to deal with English situations, but *Strayaways* includes two comments on English life, *The Waters of Babylon* (1895) and *In the Fighting Line* (1913). The former is a sketch of the moment of weak sentiment which led Martin to see off friends sailing to the East from Albert Dock, and her relief at returning to the homeliness of Liverpool Street Station: 'How friendly, subsequently, seemed the buses, how national the hansoms, how maternal, how immutable the Strand.' *In the Fighting Line* is a reminiscence of East Anglia,

G

where Edith and Martin had canvassed for an election. Martin
pointed out the irrationality of those who entrusted two women
with the task of expounding political theories to elderly gentlemen, while considering any woman incompetent to vote on
the same subjects.

Four studies called *Quartier Latinities* were the results of
Martin's meditations on the sand dunes at Étaples on the theme
of bohemian life as practised by Edith, the art student. The
crémerie, undeservedly popular for meals, was later described
by Edith in *French Leave*. After dealing with its menu of
'amaranthine *côtelette aux pommes frites*, only varied by *tête de
veau à la sauce Ravigotte*, which resembled 'the unshaven cheek
of an elderly gentleman', Martin was left with an unanswered
question. Instead of frowsting in this devil's kitchen, why did
no one patronize either of the two adjacent cafés, clean,
pleasantly shaded, beautifully christened *Le Restaurant au
Paradis des Cochers*, and *Le Rendezvous des bons Gymnasiarques*?
Apparently nothing would shake the loyalty of the *crémerie*'s
clientele, the masochism of their lives being gastronomical as
well as artistic.

As Martin saw the female art student (in *Quartier Latinities
II*), she was a single-minded fanatic, dressed in an unhappy
compromise between the styles favoured by Burne-Jones and
Puvis de Chavannes, topped by an irrelevant flowered head-
piece from the Bon Marché. Her total lack of assimilation to
Parisian life gave her, however, one advantage. When she
stormed the stairs of the Châtelet for a Grieg concert, conducted by the master, her imperviousness allowed her to drive
untouched through the clamouring ranks of the box-openers.
Martin then moved on to the Luxembourg gardens, describing
a scene more suitable to be painted by Douanier Rousseau than
by Edith. Grown-ups, bearded and buttoned into frock coats,
or shrouded in widow's weeds, not only watched the Guignol
with delighted seriousness, but were prepared to play endlessly
with hoops, battledores and balloons. Martin watched, and
wondered at this gay preoccupation with toys, among the
hawthorn blossoms and chestnuts, on the spot where, in the
lifetime of the players, the Communards had been brought out
and shot *en masse*, 'while the long daylight lasted, men and
women, black with powder and the soot of conflagration'.

Fastidiously revolted though she was by insanitary circumstances, Martin brought herself to examine the domestic marketing of the Latin Quarter, where, she wrote, 'the franc has a sinecure as a mere parent of coppers'. Shaky old ladies might complain of being cheated of their fair share of grease on the two sous' worth of soup ladled from a vat in the butcher's back kitchen, but Martin maintained that no one could complain that full value for a sou was not given by Parisian newspapers, with their unfailing supply of murders by a jealous husband, whose rival was invariably *un brave garçon aux grands yeux bleus*.

Edith, editing *Strayaways*, has been quoted as saying that Martin's writings, there collected, gave an opportunity to examine her individual point of view. This examination reveals more of Martin's mind than Edith, perhaps, realized, her devotion to Martin bringing with it a certain lack of objectivity. Edith tackled the love-relationships in her later novels, when they were necessary to the development of the story, rather as a fox makes his point crossing difficult country, bravely, but with no time to spare for by-ways. Martin, in her watch with Anastasia, could speculate on passion. She could also recognize the truth of the advice '*Non fate guerra al Maggio*', acknowledging that the month of May which had covered the laburnum with gold was pulsing through the body of the catspaw servant girl. In their writing together Edith contributed her full share of wit, and perhaps more than her full share of physical energy, a quality often overlooked as an essential to the practice of literature, but she dug less deeply than Martin into the lodes of human experience.

Edith's contributions to *Strayaways* were fewer and less serious than Martin's. *En Costume de Ville* is a gay account of the complications of an extra-mural life class, where the amateur models, required to appear in their everyday clothes, have to be trapped like rare animals. Many of the experiments with the psychic, described in *Extra Mundane Communications*, have been considered as part of the history of Edith's family, but she ended with a quotation from Frederic Myers on the Blessed Dead which shows more of her heart than she usually uncovers. 'Nay, it may be that our response, our devotion, is a needful element in their ascending joy.'

Attacked by the unfairly inherited evil of gout, an evil added
to the rheumatic pains that plagued her later years, Edith went
to be baked and sluiced at Aix-les-Bains. She wrote a sketch,
The Pool of Siloam, about her sufferings, and it is regrettable to
think that she probably never met with Joyce's pun about
Aches-les-Pains. Two hunting pieces, *A Foxhunt in the Southern
Hills* and *Not the Woman's Place*, are also filled with their
special suffering. They are stories of war-time hunts, with bog
drains that look as if 'dug out of wedding cake and filled with
treacle', mysterious mountain doors under which a fox can
take refuge, and, most painful of all, the struggles of a female
M.F.H. to keep the hunt going in war-time. Obstacles are
formidable, but Edith reflects that Florence Nightingale had
also met with prejudice. She happened to have encountered a
contemporary of Miss Nightingale's who had retained her
original opinion, unamended by later developments. ' "Florence Nightingale?" said this little old lady, buried in a big
chair, looking like a tiny shrivelled white mouse with bright
blue eyes and grey mittens. "Ah! yes, I knew her well. A
beautiful woman, my dear; but she had that curious fancy for
washing dirty men." '

Ireland Then and Now and *Stage Irishmen and Others* were two
further essays in which Edith attacked the picture of Ireland
which Irish and English had combined to miscreate. In the first
she based her thesis on the *Recollections of Sir Jonah Barrington*,
whose career, it might be suggested, was a travesty of the
noble life of Charles Kendal Bushe. Having learnt by prudent
inquiry that the regiment in which he had the offer of a commission was due to sail on active service to America, he
refused the offer and took to the law and politics. Opposing
the Union, he lost not only the promise of the post of Solicitor
General, but the profitable sinecure he already held. However, with an ambivalence which the *Dictionary of National
Biography* finds disconcerting, he thought it no inconsistency
to act as a go-between among those prepared to sell their
support of the Act. Later he used funds paid into his own
court to settle his private financial troubles and, deprived of
his judgeship and his Parliamentary seat, left the country to die
at Versailles.

Edith wrote about Barrington in 1918, when it seemed to

her that the Irish Republican Party had worked itself into a
state of bigoted insularity which disqualified all, except themselves, from the right to be called the people of Ireland. The
Rakes of Mallow, 'Always raking/Never thinking,' would
have been rejected along with Barrington's seven sportsmen,
who whiled away a week of frost shut up in a huntsman's
cottage, with the carcase of a cow and a hogshead of claret.
Cheered by the family piper, at the end of the seven days they
had eaten the cow to the bare bones, and emptied the hogshead, which would normally yield over two hundred and
eighty bottles. Edith stifled her regard for the good old days,
and went on to point out that the pessimistic romancer,
Barrington, and the optimistic educational reformer, Richard
Edgeworth, father of Maria, agreed that the handicap of the
Irish people was lack of education.

To her appreciation of Barrington Edith added, two years
later, a review of three volumes from *Every Irishman's Library*,
William Carleton's *Stories of Irish Life*, *The Collegians*, by Gerald
Griffin, and *Selections from the Works of Maria Edgeworth*.
Carleton, she found hard to forgive, both for his creation of
the Stage Irishman, Phelim O'Toole, with his chorus of Stage
Colleens, and for his inability to convey the tone of voice used
by the country people from whom he came. Gerald Griffin,
more highly educated, she found to have had an ear of far
greater delicacy for such speech. 'It was', she wrote, 'the convention of Griffin's period that the higher the birth, the taller
the talk.' Consequently the priggish conversation of the young
gentleman collapses into bathos beside the vivid description
of his servant. A fat neighbour, for example, was recognized a
fortnight after his funeral in the shape of a drove of young pigs.

Edith was, habitually, a good-natured reviewer, but she was
justly outraged at the editorial policy of *Every Irishman's
Library*, which could publish, unabridged, the longueurs of
Carleton and Griffin, while presenting Maria Edgeworth only
in selections. She had the deepest admiration for *Castle Rackrent*, both as a work of art and an innovation in fiction. '*Castle
Rackrent* was published in the year 1800, and in treatment might
have been written by any realist of today. Its effortless composure, its tranquil reliance on idiom and mental outlook,
rather than on mis-spellings and expletives, might have been

a lesson to its successors, had they had the intelligence to perceive and the wisdom to accept the example it offered.'

Edith added that *Castle Rackrent* was in a class by itself in its realization of the narrator's point of view, as far as anyone 'save Thady Quirk himself' could judge. Thady Quirk was the steward at Castle Rackrent, of which the original was said to have been Donore, the home of a Catholic family of Nugent, on the shore of Lough Derravaragh in Co. Westmeath. This was not far from Edgeworthstown, where Maria had listened to local legends told by her own father's steward John Langan. Fortunately Charlotte Edgeworth, one of Maria's many sisters, had a talent for painting, and she has left a faithful record of John Langan benignly watching a sheep-shearing, while two of the little sisters who swarmed at Edgeworthstown roost at his feet. Had she seen this picture Edith would have recognized it as a representation of Irish life as she knew it, Langan's face displaying the wit and understatement which was, to her, the triumph of Maria Edgeworth's style. To give an example of Miss Edgeworth's perfect timing, Edith ended her review by quoting the account of the death of Sir Condy. Last of the Rackrents, he had, shortly before, organized a fake funeral for himself, only to be disappointed by the lack of interest shown in him by the mourners.

' "... Brought to this by drink," says he. "Where are all the friends?—where's Judy? Gone, hey? Ay, Sir Condy has been a fool all his days," says he; and there was the last word he spoke, and died. He had but a very poor funeral after all.'

The Irish World and American Industrial Life, in a leading article in June 1910, gave considerable praise to a review which had originally appeared in 'our friend the enemy', the London *Times*. The *Irish World* was balanced between the intelligent critical standards of its leading articles (supporting the Gaelic League by a headline in Irish) and the parish magazine prose of its reports from far-flung Catholic communities at San Francisco or Little Rock, Arkansas. The review, which had reached *The Irish World* by the indirect route of *The Literary Digest*, still retained its Timesian anonymity, but it was, in fact, the work of Somerville and Ross. The subject of the review was a book by Doctor P. W. Joyce, with the slightly laborious title *English as We Speak it in Ireland*. Edith and Martin reproached Doctor Joyce for his unawareness of the nuances in the phraseology used at different social levels and for his omission of the poetical twists in everyday Irish conversation, though they praised his dedication to his subject. Eventually Edith included the review in *Strayaways*, calling it *The Anglo-Irish Language*. The point made, particularly applauded by the *Irish World*, was that the Irish speakers of the South and West had learnt their English from the classically educated gentry, until this acquired tongue, pliant and subtle, was adulterated by commercial invasion from England on one hand, and by emigrants returning from America on the other. These views show how deeply Somerville and Ross had pondered on the language in which so much of their dialogue was written. Their conclusions could be respectfully accepted by an Irish American Catholic journalist, when anonymity allowed for impartial judgement.

16
Trop de zèle

WHEN Edith met and made friends with Dame Ethel
Smyth, some of the gaiety which she had lost with
Martin came back into her life, while from the Unseen World,
Martin sent messages that she rejoiced at this new comfort.
The meeting took place in September, 1919, Edith's friend
Lady Kenmare having asked both redoubtable women to meet
at her home in Killarney. Maurice Baring, already the author
of many books and the brother of the hostess, was also in the
party. He, too, became a friend and correspondent of Edith,
sometimes inviting her to join him in grumbles at Ethel Smyth's
high-handed behaviour. 'Ethel is certainly a treat,' he wrote a
few years later, following-up in his next letter, 'I repeat that
Ethel is a treat.'

This piece of period slang may seem mild when applied to
Ethel Smyth's career, which was violent, both as a musician
and in her personal relationships. For example on a provincial,
concert tour, Constant Lambert, then a young musician, was
detailed to turn over for Dame Ethel at the piano. He used to
relate how she greeted him warmly, expatiating on how much
she disliked receiving this assistance from a woman, and complaining, 'I haven't had a man since Carlisle.'

This new friend was invited to Drishane where she joined
in the séances. She also introduced Edith to a wider circle in
London, and arranged for the first show of paintings by
E. Œ. Somerville. The exhibition was followed by a holiday
in Sicily, remembered with gaiety in *Happy Days!*, Edith's
penultimate book. The relationship had, however, its difficult
moments, for both women were in their early sixties and
accustomed, for many years, to dominate their surroundings.
Edith's brother, Colonel Cameron Somerville, had by now
retired to Drishane, but he was a gentle bachelor, content to
leave most matters in her hands. In June, 1920, Ethel Smyth

wrote one of many affectionate letters to Edith, but included, also, some passages that were expostulatory and almost exasperated. Mr Maurice Collis has suggested that, as Ethel Smyth had bisexual tendencies, the letter was written in the disappointment of realizing that she could expect no physical response from Edith. On the other hand, Edith's family and friends have remarked that she was unusually reticent and reserved about all physical contacts, and she would be unlikely to have conveyed any other impression to a woman of Ethel Smyth's range of experience. In the letter in question Dame Ethel chides her friend as 'you cloudy aloofer', and it appears that Edith has objected to Ethel Smyth's free-spoken tongue, and to the free-love lives of some of her friends. Dame Ethel makes a conscious effort to combat the 'governessy' side of Edith's nature, while admitting that Edith's charm was to be 'fastidious . . . and rather virginal'. This last was not an accusation to be made against Ethel Smyth, but Edith, riding on a more even emotional keel, accepted the incongruities of their friendship. A year or so later she noted in her diary. 'March 24. E. S. and I walked across the Park to Lady Troubridge and Radclyffe Hall. Latter in bed. Lady Troubridge young and nice-looking. Talked psychic things.' The occasion might have been more animated had Martin been there to shriek like a dog with its tail caught in a door.

Nineteen-twenty was a year when Edith needed help and comfort. She suffered from a crippling attack of rheumatism, and when she returned to Drishane, after treatment in England and France, she found that Co. Cork, swarming with the Irish Republican Army, had been given over to lawless violence. The Crown forces, unable to maintain order to protect those supposedly under their care, committed outrages which led to reprisals and counter-reprisals, until the situation degenerated in a spiral of murder, looting and arson. Edith's courage was unflinching, and she struggled to finish a novel, with a background of the troubled times around her. With *An Enthusiast*, written 'In collaboration with Martin Ross' and dedicated to 'My Collaborator', Edith reached the end of the road on which she had started with Martin when they began to write The Shocker. Although her spirit was still eager for novelty and adventure, historically she called a halt, in future drawing only on the resources garnered in the past she had shared with Martin.

An Enthusiast opens with a set-piece, the burial of Colonel Palliser, a memory of the funeral of Edith's own father, with the coffin covered by a Union Jack on which lay the Crimean sabre and shako. '[Eileen Caulfield] placed an immense cross of blazing yellow daffodils upon the gaudy flag that intensified, if that were possible, its gaudiness.' As the country women raise the *caoine*, the brilliant coffin is carried away among a crowd of horsemen nearly a hundred strong, who are following the funeral not of one man but of a dynasty of paternal landlords. The heir, Dan Palliser, is an innocent young man, anxious only to improve local prosperity by the introduction of co-operation and modern farming techniques. He is handicapped by a grimly bossy mother, and a gang of uncles fulminating against the state of the country. He is also handicapped by the vested interest in keeping a profitable *status quo* among such manipulators as 'Baby' Coyne, a vast old man described with the sureness of touch that recalls *Holy Island* and *The Shooting of Shinroe*. The Baby, who has '. . . the thirstiness of mouth, and the goggling malevolence of eye, of extreme infancy' lays down his principle when his vote is solicited for a local government appointment, '. . . if it was only half-a-crown I should have it for the principle of the thing. It was I introduced this method of obtaining votes into this Union, and I may say . . . it has worked exceedingly well.' Dan imports a tractor which has trouble with first appearance nerves, and the prejudices of the farm-workers. Their attitude can be found somewhere about the fifteen-hundredth page of *War and Peace*, where Tolstoy touches on the subject of steam engines. 'A steam engine moves. The question is asked, How is it moved? A peasant answers, It is the devil moving it.'

Dan Palliser's failure in his honest attempts for the public good is the real tragedy of this sad almost bitter book, but there also is a love disaster. Dan falls in love with Car Ducarrig, the young wife of a retired Colonial Governor, a man of such incredible unpleasantness that he overbalances into the ridiculous. Car Ducarrig has the musical gifts of Ethel Smyth, and possibly some of her other characteristics, '. . . many, both men and women, had fallen before her and, more often than not, the initiating feature of their overthrow had been Car's dilettante interest in human beings'. In the novel this dilettante interest leads Car to behave with a compulsive bitchiness which is the most convincing feature of her character. She is at her most tolerable when she sees, from a window, her husband surreptitiously improving the lie of a croquet ball played by Dan's cousin, Eileen Caulfield, and realizes that Lord Ducarrig is beginning yet another affair. Dan's uncle, Admiral Caulfield, and his fellow Unionists, are dusted down by Edith as relentlessly as the corrupt 'Baby' Coyne. As they conduct an auction of bloodthirsty suggestions for dealing with the I.R.A. the Admiral is particularly savage, though he mellows later with pleasure at the poor haul the raiders make at his own house—' "Two of my South Pacific spears, made of human shin bones, and a Malay kris." '

Dan and Car fall in love, an affair that suffers, like Larry and Christian's, from being observed too closely from the male point of view. The final disaster comes when Dan is picked off accidentally by Lord Ducarrig, in an attack on the house, which the ever-unfortunate Dan has managed to drive back by wielding his father's Crimea sabre. This symbolical death of the enthusiast takes place just after Car admits to herself that she can at least admire her husband in his capacity as a man of action.

In the Civil War which followed the Treaty between England and Ireland, Cork was again in a state of anarchy. Now instead of Auxiliaries and Black-and-Tans, to whom any man in a mackintosh might be a gunman, the Army of the new-born Free State was fighting to subdue the Republicans. Edith still faced the situation with her natural courage, and the confidence that Castletownshend was under the protection of Martin's love, and the invisible swords of the Crimean hero, her father, and the Mutiny hero, her uncle Kendal Coghill. In August, 1922, the situation was still precarious in Castletownshend, though in July a raiding party of Republicans had been seen off by Father Lamb, a small but indomitable priest. He had routed an attempt to force the inhabitants to pull down the pier, on which the livelihood of the fishermen depended. Edith and Jem Barlow, with admirable coolness, watched at the Two Trees, focal point of the main street, while Father Lamb snatched and broke the Republicans' rifles.

Hearing that Michael Collins, the Free State General, was expected at Skibbereen, Edith and her brother Cameron drove there on August 22nd, to ask for more protection for Castletownshend. Edith wrote in her diary that Cameron had gone into the hotel and talked to Collins, whom he had liked, but who had been unable to spare any soldiers. The next entry recorded the shattering news that Collins had been shot in a skirmish between Skibbereen and Cork. Although he was a popular hero, there were many people who had scores to settle with him. To read that one of the last persons to whom he talked was Colonel Cameron Somerville is a strange sensation for those who remember the Civil War as a background of childhood, a curious mingling of the everyday and the historical.

The emergency which had made Dan Palliser a martyr to his own zeal came to an end. Edith, in a world that would have been incredible to her parents, published another autobiographical collection under the name of *Wheel-tracks*, from the wobbling tracks of the donkey carts in the mud roads of Cork, which are quickly obliterated by time and weather. The material was mostly what she had discarded as superfluous in *Irish Memories*, and sudden flashes illuminate her family from unexpected angles. Her Somerville grandfather, for instance, although a man of sincerely pious habits, if required to swear deponents in emergency cases would do so on an early leather-bound copy of Bradshaw's *Railway Guide*. He also raised a pillar on a small hill, with no other reason than the wish to puzzle posterity. These freaks of behaviour in her ancestor may have descended to Edith, and given an extra twist to the talents contributed by the Bushes and the Coghills.

Dealing with her own family in reminiscence, Edith was looking over her shoulder into the golden country of her childhood, a country which, attached as she was to the rock of Castletownshend, she never entirely left. The past was particularly remote in the case of her Somerville grandmother, who had been born a Townshend two years before the Fall of the Bastille. As her eldest grand-daughter, Edith, lived for four years after Hitler's suicide in the ruins of Berlin, their lives covered one hundred and seventy years between two climaxes of national disintegration. It was the voice of the eighteenth-century which summoned Edith indoors, when she was seen to be listening entranced to a story of haunting by local fairies, told by the man who was mowing the lawn. Bidding the man get on with his mowing, Edith's grandmother told her that she was not to talk to the men on the place as this might make her a little 'brouganeer', the family phrase for speaking with an Irish accent. Neither Edith, nor the man who came to mow, allowed ancient prejudices to limit their talks, which laid the foundation for the work she was to share with Martin.

Their notes of the talk they heard around them did not make 'brouganeers' of Edith and Martin, but kept them alert in such places as teashops and railway-carriages. Edith wrote in *Eavesdrops* of a rich haul Martin made in a teashop, where she overheard a lady saying, with philosophical detachment, ' "I often think the idea of tea is better than the reality." ' With a friend this pessimist went on to discuss Willy, who was in jail—he was always unfortunate—just for taking some money out of the bank he was a clerk in. ' "And look at Mr Brown! . . . when he got married, in Westland Row Chapel, he agreed to give the priest three pounds and when he gave the roll of notes to the priest what was it only paper! And of course the priest was too polite to look into it—only put it straight in his pocket—and away with me brave bridegroom out of the country!" ' Except for the polite scruple of the priest, the surge and thunder of *Ulysses* is clearly audible. In more rural circumstances Edith was held riveted by the badinage of a farmer and various lady friends, travelling by train to Waterford Races. A complicated cut-and-thrust of flirtation was only brushed aside to allow everyone to consider the case of a cow treated for a swollen throat with a red-hot hay fork. The cow, however, died.

Much of the autobiographical matter in *Wheel-tracks* has been dealt with in its place in Edith's life, but she included a short, affectionate memoir, *Of an Uncle*, a memorial to the most flamboyant of her mother's brothers, Colonel Kendal Coghill. The Colonel's teeth made his niece think of a Bengal tiger, and his fierceness in battle was in keeping with his appearance. Edith omitted the more terrible descriptions from his letters, written as a young man at the Siege of Delhi, but they are still

harrowing reading, with their history of angry vengeance for
savage atrocities. Surviving battles and cholera, Kendal Coghill retired to Castletownshend, where, to his family circle, he
remained an unpredictable but fascinating phenomenon. He
had also an operatic quality which excited Edith to adoration,
when, as a small girl, she heard him sing at a concert. He sang,
'Je suis soldat, s–oldat du Roi', in a high tenor voice like a
cavalry trumpet, an attribute passed on by Edith to Major
Talbot-Lowry of Mount Music.

17
The flesh on the skeleton plot

The Big House of Inver was published in 1925, and dedicated 'To Our Intention, 1912–1925', with a note that,
as the firm was still in business, Edith felt justified in linking
her name with Martin's. The dedication was explained by
another note on the last page of the book.

'Extract from a letter to E. Œ. S. from Martin Ross.
'March 18th 1912.
'Yesterday I drove to see X—— House. A great cut-stone
house of three stories.
'Perfectly empty . . . It is on a long promontory by the sea,
and there rioted three or four generations of X——s, living
with country women, occasionally marrying them, all illegitimate four times over . . . About one hundred and fifty years
ago a very grand Lady —— married the head of the family and
lived there and was so corroded with pride that she would not
allow her two daughters to associate with the neighbours of
their own class. She lived to see them marry two of the men
in the yard . . . Yesterday as we left, an old Miss X——,
daughter of the last owner, was at the door in a little donkey
trap. She lives near in an old castle, and since her people died
she will not go into X—— House, or into the enormous yard,
or the beautiful old garden. She was a strange mixture of
distinction and common-ness, like her breeding, and it was
very sad to see her at the door of that great house.
'If we dared to write up that subject——!
'Yours ever Martin.'

Given this skeleton of a plot by Martin, some of the gusto with
which she had illustrated *A Patrick Day's Hunt* returned to
Edith in a literary form. She put flesh on the skeleton and
dressed it richly in historical fancy dress.

In *The Big House of Inver*, Edith pared away the Anglo-Irish point of view so that it is hardly a factor in the story. Peggy Weldon has an English mother and she marries a newly-rich English baronet, but neither her mother nor her husband have the strain of the double loyalty, inherited by such families as the Somervilles and Martins. This marriage completes the moral and physical destruction of the family of Prendeville, the name chosen by Edith for the family whose decline had been outlined by Martin.

The apex from which the Prendeville family's decline begins is the building of the Big House and the marriage, in the next generation, of 'Beauty Kit' to the grand Lady Isabella. Edith described the house, three stories, curving wings and pillared portico, remarking that it was such houses still standing that justified Ireland's claim to be considered a civilized country. Although she gives a date fifty years too early, the Big House has a strong resemblance to the houses built by Davis Duckart, such as Kilshannig, Co. Cork, which Edith might have seen. A mistake in dates would not be difficult for someone who only in later life had come to appreciate the architectural splendours of her country. Lady Isabella brings Italian plaster-workers from Dublin to make the ceilings of the Big House a wonder to the neighbourhood and a pride to herself. Puffed-up with this pride, Lady Isabella lives in a social isolation, which leads to her son and daughters marrying among the country people on the estate. At the time of the terrible increase in the population, which so overloaded the land that it could no longer feed its children, the neighbourhood of Inver is swarming with the illegitimate spawn of the Prendevilles, whose origin is testified by the cognomen of Pindy.

After the famine, Jasper, the reigning Prendeville, retires from the army, on account of his drunken habits, which are also extreme enough to cut him off from the far from temperate local society. Relying for companionship on thirsty hangers-on in the village, a certain stability is given to his home life by his illegitimate daughter. This handsome by-blow, the child of Captain Jasper and a country girl who died at her birth, goes by the name of Shibby, the tavern variant of the proud name of Isabella. She keeps house for her father with a mixture of devotion to the idea of the Prendeville family and contempt for the licentiousness that has led to her own begetting. By now the Big House has been stripped of its furniture and the family live in rough comfort in the old Tower of Inver. The demesne has also been stripped from the Prendevilles by a sharp deal on the part of the steward John Weldon, who does not allow his feudal feelings to prevent him from feathering his nest at his employer's expense. The feudal feelings are uppermost when John Weldon finds an amenable young wife for the middle-aged captain, who fulfils the purpose of her marriage, heir-thwarting, by producing a son, Kit. A daughter is born, and then, at the birth of a second son, mother and child die. Even allowing for Edith having grown up in an age with a high rate of maternal mortality, it might be thought that, in her later books, she was over-willing to use death in child-bed to create the situation she required.

After these preliminaries Edith arrives at the main story of her book, and it must be admitted that the early complications have made a heavy demand on the fine edge of the reader's response. Now, however, the plot begins to move with the return of Peggy Weldon from her education abroad, which has made her too cultivated for her own home. Her grandfather, 'Old John Weldon', the steward, over ninety, is still alert mentally, though of the same vast size which Edith had noticed almost as a moral characteristic when she described 'Baby' Coyne. Peggy's father, 'Young Johnny' Weldon, as a stripling of sixty, resents his father's unrelaxed grasp on affairs, which handicaps 'Young Johnny's' own operations as an adroit solicitor. Peggy's mother, an English governess, still somewhat at sea in the world into which she has married, has a strenuous life as a buffer, amid the clash of personalities under her roof.

Captain Jasper is now a senile eighty-eight, confusedly fearful of Shibby, but relying on his daughter Nessie, the gentle slave of the family. Among the bitter blows of Shibby's life has been the sale of the demesne, the inheritance of Kit, on whom she has poured out the love for which the shame and pride of her birth has left her no other outlet. As good-looking as his forebear, 'Beauty Kit', and only less profligate from lack of means, Kit is destined, in Shibby's schemes, to fascinate an heiress, who will buy back the demesne and reign with Kit in the Big House. Against this happy day Shibby is painfully re-furnishing the house, with grotesque goods bought at local auctions and paid for by the penny-pinched profits of her hens and pigs.

Kit, with an early acquired taste for whiskey, and a knowledge of his power over women, indulges both these propensities at the Connor's public house. He spends there the money he makes, by his skill in training horses, on drink and on Foxy Mag Connor. The girl becomes pregnant, but even before this is known her brother bullies and fawns on Kit, until in a moment of drunken irritation Kit agrees to ride a 'fixed' race. In the meantime Kit has begun a courtship of Peggy Weldon, who he meets on the sandy bay, when he is schooling a young mare. Peggy, a large, attractive girl, though an incompetent rider, is being bolted with by a horse she has taken without permission from her father's stable. At that moment Kit is allowed the virtues of those earlier horsemen, Willie Sarsfield and John Michael, of which Edith and Martin so well understood the fascination. His love for the filly is almost unselfish, and her confidence in him is complete, in spite of her dread of the sea, as 'the foamy terror that ran beside her, so thin, and swift and noiseless, stole nearer'.

Shibby's plans begin to succeed when she makes a pact with 'Old John' Weldon that she will persuade Kit to marry Peggy if 'Old John' will bequeath the demesne to his grand-daughter. Peggy is succumbing to Kit when the English baronet appears. 'Young Johnny' immediately sees the possibilities of Sir Harold Burgrave as a son-in-law, but he has to cope with Peggy's obstinate passion for Kit, while entertaining his important guest amid the discomforts that Somerville and Ross used to heap upon Major Yeates. Anxiously placatory, Mr Weldon keeps his finger on the bell of the railway refreshment room, where he is attempting to give luncheon to a crossly hungry Sir Harold.

' "Who rang that bell?" said the old waiter, emerging suddenly from a distant lair behind a screen.

' "I did!" replied Mr Weldon, with violence, "Why——"

' "Well, don't do it again!" interrupted the old waiter angrily.'

Even greater sufferings come to Mr Weldon, when, having

lured Sir Harold into the Big House with a hint that it is for sale, he finds himself staggering through every room. The dignity of the house has survived a sequence of Pindy squatters, who had 'left the sign manual of brutalized human creatures, a deliberate destruction . . . one that neither cattle nor swine can equal'. In agonies of dyspepsia, Mr Weldon is blind to the architectural details which fascinate Sir Harold, and, having hooked his fish, is almost too exhausted to land it.

A mental collapse of Mag Connor, and blackmailing demands from her brother threaten Shibby's schemes, but, with a ruthlessness equal to Charlotte Mullen's, she bribes and threatens Jo Connor into promising to emigrate. Foxy Mag is, however, recalcitrant in her dementia, and Shibby meeting her on a rock, Kit's trysting place, by the river has a struggle to hold her. Suddenly Mag Connor has gone from Shibby's grasp. The voice within the mind of the dedicated priestess of the Prendevilles, urging her to let the girl go, has been so strong that she can only say to herself that she will take what God knows is owing to her. In any case the situation is beyond redemption, even by Shibby's iron will. Jo Connor has told the tale of Mag's seduction and of the 'fixed race', leaving Peggy to turn to Sir Harold. Kit strikes the next blow. With facile delight at the idea of ready cash, he tells Shibby that Young Johnny has arranged the sale of the Big House to Sir Harold, taking advantage of Shibby's absence to get Kit's support in putting the deal through with Jas. Now even the infinite tolerance of Shibby's love turns to contempt.

' "The curse of God is on me," she said in a low voice, "what use is there to strive? Laugh away, boy. You're easy pleased! Your sweetheart has left you for another man, and your fancy girl is drowned, and now your house is sold." '

Shibby knows it will be useless to reproach Jas for this latest betrayal, but there is yet one more act of destruction, what Professor Fehlmann calls, '*une récherche systématique du suicide*', for Jas to accomplish.

Seeking him in the Big House, where it had often been only the smell of his old pipe that told her where to find him, Shibby finds flames and smoke raging through the splendid rooms. In the obscurity someone comes to her aid, and between them they drag the Captain's body out of the great front door. Only then does Shibby realize that she and Young Johnny are facing each other across Jas' corpse lying on the gravel.

The Big House of Inver is a novel in which the last paragraph of the last page carries a perfectly timed punch.

'The story of the Big House of Inver is finished. The only noteworthy observation that needs still to be told is that of Mr John Weldon.

' "Sure I had it insured, to be sure! On the same day we paid the money—and all that's in it, too, thank God!

' "I'm an insurance agent, don't ye know!" '

The house that Martin described to Edith was Tyrone House, belonging to the St George family and burnt down during the Civil War. Edith saw it afterwards, a windowless ruin, as she had felt was its destiny. The implications of Martin's skeleton plot, what Shibby called 'too much pride and wickedness', were faced unflinchingly by Edith. Drunkenness and sharp practice in horse-dealing had been always part of the life around her, but for the first time since the old days of *An Irish Cousin* she returned to the theme of a family's moral decay. More experienced as a woman and an author, she wrote in plainer terms, but her thought was the same.

'An old stock, isolated from the world at large, wearing itself out in those excesses that are a protest of human nature against unnatural conditions, dies at last with its victims round its death-bed.'

18

The vanished hand

THERE are direct traces of Martin's hand to be found in
The Big House of Inver. In a sentence, not reproduced by
Edith, she had said that Tyrone, though built more grandly,
had reminded her of Ross. Edith gave the Prendevilles the
marriage stones, blue-black slabs of slate with names spelt
haphazard, that had belonged to the early Martins of Ross.
The old Tower of Inver, where Shibby strives to rule her
unstable and treacherous male kin, might have been any one
of the Norman towers which still stand aggressively in Co.
Galway. As Yeats wrote in *My House*:

> 'An ancient bridge, and a more ancient tower,
> A farmhouse that is sheltered by its wall,
> An acre of stony ground,
> Where the symbolic rose can break in flower,
> Old ragged elms, old thorns innumerable,
> The sound of the rain or sound
> Of every wind that blows.'

The Big House of Inver distressed those of Somerville and
Ross' followers who had ignored every aspect of their writing
except its most obvious humour. A younger generation of
reader, perhaps fed too assiduously by their elders on a diet of
Major Yeates, to the exclusion of *The Real Charlotte*, had not
much inclination for the Vicissitudes of a Norman-Irish Family.
Dame Ivy Compton-Burnett, whose *Pastors and Masters* appeared in the same year, thought *The Big House of Inver* 'a very
good book', but this was a writer whose regard for *The Real
Charlotte* as a novel, and for Charlotte Mullen as a creation,
was responsible for making Somerville and Ross converts
among younger generations.

Edith's last two novels, *French Leave* and *Sarah's Youth*
appeared, respectively, in 1928 and 1938. That is to say when

she was seventy and eighty years of age. Martin's vanished hand has little part in either, except for the art student chapters in *French Leave*, which have their roots in *Quartier Latinities*, and the episode when the heroine of *Sarah's Youth*, on the sofa after a hunting accident, is described in loving detail, as Edith might be recalling Martin's convalescence forty years before.

French Leave is a jovial version of *Mount Music*, omitting politics, religion, and the study of character in depth. It opens with Patsey Kirwan, a prettyfied Edith in a bonnet and a bustle, running herself close to a collapse of the lungs to reach the church in time to play the organ at a step-sister's wedding. This mad rush in constricting wedding garments may well have happened to Edith, but, unlike Patsey, she never found an eligible young Lord Corran already playing Löhengrin in the organ loft. Incidentally, *Musical Opinion* printed an indignant letter, complaining that the account of the organ and its behaviour was a major 'novelist's blunder', which seems strange if Edith's long service as an organist is considered. Patsey's father, Sir Ingram, is a less pathetic and generally more dislikeable version of Major Talbot-Lowry. There is a kind of parody of the Mangan family in 'Holy George' Lester, a rich Protestant farmer, and his son George (who shares Patsey's ambition to study painting), though their home, where imperfectly cured goatskins cover the holes in the drugget, has none of the lush comfort of the Mangan establishment. Patsey and George bolt, separately, to Paris, where Patsey 'falls in love' with a pretty American girl, 'a growing passion', Edith wrote, 'which can be as occupying as a profession'. But this crush has no significant undertones, being merely part of the excitement of a plunge into Bohemian life, and the American girl provides a solution for disposing of George Lester, who obviously cannot be allowed to marry Patsey. Her fate is to marry Lord Corran, whose house stands in a wide flat plain, criss-crossed with stone walls, and populated by enough sporting foxes to console Patsey for its remoteness from the *rue de la Grande Chaumière*.

The same problem of unsuitable marriages crops up in *Sarah's Youth*, though much of the book is a fantasy of Edith's young self being adopted by Edith's middle-aged self. In a letter to Mr John Gore she called *Sarah's Youth* the great-grand-daughter of *The Real Charlotte*, but *An Irish Cousin* was more truly its progenitor. Captain Heritage, retired from the Militia, which has taken him to 'Foreign Service' on Salisbury Plain, could easily have danced with Theo Sarsfield at the squireen's ball, but there is no doom about the story of *Sarah's Youth*. Sarah is the daughter of Captain Heritage and a down-trodden heiress, Miss Dixon, who dies at Sarah's birth. This leaves Captain Heritage free from a marriage, which had been arranged by his battle-axe of a mother, and able to marry his mother's pretty house-slave, who is allowed to survive the birth of another daughter, Kathleen.

Sarah's tantrums and Kathleen's second-sight make for disturbances at home, but both are united in devotion for Tim Kavanagh, the last fascinating horseman that Edith was to create. After the failure of an attempt to civilize Sarah at an English boarding school, in which readers of Angela Brazil will find an echo of *The New Girl at St. Chad's*, she becomes a protégée of the Master of the Castle Ower Hounds. This position is held by Miss Mary Lorimer, and, recollecting Edith's accounts of her own struggles with hounds, huntsmen and Fowl Funds, there is a wistful quality in the portrait of a female M.F.H. whose father pays the bills, and who controls both her kennels and her Field with benevolent firmness. Tim Kava-nagh, green-fingered for animals, has been taken on to help in the kennels, and grows up with ambitions to become a veterinary surgeon. He is still pursued by Sarah, but Miss Mary does her best to promote her own nephew. (There is a slight confusion about the Lorimer family, Lady Harriet, an-other childbed victim, being described once as dying at the birth of a son, and once from the birth of Miss Mary.) The situation is resolved by Tim marrying an illegitimate daughter of Captain Heritage, which leaves Sarah to take on the job of amateur whip to Miss Mary's hounds. Kathleen, of the second sight, has, fortunately, also a gift for music, which removes her from hampering Sarah's every move by prophecies of woe, invariably fulfilled.

In November, 1938, *The Observer* reviewed *Sarah's Youth* in a pre-Christmas round-up of fifteen somewhat incongruous books. Strange bed-fellows for the last novel of Somerville and Ross, and for each other, this list included works by Enid Bagnold, Hall Caine, G. M. Trevelyan, and P. G. Wodehouse.

In the nineteen-thirties Elizabeth Hudson, an American friend whose visits to Drishane were always a delight to Edith, suggested that a bibliography of the first editions of Somerville and Ross would be suitably published by A. J. A. Symons' First Edition Club. This plan was delayed both by Symons' death and the outbreak of war, an unfortunate postponement, for, had the Somerville and Ross bibliography appeared under the imprimatur of the First Edition Club, it might have done something to cure the blighting reputation of being writers concerned solely with hunting against a comic Irish background. Among the miscellaneous items in the bibliography the *Mark Twain Birthday Book*, compiled by Edith and published in 1885, should not be overlooked. Mark Twain himself admitted that he had been defeated when he had contracted to make a birthday book from his own works, 'my books grew suddenly and disastrously barren and empty'. Edith described the book both as an outlet for her admiration for Mark Twain and an opportunity to adjust the quotations for her own circle 'in a manner at once appropriate and wounding'. Knowledge as well as admiration must have been essential to compile such a book. Edith had not yet met Martin, and it would appear that Edith's individual outlook and literary education had their foundations in *Tom Sawyer* and *Huckleberry Finn*.

Edith, and her sister Hildegarde, visited America in 1929, as a result of the private printing, in 1927, of the Hitchcock Edition of Somerville and Ross. The reception of the seven sumptuous volumes confirmed that she would be welcome as a lecturer and that there would be a market for her paintings. Her American public among the Hunt Clubs, remote from her old admirer *The Irish World and American Industrial Life*, lapped her in luxury and charmed her with Negro serenades. The tour took Edith to the Southern States, New England and New York City, and if some of the horses she had bred had forgotten her in their new homes, she was happy to meet a parlourmaid with kind memories of Drishane.

A record of her travels, *The States through Irish Eyes*, was published, uniquely, as by E. Œ. Somerville; separated from the friend through whom she received messages from Martin, Edith did not feel that she could include Martin's name on the title-page of her American diary. Her next book, *An In-corruptible Irishman*, was a work of family piety, its creation shared by Martin, and its subject, 'The Chief', himself assisting from the unseen world to which he had gone nearly a century before. Compared with most ancestors, Charles Kendal Bushe, and his wife Nancy Crampton, were like the McRory trifle to more conventional recipes, 'a mountainous dish . . . in whose veins ran honey instead of jam, and to whose enlivenment at least a bottle of whisky had been dedicated'. Edith had a quantity of letters and a store of family legend on which to draw, but with the help of her friend and first biographer, Geraldine Cummins, she established an even closer connection with her subject. Through the medium of Geraldine Cummins, and Astor, her control, Martin brought 'The Chief' to Edith, who found him happy to greet her as a worthy descendant, and to answer questions about his own life. Mr Collis writes that Edith, in her diary, questioned the propriety of including supernatural communications in an historical work, but as Martin, in automatic writing, had declared that she had found Bushe, Edith felt compelled to accept the material as authentic. Although a book by Edith about Bushe, an essentially un-tedious subject, could not fail to charm, as in *Irish Memories* she did not recognize the need for a coherent scheme. The result is the kind of picture which was known in the nineteenth century as a 'fancy head'. *An Incorruptible Irishman* lies outside the canon of the Somerville and Ross collaboration, but two of 'The Chief's' jokes may be quoted for the flavour of the two centuries in which he lived. Of some of his female descendants he remarked that 'no one could doubt the solidity of their understandings', an euphemism for legs which lasted through-out the Victorian period. In the broader mood of his eighteenth-century youth, he was seen to follow with his eyes a peculiarly décolletée lady. ' "Did you ever see the like of that before, Chief?" someone asked. "Not since I was weaned," said Bushe.'

There is a story of Kipling's, *Uncovenanted Mercies*, in which sinners expiate their sins by permanently haunting a perfectly reproduced railway station, where they continually fail to meet those with whom they have made assignations after death. The Unseen World, as Martin conveyed its circumstances to Edith, had apparently something of the atmosphere of a

terminus, happier than Kipling's, the waiting rooms crowded
with kinsfolk, friends and Edith's dogs, all alert for a call from
Martin to muster in loving protection round Drishane. This
guardian band of Somervilles and Coghills was particularly
potent, Edith believed, at the time of the Troubles, but she felt
its influence in every corner of her life. When, on June 29th,
1932, Edith Œnone Somerville had conferred on her the
Honorary Degree of Doctor of Letters, at Trinity College,
Dublin, the Public Orator spoke no more than the truth, when,
asking that Martin's memory should also be venerated, he
declared that Edith cherished her cousin with 'no less love
than if she were present and helping'.

This honour filled Edith with the pleasure given by any
long-delayed recognition. It also gave her a status which,
though honorary, brought her nearer to her friend Dame Ethel.
She does not seem to have complained that she had lacked
formal education in her youth, but she may have felt that
respect for academic accolade which was often an attribute of
the suffragist soul. In the same year W. B. Yeats invited her to
become a founder member of the Irish Academy of Letters,
bringing her into the literary world which Martin had known.
Later, the Academy made her a Fellow and awarded her the
Gregory Gold Medal, an honour which commemorated
Martin's old friend Augusta.

The two collections of essays, *The Smile and the Tear* and *The
Sweet Cry of Hounds*, published in 1933 and 1936, were divided
by a family tragedy of peculiar and senseless horror. Edith's
brother Boyle, who had retired as a Vice-Admiral to The Point,
Castletownshend, answering a knock on his front door on a
night in March, 1936, was shot dead by a shadowy gunman.
Applications to the Admiral from local boys, who wished for
certificates of good character to enable them to join the Royal
Navy, seem to have been built up by political extremists into
an accusation that he was engaged in recruiting. Doctor Casey,
Roman Catholic Bishop of Ross, expressed something of the horrified grief felt in the country when he wrote in a pastoral letter.

'It is a sad commentary on our notions of public duty that
men are to be found who profess to believe that the public
good can be promoted by crime; but it is worse to think that
there are men who are persuaded, or persuade themselves, that

crime ceases to be crime when clothed with a mantle of pseudo-patriotism.'

Messages soon came to Edith to tell her that Boyle had joined Martin in the world of light, and, thus fortified, she finished the *Records of the Somerville Family of Castlehaven and Drishane*, which had been one of the occupations of his busy retirement. A memorial, most touching in charity and lack of bitterness, are the essays which concern Boyle in *Notions in Garrison*, published in 1941. In these he appears as a delightful enthusiast, whether rising at 4 a.m. to test theories of three local monoliths' significance at the summer solstice, or helping Edith to make a pond, that sank back into the jungle from which it had been conjured, leaving stranded the gold fish with which Boyle had stocked it.

This was not Edith's last book. In 1946 she brought forth more reminiscent essays under the cheerfully defiant title *Happy Days!* Despite great age, illness and financial stringency, her spirit could still delight in the landscape of the past, the days dominated by the heroic tribe of her aunts, the birth of the R.M. at Étaples, and Sicilian hardships made gay by the company of Ethel Smyth. In the year of her death, 1949, her final book, *Maria and Some Other Dogs*, closed a lifetime of writing and a lifetime of loving dogs. Words used to Edith about the end of Pedlar, son of a great favourite called Prinkie, might have found an echo in her own heart. ' "They got the Canon's little dog, dead, on the hill south. He was too old for hunting. Ah, the little wood coaxed him." '

Edith died at Tally Ho House, Castletownshend, on the eighth of October, a short step across the river, and through the curtain of mist which hid Martin's physical presence. Their masterpiece, *The Real Charlotte*, was published in *The World's Classics* in 1948. This was a rare tribute to a living author, but, though new readers were constantly won, the title was later, and somewhat inexplicably, dropped. For some years an Everyman edition of *Some Experiences of an Irish R.M.* was the only survivor in print of all the descendants of *An Irish Cousin*, a frail bridge along which new readers would have to find their way.

Edith and Martin are buried side by side in the Churchyard of Saint Barrahane, 'on the edge of Europe'. The truth with which they wrote about Ireland was, at moments, unpalatable, both to those who shared their views and to those who opposed them. Their legacy to the country they loved, and the language in which they wrote, is the gift of the perfect word picture.

Index